Jung on Evil

In the course of his long and productive life, Jung said a great deal about evil but relatively seldom in one place and never in the form of a single essay on the subject. His position must therefore be pieced together from many writings. However, Jung did have a consistent position on evil, which is clearly apparent in this collection.

In his early work on the unconscious, Jung considered the role of evil in the mental processes of the severely disturbed. Later, he viewed the question of moral choices within the framework of his ideas about archetypes and the shadow. Murray Stein's selection and introduction show how Jung's thoughts on evil are related to these other facets of his wide-ranging thinking. *Jung on Evil* will appeal to all those interested in Jung, as well as students of religion, ethics and psychology.

Jung on Evil

C. G. Jung

Edited and with an introduction by
Murray Stein

London

First published 1995
by Routledge
11 New Fetter Lane, London EC4P 4EE

Simultaneously published in the USA and Canada
by Princeton University Press

Typeset in Times by
Ponting–Green Publishing Services, Chesham, Bucks

Printed and bound in Great Britain by
Biddles Ltd, Guildford and King's Lynn

British Library Cataloguing in Publication Data
A catalogue record for this book is available from the British Library.

Library of Congress Cataloguing in Publication Data
A catalogue record for this book is available on request.

ISBN   0–415–08970–0

Contents

Introduction

> We need more understanding of human nature, because the only real danger that exists is man himself. He is the great danger, and we are pitifully unaware of it. We know nothing of man, far too little. His psyche should be studied, because we are the origin of all coming evil.
>
> (Jung 1977: 436)

The problem of evil is a perennial one. Theodicies abound throughout history, explaining God's purposes in tolerating evil and allowing it to exist. Mythological and theological dualisms try to explain evil by asserting its metaphysical status and grounding and the eternal conflict between evil and good. More psychological theories locate evil in humanity and in psychopathology. Probably humans have forever wrestled with questions like these: Who is responsible for evil? Where does evil come from? Why does evil exist? Or they have denied its reality in the hope, perhaps, of diminishing its force in human affairs.

The fact of evil's existence and discussions about it have certainly not been absent from our own century. In fact, one could argue that despite all the technical progress of the last several thousand years, moral progress has been absent, and that, if anything, evil is a greater problem in the twentieth century than in most. Certainly all serious thinkers of this century have had to consider the problem of evil, and in some sense it could be considered the dominant historical and intellectual theme of our now fast closing century.

More than most other intellectual giants of this century, Jung confronted the problem of evil in his daily work as a practicing psychiatrist and in his many published writings. He wrote a great deal about evil, even if not systematically or especially consistently. The theme of evil is heavily larded throughout the entire body of his works, and particularly so in the major pieces of his later years. A constant preoccupation that would not leave him alone, the subject of evil intrudes again and again into his writings, formal and informal. In this sense, he was truly a man of this century.

As indicated by the quotation given above, which occurs in his famous BBC interview with John Freeman in 1959, two years before he died, Jung was passionately concerned with the survival of the human race. This depended, in his view, upon grasping more firmly the human potential for evil and destruction. No topic could be more relevant or crucial for modern men and women to engage and understand.

While Jung wrote a great deal about evil, it would be deceptive to try to make him look more systematic and consistent on this than he actually was. His published writings, which include nineteen volumes of the *Collected Works* (hereafter referred to as *CW*), the three volumes of letters, the four volumes of seminars, the autobiography *Memories, Dreams, Reflections*, and the collection of interviews and casual writings in *C. G. Jung Speaking*, reveal a rich complexity of reflections on the subject of evil. To straighten these thoughts out and try to make a tight theory out of them would be not only deceptive but foolhardy and contrary to the spirit of Jung's work as a whole.

It does seem appropriate, however, to introduce this selection of writings from Jung's oeuvre by posing some questions whose answers will indicate at least the main outlines of Jung's thought about the problem of evil. I hope, too, that this approach will prepare the reader to enter more deeply into the texts that follow and to watch Jung as he struggles with the problem of evil, also to engage personally the issue of evil, and finally to grapple with Jung critically. If this happens, this volume's purpose will be well served. Jung would be pleased, too, I believe.

While it is true that Jung says many things about evil, and that what he says is not always consistent with what he has already said elsewhere or will say later, it is also the case that he returns to several key concerns and themes time and time again. There is consistency in his choice of themes, and there is also considerable consistency in what he says about each theme. It is only when one tries to put it all together that contradictions and paradoxes appear and threaten to unravel the vision as a whole. We may agree with Henry Thoreau that consistency is the hobgoblin of small minds, but it is still necessary to register the exact nature of these contradictions in order to understand Jung's fundamental position. For he does take a position on evil. That is to say, he offers more than a methodology for studying the phenomenology of evil. He actually puts forward views on the subject of evil that show that he came to several conclusions about it.

It is also extremely important to understand what sorts of positions he was trying to avoid or to challenge. In doing so he may have fallen into logical inconsistency in order to retain a larger integrity.

To approach Jung's understanding of the problem of evil, I will ask four basic questions. In addressing them, I will, I hope, cover in a fashion all of his major points and concerns. By considering these questions I will cover the ground necessary to come to an understanding of Jung's main positions and to appreciate the most salient features of his conclusions. In the order taken up, these questions are:

1 Is the unconscious evil?
2 What is the source of evil?
3 What is the relation between good and evil?
4 How should human beings deal with evil?

These questions represent intellectual territory that Jung returns to repeatedly in his writings. The first is a question he had to grapple with because of his profession, psychiatry, and his early interest in investigating and working with the unconscious. The other three questions are familiar to all who have tried to think seriously about the subject of evil, be they intellectuals, politicians, or just plain folk whose fate has brought them up against the hard reality of evil.

IS THE UNCONSCIOUS EVIL?

Jung spent much of his adult life investigating the bewildering contents and tempestuous energies of the unconscious mind. Among his earliest studies as a psychological researcher were his empirical investigations of the complexes (cf. Jung 1973), which he conceived of as energized and structured mental nuclei that reside beneath the threshold of conscious will and perception.

The complexes interfere with intentionality, and they often trip up the best laid plans of noble and base individuals and groups alike. One wants to offer a compliment and instead comes out with an insult. One does one's best to put an injury to one's self-esteem behind one and forget it, only to find that one has inadvertently paid back the insult with interest. The law of an eye for an eye and a tooth for a tooth (the talion law) seems to remain in control despite our best conscious efforts and intentions. Compulsions drive humans to do that which they would not do and not to do that which they would, to paraphrase St Paul.

The unconscious complexes appear to have wills of their own, which do not easily conform to the desires of the conscious person. Jung quickly exploited the obvious relation of these findings to psychopathology. With the theory of complexes, he could explain phenomena of mental illness that many others had observed but could only describe and categorize without understanding. These were Jung's first major discoveries about the unconscious, and they formed the intellectual basis for his relationship with Freud, who had made some startlingly similar observations about the unconscious.

Later in his researches and efforts to understand the psychic make-up of the severely disturbed patients in his care, Jung came upon even larger, more primitive, and deeper forces and structures of the psyche that can act like psychic magnets and pull the conscious mind into their orbits. These he named archetypes. They are distinguished from complexes by their innateness, their universality, and their impersonal nature. These, together with the instinct groups, make up the most basic and primitive elements of the psyche and constitute the sources of psychic energy.

Like the instincts, which Freud was investigating in his analysis of the vicissitudes of the sexual drive in the psychic life of the individual, the archetypes can overcome and possess people and create in them obsessions, compulsions, and psychotic states. Jung would call such mental states by their traditional term, "states of possession." An idea or image from the unconscious takes over the individual's ego and conscious identity and creates a psychotic inflation or depression, which leads to temporary or chronic insanity. The fantasies and visions of Miss Miller, which formed the basis for Jung's treatise, *The Symbols and Transformations of Libido*, published in 1912–13 (later revised and published as 'Symbols of Transformation' in *CW*), offered a case in point. Here was a young woman being literally driven mad by her unconscious fantasies.

On the other hand, however, Jung was at times also caught up in a more romantic view of the unconscious as the repository of what he called, in a letter to Freud, the "holiness of an animal" (McGuire 1974: 294, see below). Freudian psychoanalysis promised to allow people to overcome inhibitions and repressions that had been created by religion and society, and thus to dismantle the complicated network of artificial barriers to the joy of living that inhibited so many modern people. Through analytic treatment the individual would be released from these constraints of civilization and once again be able to enjoy the blessings of natural instinctual life. The cultural task that Jung envisaged for psychoanalysis was to transform the dominant religion of the West, Christianity, into a more life-affirming program of action. "I imagine a far finer and more comprehensive task for psychoanalysis than alliance with an ethical fraternity," he wrote Freud, sounding more than a little like Nietzsche.

> I think we must give it time to infiltrate into people from many centres, to revivify among intellectuals a feeling for symbol and myth, ever so gently to transform Christ back into the soothsaying god of the vine, which he was, and in this way to absorb those ecstatic instinctual forces of Christianity for the one purpose of making the cult and the sacred myth what they once were – a drunken feast of joy where man regained the ethos and holiness of an animal.
>
> (McGuire 1974: 294)

So, while the contents of the unconscious – the complexes and archetypal images and instinct groups – can and do disturb consciousness and even in some cases lead to serious chronic mental illnesses, the release of the unconscious through undoing repression can also lead to psychological transformation and the affirmation of life. At least this is what Jung thought in 1910, when he wrote down these reflections as a young man of thirty-five and sent them to Freud, his senior and mentor who was, however, a good bit less optimistic and enthusiastic about the unconscious.

In its early years, psychoanalysis had not yet sorted out the contents of the unconscious, nor had culture sorted out its view of what psychoanalysis was all about and what it was proposing. Would this novel medical technique lift the lid on a Pandora's box of human pathology and release a new flood of misery into the world? Would it lead to sexual license in all social strata by analyzing away the inhibitions that keep fathers from raping their daughters and mothers from seducing their sons? Would returning Christ to a god of the vine, in the spirit of Dionysus, lead to a religion that encouraged drunkenness and accepted alcoholism as a fine feature of the godly? What could one expect if one delved deeply into the unconscious and unleashed the forces hidden away and trapped there? Perhaps this would turn out to be a major new contributor to the ghastly amount of evil already loose in the world rather than what it purported to be, a remedy for human ills. Such were some of the anxieties about psychoanalysis in its early days at the turn of the century.

Is the unconscious good or evil? This was a basic question for the early psychoanalysts. Freud's later theory proposed an answer to the question of the nature of the unconscious – good or evil? – by viewing it as fundamentally driven by two instincts, Eros and Thanatos, the pleasure drive and the death wish. These summarized all unconscious motives for Freud, and of these the second could be considered destructive and therefore evil. Melanie Klein would follow Freud in this two-instinct theory and assign such emotions as innate envy to the death instinct. Eros, on the other hand, was not seen as essentially destructive, even if the drive's fulfillment might sometimes lead to destruction "accidentally," as in Romeo and Juliet for instance.

From this Freudian theorizing it was not far to the over-simplification which holds that the id (i.e. the Freudian unconscious) is essentially made up of sex and aggression. Certainly from a Puritanical viewpoint this would look like a witch's brew out of which nothing much but evil could possibly come. The id had to be repressed and sublimated in order to make life tolerable and civil life possible. Philip Rieff would (much later) extol the superego and the civic value of repression!

If Freud saw his cultural task as unmasking human pretension and dealing a fatal blow to narcissistic self-evaluation, Jung would conceive of his work as an attempt to produce a reconciliation between the warring opposites within the human psyche. On the one hand, humans have noble aspirations and ideals, which are rendered palpable and visible in images like the dogmatic Christ symbol of the Christian religion. On the other hand, the same people who ascribe to these virtues and try to identify with such ideal figures commit atrocities great and small. In the name of religion countless wars have been fought and pogroms promulgated. The brighter the ideal, the baser seems to be the shadow. And it is this shadow feature of the personality, Jung felt, that Freud had fixed upon and dedicated himself to exposing. But is this the last word about the unconscious? Is the unconscious to be simply equated with the shadow and therefore with the precise contrary of the ego's ideals and finer aspirations? This would mean that the unconscious is to be regarded as essentially evil, or if not evil at least as pressing toward what one would judge as evil if enacted fully.

From his extensive investigations into the nature of the deeper levels of the unconscious psyche, which he called the collective unconscious, Jung concluded that the unconscious is duplicitous and dangerous, but not in and of itself essentially destructive or evil. Jung's deepest and most exhaustive research and reflection on the nature of the unconscious psyche were carried out in the last thirty years of his life (he lived to eighty-six), after he had developed the theoretical framework he would use to sort and interpret his findings. These later works centered largely on cultural and religious themes, with particular reference to the Christian West and a special interest in the subject of alchemy and its relation to the structures of collective consciousness in the cultures where it sprang up and flourished. For Jung, alchemy was a treasure trove of information about the collective unconscious of the Western psyche. He treated the thoughts and images of the alchemists as projective materials, and he analyzed them with an eye to the archetypal images and structures revealed in them. He saw alchemy as a dream-like statement about the Christian culture in which it was practiced, representing the compensatory function of the unconscious in reaction to the dominant structures and images of collective consciousness (see Chapter 2).

One of the most fascinating figures in alchemy was, for Jung, Mercurius. As Jung interpreted this figure, Mercurius represented the essential spirit of the unconscious (see Chapter 3). In their meditations and projective thoughts about the mysteries of nature and matter and in the revelations they beheld in their alembic vessels, the alchemists described a spirit who controlled the work, who was present at its beginning and its end, and who functioned as the presiding and necessary presence throughout the work from start to finish. This was Mercurius. As Jung concluded, Mercurius represented the spirit of the unconscious psyche, and by investigating his attributes carefully and sensitively it would be possible to decide if the spirit of the unconscious is evil or of a nature more constructive and benign.

Mercurius certainly did show signs of destructive potential. He was a dangerous spirit, and he was also duplicitous and deceptive, sexually active and even promiscuous, dual in gender identity, and a sort of Luciferean ("light-bringer") figure. But, Jung also realized, Mercurius is not to be identified with the Christian devil, who represents the absolute contrary of goodness, who is evil personified. From this extensive research, Jung's conclusion was that although the unconscious is mercurial and tricky (cf. also "On the psychology of the trickster" *CW* 9/1, paras 456–88), liable to upset the apple-cart of the conscious person's intentions and wishes, and at times perverse and extremely volatile and difficult to contain, it is not essentially evil. Rather, it is compensatory to the conscious personality and to its normal Judeo-Christian attachment to ideals of righteousness and virtue. If Christ is the archetypal dominant of collective consciousness in the Christian West, Mercurius is the shadow brother of Christ, and as such he is compensatory and not an absolute opposite.

The unconscious is not evil, therefore. Its moral quality depends upon consciousness and stands in compensatory relation to it. The unconscious could therefore be taken as a resource for inspiration and transformation, but it also had to be handled with extreme care and regard. It was not seen by Jung as evil per se, but it could easily become volatile and turn against the ideals of goodness proposed by a one-sided ego position. Mercurius was the yin to Christ's yang, the unconscious compliment to the Western dominant of consciousness, and as such should ideally be brought into relation with the Christ figure and held there (see Chapter 4).

WHAT IS THE SOURCE OF EVIL?

If the unconscious is not the source of evil, then where does evil come from? Or perhaps evil is not real at all, and therefore this is a nonsensical question to begin with. Perhaps evil is only the absence of good, or merely the product of a point of view.

In response to the question of evil's actual existence, Jung would answer in the affirmative that, yes, evil is real and is not to be written off as the absence of good. In his long and rather tortured argument against the Christian doctrine of evil as privatio boni (the privation, or absence, of good), an argument that at times reaches a vituperative register and is to be found in many publishing writings but is most sharply stated in his correspondence with Father Victor White (see Chapter 5), Jung wanted to affirm the value of treating evil as "real," as a genuine force to be reckoned with in the world. He felt that a view like that espoused by traditional Christianity in its doctrine of privatio boni underestimated the problem of evil. Jung did not want to be soft on evil.

And yet, paradoxically, Jung did not want to see evil as an independent, self-standing and inherent part of nature, psychological, physical or metaphysical. This would lead to dualism. Evil is not quite, or not always, archetypal for Jung, and he did not write a paper on the archetype of evil as he did on the archetype of the mother or other similar themes. So he does end up being somewhat soft on evil after all.

Evil is for Jung most primarily a category of conscious thought, a judgment of the ego, and is therefore dependent for its existence upon consciousness (see Chapter 6).

> With no human consciousness to reflect themselves in, good and evil simply happen, or rather, there is no good and evil, but only a sequence of neutral events, or what the Buddhists call the Nidhanachain, the uninterrupted causal concatenation leading to suffering, old age, sickness, and death.
>
> (Jung 1975: 311)

This is a view often expressed in Jung's writings.

Yet evil is an essential adjective, an absolutely necessary category of human thought. Human consciousness cannot function qua human without utilizing this category of thought. But as a category of thought, evil is not a product of nature, psychical or physical or metaphysical; it is a product of consciousness. In a sense, evil comes into being only when someone makes the judgment that some act or thought is evil. Until that point, there exists only the "raw fact" and the pre-ethical perception of it.

Jung discusses the issue of types of "levels" of consciousness briefly in his essay on the spirit Mercurius ('Alchemical studies', *CW* 13, paras 247–8). At the most primitive level, which he calls participation mystique, using the terminology of the French anthropologist Levi-Bruhl, subject and object are wed in such a way that experience is possible but not any form of judgment about it. There is no distinction between an object and the psychic material a person is investing in it. At this level, for instance, there is an atrocity and there is one's participation in it, but there is no judgment about it one way or another. For the primitive, Jung says, the tree and the spirit of the tree are one and the same, object and psyche are wed. This is raw, unreflective experience, practically not yet even conscious, certainly not reflectively so.

At the next stage of consciousness, a distinction can be made between subject and object, but there is still no moral judgment. Here the psychic aspect of an experience becomes somewhat separated from the event itself. A person feels some distance now from the event of an atrocity, say, and has some objectivity about the feelings and thoughts involved in it. It is possible to describe the event as separate from one's involvement in it and to begin digesting it. The psychic content is still strongly associated with an object but is no longer identical with it. At this stage, Jung writes, the spirit lives in the tree but is no longer at one with it.

At the third stage, consciousness becomes capable of making a judgment about the psychic content. Here a person is able to find his or her participation in the atrocity reprehensible, or, conversely, morally defensible for certain reasons. Now, Jung writes, the spirit who lives in the tree is seen as a good spirit or a bad one. Here the possibility of evil enters the picture for the first time. At this stage of consciousness, we meet Adam and Eve wearing fig leaves, having achieved the knowledge of good and evil.

In early development, the first stage of consciousness is experienced by the infant as unity between self and mother. In this experience the actual mother and the projection of the mother archetype join seamlessly and become one thing. In the second stage, the developing child can make a distinction between the image of the mother and the mother herself and can retain an image even in the absence of the actual person. There is a dawning awareness that image and object are not the same. A gap opens up between subject and object. The infant can imagine the mother differently than she turns out to be when she arrives. In the third stage, the child can think of the mother, or of the mother's parts, as good or bad. The "bad mother" or the "bad breast" does not suddenly begin to exist at that point, but a judgment about her behavior (she is absent, for instance) is registered and acted upon. Now the possibility of badness (i.e. evil) has entered the world.

This view of evil – that it is a judgment of consciousness, that it is a necessary category of thought, and that human consciousness depends upon having this category for its on-going functioning – generates many further important implications. One of them is that when this category of conscious discrimination is applied to the self, it creates a psychological entity that Jung named the "shadow." The shadow is a portion of the natural whole self that the ego calls bad, or evil, for reasons of shame, social pressure, family and societal attitudes about certain aspects of human nature, etc. (see Chapter 7). Those aspects of the self that fall under this rubric are subjected to an ego-defensive operation that either suppresses them or represses them if suppression is unsuccessful. In short, one hides the shadow away and tries to become and remain unconscious of it. It is shameful and embarrassing.

Jung provides a striking illustration of discovering a piece of his own shadow in his account of traveling to Tunisia for the first time (see Chapter 8). From this experience he extracts the observation that the

> rationalistic European finds much that is human alien to him, and he prides himself on this without realizing that his rationality is won at the expense of his vitality, and that the primitive part of his personality is consequently condemned to a more or less underground existence.
>
> (Jung 1961: 245)

It is this piece of personality that the cultivated European typically bottles up in the shadow and condemns violently when it is located in others. The magnificent film *Passage to India* depicts such projection of shadow qualities with exquisite precision. Jung would experience the full force of shadow unawareness and projection in the Nazi period and in World War Two.

Because the human psyche is capable of projecting parts of itself into the environment and experiencing them as though they were percepts, the judgment that something is evil is psychologically problematic. The stand-point of the judge is all-important: Is the one making a judgment of evil perceiving clearly and without projection, or is the judge's perception clouded by personal interest and projection-enhanced spectacles? Since evil is a category of thought and conscious discernment, it can be misused, and in the hands of a relatively unconscious or unscrupulous person it can itself become the cause of ethics problems. Is the judge corrupt, or evil? This would require another judgment to be made by someone else, and this judgment could in turn be the subject of yet another judgment, ad infinitum. There is no Archimedean vertex from which a final, absolute judgment on good and evil can be made.

Despite staking out his ground here, which could easily lead to utter moral relativism, Jung did not move in that direction. Just because the categories of good and evil are the product and tool of consciousness does not mean that they are arbitrary and can be assigned to actions, persons, or parts of persons without heavy consequence. Ego discrimination is an essential aspect of adaptation and consequently is vital to survival itself. Ego consciousness must take responsibility for assigning such categories of judgment as good and evil accurately or they will lose their adaptive function. If the ego discriminates incorrectly for very long, reality will exact a high price.

In order for consciousness to perform its function of moral discrimination adaptively and accurately, it must increase awareness of personal and collective shadow motivations, take back projections to the maximum extent possible, and test for validity. Time and time again Jung cries out for people to recognize their shadow parts. Questions of morals and ethics must become the subject of serious debate, of inner and outer consideration and argument, and of continual refinement. The conscious struggle to come to a moral decision is for Jung the prerequisite for what he calls ethics, the action of the whole person, the self (see Chapter 9). If this work is left undone, the individual and society as a whole will suffer.

As opposed to a theorist who would root the reality of good and evil in metaphysical nature itself and then rely on inspiration, intuition, or revelation to decide upon what is actually good and what is evil, Jung puts forward a theory that places the burden for making this judgment squarely upon ego consciousness itself. To be ethical is work, and it is the essential human task. Human beings cannot look "above" for what is right and wrong, good and evil; we must struggle with these questions and recognize that, while there are no clear answers, it is still crucial to continue probing further and refining our judgments more precisely. This is an endless process of moral reflection. And the price for getting it wrong can be catastrophic (see Chapter 11).

Because Jung considered this to be perhaps the central human task, he ventured even into the risky project of making such judgments about God Himself. Is God good or evil, or both? These are questions that Jung addresses in his impassioned engagement with the Biblical tradition, and especially in his late work 'Answer to Job' (see Chapter 10).

To ask if God is good or evil, or both, is for Jung the equivalent of asking this question about the nature of reality. Is reality good? Yes. Is it evil? Yes, it is evil as well. But this judgment rests upon the human, or perhaps even upon the individual, point of view. Nature, for example, is judged to be good when it is harmonious and stable and works in our (human) interest. But when it is tumultuous, when it produces and feeds our diseases, when its ways thwart the goals of human life and well-being, then we judge it to be evil. From a more disinterested vertex, however, it simply is what it is.

When humans adopt a more disinterested viewpoint, they transcend the categories of good and evil to an extent and view human life, human behavior, and human motivation from a vertex that sees it all as "just so." Human beings love each other, and we hate each other. We sacrifice for each other and destroy each other. We are noble and base. And all of this belongs to human nature. The judgments we make about good and evil are bound to be biased by our own interests and tilted in favor of our pet tendencies and traits.

This opens the door, then, to investigate in a more impartial way the sources of those trends in human affairs and character development that human beings would usually judge to be evil. Without giving up the categories of good and evil as tools of conscious discrimination and re-flection, we can avoid the blindness of righteous indignation and moral outrage that might otherwise overwhelm consciousness. We can ask for explanations for behavior. Why do the Serbs rape and mutilate the Moslem

Bosnian women? Why did Hitler want to eliminate the Jews? Why did Herod slaughter the innocent children? Why do I commit atrocities, albeit on a lesser scale, in my personal life? Without in any way shrinking back from the judgment that these are instances of evil, one can go on to ask the questions of psychological and social motivation that lead up to and support the attitudes and behavior that we judge to be evil. Explanations do not exonerate the perpetrators, nor do they have any bearing whatsoever on the question of punishment or the consequences for evil acts. This is not rationalization or excuse-making, but investigation. Jung's position does provide an opening for exploring reasons and causes and therefore also for finding ways to prevent such acts in the future by understanding what brings them about.

It is a great advantage to be able to say that essential evil is not rooted in reality itself, for if it were then one could do nothing about it. In Jung's understanding, evil is a category of judgment that can lead to scientific investigation and political action. If evil were real in a more ontological sense – if Satan really did exist as a being apart from God and controlled human events – then the possibilities of human engagement and intervention would be much diminished. Jung's position also allows one to remain optimistic to a certain extent about the rehabilitation of perpetrators. If it is not the case that the perpetrator is intrinsically evil, then it follows that a spark of hope remains for change and for a reversal of the traits and qualities that led to the evil act. Criminals bear the weight of shadow projection for society, but in Jung's view the criminal remains a member of the human community and represents an aspect of everyone. Those traits one condemns in the perpetrator also belong to oneself, albeit usually in a less blatant form.

One of the goals of a personal psychological analysis is, in Jung's view, to make an inventory of psychic contents that includes shadow material. Once this is done and the shadow is acknowledged and felt as an inner fact of one's own personality, there is less chance of projection and greater likelihood that perception and judgment will be accurate. This does not eliminate making judgments about evil, for this category remains in consciousness as a tool for discriminating reality, but it does allow for less impulsive and emotionally charged, blind attribution of evil in cases where serious ambiguity exists.

Still, if evil is an adjective, applied by ego consciousness to actions and events in the course of discriminating and judging reality, this fails to explain the source of the behavior, the acts, and the thoughts that are judged to be evil. What is the source of the deed, the "raw fact," which one judges to be evil?

For example, war is a common human event that is often judged to be evil. Is war-making native to the human species? It would seem that war-making is intrinsic to part of human nature. There are mythological figures, both male and female, who represent the spirit of war and the human enthusiasm for it. Human beings seem to have a kind of aggressiveness toward one another and a tendency to seek domination over others, as well as a strong desire to protect their own possessions and families or their tribal integrity, which added together lead inevitably to conflict and to war. Some would say that war is a natural condition of humanity as a species, and it would be hard to dispute this from the historical record. Is making war not archetypal? Does this not mean that evil is deeply woven into the fabric of human existence?

It is one thing to say that the tendency to go to war is endemic in human affairs, however, and another to say that evil is therefore also a part of human nature. War is an event, and each instance of it must be evaluated by consciousness in order to be condemned as evil. Conscious reflection upon warfare has found that some wars are evil and others not, or that some wars are more evil than others. Theologians have elaborated a theory of the just war. In itself war can be considered morally neutral, a tool that can be used for good or evil. So while it may be claimed that the source of the behavior that will later be condemned as evil is an inherent part of human nature, this still does not mean that evil is archetypal.

Going deeper, though, can we frame the question more precisely to tease out those aspects of human behavior that are universally condemned as evil and ask if they are inherent in human existence? Can it be shown that human beings naturally and inevitably commit acts that would universally be judged as evil? And if so, how are we to understand the source of these acts? How does the evil deed happen? For we know that evil does occur throughout human history and experience.

Jung's own major confrontation with evil on a large scale was Nazi Germany. Much that the Nazis did individually and collectively has been judged as evil. Jung was close enough to the center of this political phenomenon to observe it unfolding right before his eyes, to feel its energy and to know its threat personally. He was fascinated by the mythic dimensions of German Nazism and for a time by its energy. In the early 1930s he wrote things that show he believed that the collective unconscious in Germany was pregnant with a new future. Perhaps, he thought, some good could come out of it, perhaps the unconscious was giving birth to a new era that would lead humanity forward. Mercurius is ambiguous, and the products of the creative unconscious are sometimes bizarre in their first appearance. Jung most definitely underestimated at first the Nazis' potential for evil.

What he did observe by the mid-1930s, however, was a sort of collective psychosis taking hold in Germany, a society-wide state of psychic possession. In his essay on Wotan (*CW* 10, paras 371–99) he writes of this phenomenon. An archetypal image from ancient Germanic religion and myth, Wotan was stirring again in the German soul, and this was generating martial enthusiasm and battle-frenzy throughout the population. Wotan was a war god, and the German people were now showing the signs of irrational possession by battle-eagerness that is seen in warriors preparing for battle. This state of possession was disturbing normal ego consciousness among the Germans and their sympathizers to the point of clouding normal moral judgment. Under these conditions the psyche is ripe for releasing behavior that is primitive, irrationally driven, and highly charged with affect and emotion. Jung predicted that the German people were getting ready to act out a Wotanic possession.

What had brought this archetypal constellation into historical reality? The enactment of the Wotanic fury in modern Germany needs to be explained by referring to historical events and patterns: Germany's humiliation after World War One, the national degradation and political and economic turmoil of the 1920s, the compensatory politics of arrogance and revenge espoused by the Nazi leaders and bought wholesale by the populace. The appearance of the Wotan archetype in the collective consciousness of the German nation could be interpreted as a psychological compensation for a national mood of humiliation and loss of self-worth, the archetypal basis for a sort of narcissistic rage reaction.

In Jung's psychological theory, the regression of psychic energy to primitive levels of the collective unconscious constellates a compensatory archetypal symbol, which galvanizes the will and brings about a new flow of energy into the system, along with a strong sense of meaning and purpose. But this is also often accompanied by ego inflation and identification with primitive energies and impulses. What is created is a "mana personality" (cf. 'Two essays on analytical psychology', *CW* 7, paras 374ff.). There are no guarantees that what this archetypal symbol and its derivative notions and energies stand for will bear careful ethical scrutiny and inquiry. The crusader spirit of someone identified with archetypal thoughts and values will argue fiercely that the ends justify the means and will overlook all countervailing considerations. This person may look like a moral leader when in fact what is being espoused is an abdication of moral reflection. The crusader for liberation or equality or moral rearmament may well be advocating at the same time *abaissement du niveau mental*.

A strong influx of archetypal energy and content from the unconscious shades the light of ego consciousness and interferes with a person's ability to make moral distinctions. Now ordinary moral categories and the ego's ethical attainments are easily over-ridden in the name of "higher" (certainly stronger) values. And when these dubious higher values have become the group norm, individual and collective shadows have found a secure playground. This is how evil is unleashed on a mass scale; it is individual shadow added to shadow and then raised to the square power by group consensus, permission and pressure (see Chapter 11).

Under conditions like this, which held sway in Germany and other Nazi-dominated areas of Europe between 1933 and 1945 (see Chapter 13), kinds of behavior that would ordinarily be suppressed and repressed become acceptable. Indeed acts like betrayal of friends, robbery of personal property, lying and cheating and public humiliation of others, which would normally be condemned in civil society, may suddenly become praiseworthy. Now it is allowed and indeed encouraged to murder neighbors, to plunder their property, to rape their women, to take revenge for past slights and present envies. Even if some level of discipline remains in the ranks on the collective level, there is a strong incentive to look aside when individuals are "carried away" with enthusiasm for the cause or lose control of themselves. Thoughts and actions that were formerly condemned as evil are now condoned or overlooked.

The inflation produced by ideology and propaganda-inspired images creates a collective *abaissement du niveau mental* such that ego con-sciousness loses its ability to make considered moral judgments. The normal functioning of a personal conscience is interrupted. Everyone is swept up in the emotions of the moment, and the air is filled with urgent promptings onward. It is the rare individual who retains a personal sense of good and evil and continues to hear the voice of conscience in the midst of a collective state of possession and archetypal inflation.

The source of what we perceive as evil, then, is a mixture of psychological content (the shadow) and psychological dynamics that allow for, encourage, or require shadow enactments. This is different from saying that the shadow is evil per se. What is in the shadow may well, under certain conditions, be seen as good and useful for promoting human life and well-being. Sexuality and aggression are cases in point. Any archetypal image and any instinctual drive may yield evil action under psychological conditions of inflation and identification with primitive archetypal contents accompanied by social conditions of permission or secrecy. Used under other conditions and governed by more favorable attitudes, these same psychological contents and drives can yield benefit and goodness.

The question becomes, then, what inspires their deployment for evil? Is there something in the human psyche that can lead one consistently to choose evil over good?

In his reflections on Western religious history in *Aion* (*CW* 9/2), published in the aftermath of the Second World War in 1951, Jung interprets the history of Christianity with reference to the astrological sign of the Fishes. In this Platonic Year (the "aion" of Pisces), which has lasted for two thousand years, there has been an underlying theme of conflict between great opposing forces, which is symbolized in astrology by two fish swimming in opposite directions. As Jung delineates this history, he sees the conflict as raging between spirituality and materialism (spirit vs. body) and a parallel conflict between good and evil. These have been interwoven with the conflict between masculine (as spirit) and feminine (as materia) figures and values. So on the one side there is the line-up of spirituality, masculinity, and the good; on the other side there are materialism, femininity, and evil. The conflict between these two sides is graphically depicted in Biblical story and imagery, and it culminates in the great battles of the Book of Revelation. This same conflict has been lived out in history during the historical period of the Christian dispensation.

Now we are coming to the end of this era, we can look back and see how the dark side of the Lord of History has incarnated Himself and is continuing to do so. Materialism is the philosophy of the age, the feminine is returning in the form of the Goddess (Jung felt that the Roman Catholic doctrine of the Assumption of the Virgin, promulgated in 1952, signalled the return of the Goddess – see Chapter 10), and evil is rampant in world politics (totalitarian Communism and Fascism have dominated the present century). Toward the end of the Age of Pisces, especially, there is a strong movement from within the collective unconscious to realize and incarnate the shadow side of God, which contains these elements.

For Jung this movement toward the incarnation of God's darkness was to be seen as the most elemental source of the persistent lure to do that which consciousness judges to be evil. It is an irrational force beyond the will of the ego. The ego is drawn by the magnetism of God's need to incarnate His own dark destructiveness. This is the ultimate source of evil, its absolute home. It was this horrifying thought that inspired Jung to write 'Answer to Job' and to recognize, in *Aion* (1951), that "it is quite within the bounds of possibility for a man to recognize the relative evil of his nature, but it is a rare and shattering experience for him to gaze into the face of absolute evil" (para 19).

Doubtless there is a logical contradiction in Jung's wanting to say both that evil is adjectival and the product of conscious human judgment on the one hand, and that the persistent presence of evil in the world is due to God, who is trying to incarnate some part of His divine nature in time and space, on the other. To this challenge I am sure Jung would answer that evil is a paradox. Like the nature of light, if you look at it one way it appears to be a wave, something in the mind of the beholder; if you look at it the other way, it appears to be a particle, something emanating from the ontological ground of being. Both are true, and both are needed "in order to attain full paradoxicality and hence psychological validity" ('Alchemical studies', *CW* 2, para 256) and to give an adequate account of the phenomenon of evil.

WHAT IS THE RELATION BETWEEN GOOD AND EVIL?

What horrified Jung most was, by all accounts, irrevocable splitting. Perhaps this was rooted in his fear of madness (cf. Jung 1961: 170ff), or in his early childhood experience of strife between his mother and father. At times Jung fell victim of the dark fear that he might be so internally split that he could never find healing and would forever suffer from a psychic Amfortas wound. Whatever the personal motivation may have been, his whole psychology and psychotherapy were aimed at overcoming divisions and splits in the mind and at healing sundered psyches into operational wholes. Wholeness is the master concept of Jung's life and work, his personal myth.

Thus when it comes to discussing the relation of good and evil it is altogether consistent that Jung should oppose dualism at any cost. This was for him the worst possible way of conceiving of the relation of good and evil, to pit one against the other in eternal and irreconcilable hostility. At bottom good and evil must be united, both derivative from a single source and ultimately reconciled in and by that source. For Jung a dualistic theology would have been anathema, a dualistic psychology harmful.

Never one to shy away from using mythological or theological language, Jung would therefore strongly entertain the notion that good and evil both derive from God, that one represents God's right hand, so to speak, and the other His left. In the Biblical account of Job, Jung found confirmation of this view. Here Satan belongs to Yahweh's court. Jung sees him as Yahweh's own dark suspicious thought about his servant Job. In the New Testament, good and evil would become more harshly polarized in the images of Christ and Antichrist, but always Jung would refer Satan and Antichrist back to Lucifer, the light-bringer and the elder brother of Christ, both of them sons of Yahweh.

From the other angle of vision, both good and evil are products of conscious judgment. This is as true of good as it is of evil (cf. above). Moreover, at this level of consideration, good needs evil in order to exist at all. Each comes into being by contrast with the other. Without the judgment of evil there could be no judgment of good, and vice versa. Good and evil make up a pair of contrasting discriminations that is used by ego consciousness to differentiate experience. A complete conscious account of any situation or person must include some employment of this category of good-and-evil if it is to be a fully differentiated account.

Jung's insistence that one cannot have good without evil was a thorny point of contention between him and his theologically minded friends. Theologically educated students of Jung's psychology, such as the Dominican Father Victor White, would take strong exception to this view. For them it was not inconceivable to postulate the existence of absolute goodness without evil, since this is after all the standard Christian doctrine of God. Good does not require evil in order to subsist any more than light needs darkness in order to exist. But for Jung this was highly debatable. Pure light without any resistence or darkness could not be seen, and therefore it would not exist for human consciousness. Since he looked upon good and evil as judgments of ego consciousness, it would be impossible in his view for real persons to name such a thing as light or goodness if they had never experienced darkness or evil.

Because Jung was basing himself on a psychological view of evil – i.e. that it is a judgment of consciousness – there were endless misunderstandings with philosophers and theologians who wanted to think about the nature of evil in non-psychological terms. This could have been clarified easily enough if Jung had not also wanted to maintain the other end of the paradox about evil, that it is rooted in God's nature, in the nature of reality itself.

At this end of the discussion Jung would put forward a theory of opposites: psychic reality is made up of ordered patterns that can be spread out into spectra of polarities and tensions like good-to-evil and male-to-female. Without the energic tensions between the poles within entities like instinct groups and archetypes, there would be no movement of energy within the relatively closed system of mind/body wholeness. It is the tension within these polarities that yields dynamic movement, the fluctuations of libido in the psychic system. Jung argued that the same is true of the flow of energy in physical systems.

Evil within the psychological realm is equivalent to entropy in the physical realm: it is the tendency within a system to run down and to disintegrate, a flow of energy toward destruction. Good, by contrast, is equivalent to negentropy, the flow of energy in the opposite direction, toward building systems up into greater levels of integration and complexity. Both forces are at work in the psyche and in nature, and both are needed to produce the kind of reality we know in life and study in science. Like Whitehead, Jung saw reality as a process, an interplay of forces in a dynamic and constant stream of activity that build up and dissolve structures. Remove any force or tension in this process, and you have a different system and probably one that does not work as well or at all.

At this somewhat conspicuously metaphysical level of speculation, Jung would affirm that good and evil need each other in order for either one to exist at all. It is not here only a question of conscious discernment and judgment but a question of reality. Psychic and physical and spiritual life as we know them can best be described as constant flux, continuous transforma-tion and change, perpetual movement. Nothing stands still for very long. And this restlessness is generated by the tensions within and among opposites such as good and evil. Structures arise and dissolve in endless transformations, as the forces congealed in their organizations allow themselves to be contained for a time and then move on. This perception and conviction on Jung's part helps to account for his extraordinary fascination with alchemy and its account of the continuous transformation of elements.

HOW SHOULD HUMAN BEINGS DEAL WITH EVIL?

Jung was critical of moral crusaders, Albert Schweitzer being a case in point (cf. 'Flying saucers: a modern myth', *CW* 10, para. 783). He felt that people who become too identified with a particular cause or moral position inevitably fall into blindness regarding their own shadows. Would Schweitzer consider the shadow of his mission to the Africans? Jung was doubtful.

The first duty of the ethically-minded person is, from Jung's psychological perspective, to become as conscious as possible of his or her own shadow. The shadow is made up of the personality's tendencies, motives, and traits that a person considers shameful for one reason or another and seeks to suppress or actually represses unconsciously. If they are repressed, they are unconscious and are projected into others. When this happens, there is usually strong moral indignation and the groundwork is laid for a moral crusade. Filled with righteous indignation, persons can attack others for perceiving in them what is unconscious shadow in themselves, and a holy war ensues. This is worse than tilting at windmills, and it ends up being morally reprehensible in its own right.

A careful examination of conscience and of the personal unconscious is therefore the first requirement if one seeks seriously to do something about the problem of evil. This self-examination is itself an exercise in moral awareness. To see one's own shadow clearly and to admit its reality requires considerable moral strength in the individual. It also requires the prior attainment of moral consciousness, of the ego's ability to make moral discriminations. This is not a given. There are individuals who do not reach this level of development, and there are in each of us as well areas of unconsciousness that function in a similarly blind fashion when it comes to questions of good and evil. The capacity to make ethical judgments and the willingness to make them about oneself as well as others are prerequisites for further moral action.

Even leaving aside serious psychopathology, i.e. psychotic and debilitating neurotic conditions, the human being has a great capacity for self-deception and denial of shadow aspects. Even persons who are otherwise giants from a moral point of view can have gaping lacunae of character in certain areas. Religious and political leaders who become famous for their far-reaching moral vision and ethical sensitivity are often known to fall into the hole of acting out instinctual (for example, sexual) strivings and desires without much apparent awareness of the moral issues involved. Their acting-out may be conveniently compartmentalized and hidden away from their otherwise scrupulous moral awareness.

For the psychopath or sociopath Jung would recommend attempting to raise the level of conscious functioning to the moral level. Whether or not this is possible after a certain age has been attained or a certain level of commitment to a hardened counter-position has been made are open questions. It may well be the case that if moral conscience is not cultivated in the early years of development there is little likelihood that it will ever manifest in a fashion other than as compliance. Learning the language of moral discrimination may be a lot like learning other languages: after the age of thirteen or so it becomes increasingly difficult to learn them very well, and eventually for some it may be impossible altogether. One must begin moral education at an early age.

With respect to others who are more or less normally developed to a level of moral discrimination, further shadow realization is a matter of applying consciousness and discrimination to sectors of experience that have been walled off. These sectors generally have to do with the instinct clusters: eating, sexual behavior, addictions to activity, to reflection, or to creativity. Wherever human behavior becomes driven by unconscious needs, desires, or wishes, shadow gathers and usually remains unexamined. The missionary who destroys one culture in order to create another, the political prophet who cannot stay away from prostitutes, the feminist who suffers from an eating disorder are all familiar examples.

As a psychologist and a psychotherapist of individuals, Jung would begin addressing the practical question of what to do about evil by confronting the individual with his or her own shadow parts and areas of underdevelopment of consciousness. After this work has been started, the psychological task would become one of integrating the shadow. Integration is a term that refers to a process different from differentiation but not its opposite. Differentiation has to do with making distinctions and becoming conscious of differences, the differences between good and evil for example. Integration is a term that refers to the psychological act of ownership: that is myself! With respect to integration of the shadow, and of the evil that it contains, this means that the evil of which I was formerly unaware in myself (and probably found in someone else, a projection-carrier) I now can locate within. Moral awareness is brought to bear upon an area of attitude, thought, or behavior that had before lain in darkness.

Sometimes a whole culture will suddenly make a shift and begin looking in a new moral light at behavior that had easily passed as acceptable or harmless only a short time earlier. Sexual harassment in the work-place is one such area in recent times. The sexually explicit invitation or comment, the off-color joke or insinuation, the casual hug or pat are now suddenly regarded with a kind of moral awareness that would have been considered prudish or in bad taste only a few years ago. This is more than a change in taste and social personas: it is an expansion of moral consciousness into new territory. Suddenly the boss who grabs is not someone to be humored but someone to be prosecuted.

Obviously such moral discriminations as these can fall into the hands of unscrupulous individuals who will unethically take up a cause or make a charge for reasons of personal gain or advancement. The secretary who is about to be fired for incompetence and a poor work attitude cries foul on grounds of sexual harassment in order to forestall her unemployment. This does not mean that the advance in collective moral awareness is a mistake, but only that less morally developed individuals can always find a way to use situations to their own advantage.

Society cannot bear the full responsibility for moral consciousness or the lack of it, however. For Jung, the emphasis always returns to the individual. Rules and laws may be passed with the intention of legislating moral behavior and eradicating evil from the social system as far as possible, but moral education must still be aimed at the individual. For an unscrupulous individual can always use the system to evil ends. A good tool in the wrong hands is a dangerous weapon, was a concept often expressed by Jung.

Yet, too, from his experience with Nazi Germany, Jung would have to confront the shadow within the larger structures of society. The ways in which a society is set up, through its laws and customs, has a lot to do with how evil is handled and perceived within its precincts. "Moral man and immoral society," a concept of Reinhold Niebuhr's, would not have been foreign to Jung's consciousness after World War Two. Many scrupulous and well-intentioned individuals within the Third Reich ended up serving the

Devil by being good and obedient citizens. There is in Jung's work a strong appreciation of collective shadow as well as individual shadow.

Once the work of shadow awareness and integration has been to a large extent done by the individual, therefore, the work of confronting evil and dealing with it continues, but in the wider area of society and politics. Jung was not a quietist about evil in the larger world, in politics, in economics, or on the stage of world affairs. Perhaps his Swiss up-bringing and citizenship played a role in moving him toward a position of neutrality with regard to intervening in other people's affairs, but Jung was no pacifist with regard to confronting the evils of totalitarianism. He feared, perhaps wrongly, Communism more than Fascism in the Europe of the 1930s, and his anti-Communist and anti-Stalinist feelings were strong and often stated. He felt deeply that fanatical ideologies of any sort were demonic because they depended for their existence upon identification with archetypal images and upon grandiose inflations, which crippled individual accountability and destroyed moral consciousness. Such ideologies should therefore be confronted by psychological interpretation, which would have the benefit, if successful, of restoring consciousness to its proper human dimensions. The ideologue depends on drawing archetypal projections to himself from the populace, which in turn robs the populace of its authority and certainly robs individuals of their integrity as ethical human beings.

In principle, then, Jung would advocate a form of political activism that would bring psychological interpretation to bear upon collective human affairs. This would be to carry a version of psychotherapy out of the clinical setting into the world.

Jung himself began this kind of work, applying his psychological theory and hermeneutic to history and Western culture, in the last several decades of his life. He became, in effect, the psychotherapist of Christianity in his voluminous writings on its history, theology, and symbols (cf. Stein 1985), and in his other numerous writings about culture, art, and modernity he addressed the ills of the age. In this fashion he was engaging the issue of evil in the world at large. Many of the selections in this volume attest to this preoccupation of his and provide a clue for ways to develop this line of thought and action further.

Because of his view of the inevitable presence of shadow in human affairs, Jung could in the final analysis by no means be considered a utopian or a social idealist. "Every bowl of soup has a hair in it," was a favorite Swiss aphorism of his. Reality, God, as well as the human individual have shadow wrapped tightly into the warp and woof of their very being, and there is no means to remove it surgically. While it is important for consciousness to throw its weight on the side of good, of life, of growth and integration, it must be recognized that this is a struggle without hope for final victory. For victory would be stasis and so would spell defeat anyway from the point of view of evolution. The evolution of reality depends upon the dynamic interplay of forces that we call good and evil, and where the evolution of consciousness and spirit is finally headed is still beyond our knowledge. The best we can do is to participate in this unfolding with the greatest possible extent of consciousness. Beyond that we must reconcile ourselves to leaving the outcome up to the Power that is greater than ourselves.

REFERENCES

Jung, C.G. (1953–83) *The Collected Works of C.G. Jung*, edited by H. Read, M. Fordham and G. Adler, translated by R.F.C. Hull, London: Routledge, and Princeton: Princeton University Press.
—— (1975) *Letters*, Vol. 2, Princeton: Princeton University Press.
—— (1977) *C.G. Jung Speaking*, Princeton: Princeton University Press.
McGuire, W. (ed.) (1974) *The Freud–Jung letters*, Princeton: Princeton University Press.
Stein, M. (1985) *Jung's Treatment of Christianity*, Wilmette, Il.: Chiron Publications.

Selections for *Jung on Evil* (in the order presented):

1 A letter to Freud (from *The Freud/Jung Letters*: 293–4, letter 178J)

In this letter we see Jung at the age of thirty-five grappling with the implications of psychoanalysis for ethics, for religion, and for culture generally. Clearly he saw it as transformative, and while he betrays a rather unsure grasp of its full implications, he is convinced that the future of Western civilization can be, and most likely will be, greatly affected by it. Just how psychoanalysis and its release of unconscious energy and symbolism should be related to the present structures of society and culture remains unclear to him at this point. Still he is brimming over with enthusiasm and confidence and encourages Freud to lose his timidity.

2 Introduction to the religious and psychological problems of alchemy (from *CW* 12, paras 22–43)

Constantly in search of historical parallels to the relation of psychoanalysis to contemporary culture, Jung came upon such heresies as Gnosticism and alchemy. He became particularly fascinated by alchemy, not as a chapter in the history of science but as a point of contrast to the spiritual and moral consensus of the religious traditions of the West. He viewed alchemy as an expression of the collective unconscious of the Christian culture in which it sprang up, compensating the conscious consensus and providing access to the unconscious for its practitioners. The materials of Gnosticism and alchemy provide, in his view, an alternative way of understanding the nature of evil and its relation to the good. In this section from his important work 'Psychology and alchemy' he writes of the intimate connections between good and evil in the self, where "good and evil are indeed closer than identical twins"(para. 24) These passages, it should be noted, were written in Switzerland in the early 1940s, during the frightening early years of World War Two.

3 The spirit Mercurius (from *CW* 13, paras 247–72)

In this little gem of an essay, first presented as two lectures at the Eranos Conference, Ascona, Switzerland in 1942, Jung investigates the alchemical literature to discover the essence of what these early "depth psychologists" had to say about the nature of the unconscious. Mercurius was the guiding spirit of alchemy and, for Jung, represented the spirit of the unconscious itself. If it could be shown that Mercurius was not evil, it would mean that the unconscious did not embody the *spiritus maleficus*. Jung argues here that the unconscious can be exceedingly dangerous but is not in itself evil.

4 The problem of the fourth (from *CW* 11, paras 243–85)

This excerpt from Jung's great essay, "A psychological approach to the dogma of the trinity," places the discussion of evil within the context of classical Christian theology. Here we see Jung attempting to bring his understanding of the human psyche and especially of the unconscious into relationship with the dominant God image of the Christian period. What Jung argues against is a position that would radically split evil off from good and consign it to non-existence, a position that from the psychological viewpoint amounts to denial, a form of ego defense. What he wants to argue for is the inclusion of evil within the image of God, so as to keep evil in relation to good and to relate the God concept more fully to reality.

5 Two letters to Father Victor White (from *C.J. Jung: Letters Vol. 2*: 58–61, 163–74)

The extensive correspondence between Jung and Fr Victor White revolved largely around questions of the relation between psychology and theology. The subject of evil was a frequent topic. With Fr White Jung felt free to express himself strongly and emotionally, and his objections to the doctrine of evil as privatio boni (the absence of good) are especially vivid. Fr White, whose side of the correspondence has never been published, objected to Jung's understanding of the doctrine, but to little avail. Jung was intent on making the point that evil is real and not something to be denied. In these letters we see him struggling to explain himself to a psychologically-minded theologian who was favorably disposed to his views but could not agree with his critique of Christian doctrine.

6 Good and evil in analytical psychology (from *CW* 10, paras 858–86)

In this delightful little work, which was composed of extemporaneous comments Jung made very late in life to a group of visiting German doctors, we see the aged sage of Zurich expressing some of his pithiest comments on the subject of evil. Full of humor and wit, these remarks indicate an amazing humility in the face of such vast questions as: what is good? what is evil? After a lifetime of reflection on the subject of evil, he shows here his keen awareness of the ambiguity involved in making moral judgments and yet his grasp, too, that such judgments must be made.

7 The shadow (from *CW* 9/2, paras 13–19)

In this brief chapter from his late work, 'Aion', published in 1951 but written some years earlier (1948) for an Austrian medical journal, Jung explains in simple terms his concept of the shadow. The psychological confrontation with the shadow is "a moral problem that challenges the whole ego-personality," he writes. Recognition of the shadow means not only seeing one's own moral faults, however, but also discovering all the ways in which one creates one's own messy fate and destiny. Shadow integration is equivalent to taking responsibility for one's own life.

8 North Africa (from *Memories, Dreams, Reflections*: 238–46)

In this account of his trip to Tunisia in 1920 with a friend, Jung tells of a personal encounter with the shadow. In the Sahara, this cultivated European psychiatrist met up with an aspect of his own human nature that he did not know. His dreams and reflections upon this experience taught him a great deal about the nature of the self. Shadow projections take place between societies and peoples as well as between individuals, and what gets labelled inferior and even evil may be precisely the lost parts of one's own wholeness. This penchant of humans to project the shadow must teach caution in making judgments about evil too quickly and simplistically.

9 A psychological view of conscience (from *CW* 10, paras 825–57)

When it comes to judging right and wrong, conscience is an essential psychological factor. One cannot always consult written codes or take time for elaborate reflection and debate. Conscience is an immediate response, a gut reaction, that tells one what to do or not to do. In this essay, Jung investigates the phenomenon of conscience by citing case material, dreams, Freud's theory of the superego, and his own subjective experience. He relates conscience to a collision between ego consciousness and an archetype, which speaks for the collective patterns, the mores. Ethical behavior, by contrast, he says, depends on conscious reflection, and a true ethical act involves the whole person, conscious as well as unconscious aspects. Conscience in itself is an autonomous function of the psyche and is probably strongly related to the innate function of consciousness to make discriminations about reality. This essay was written late in Jung's life and is one of the last major works he produced.

10 Answer to Job (from *CW* 11, paras 553–608, 628–42, 649–82, 688–717, 736–47)

This is one of Jung's most controversial works. It was the straw that broke the camel's back in his relationship with Victor White, whose review of it was scorching. It was composed at fever pitch during Jung's recovery from his second heart attack, and in it he holds nothing of his emotionality in reserve. Here we see Jung at his most impassioned grappling with the Biblical image of God and with the religious tradition that formed his personal life and his culture. Personal elements and interpretations aside, however, this is also Jung's most sustained single engagement with the problem of evil as a cultural and historical phenomenon. Some people have argued that this work lays the groundwork for the next stage in the evolution of Western religion and spirituality. At any rate, it is an extremely fascinating and stimulating work and one that deserves the most careful reading.

11 The fight with the shadow (from *CW* 10, paras 444–57)

In this essay, presented originally as a broadcast on the BBC in November 1946, Jung shows a keen awareness of the evil that was set loose in Nazi Germany. Here Jung is explaining, from a psychological viewpoint, what happened in the war years, and he is also appealing for everyone in the post-war period to become conscious of their own shadows. "The world will never reach a state of order until this truth [i.e. the existence of the shadow] is realized" (para. 455), he states without qualification. To struggle with the shadow is to struggle with one's own participation in evil.

12 After the catastrophe (from *CW* 10, paras 400–43)

This essay was published in 1945 in a Swiss magazine, just as the war's devastation was being fully realized by the world at large and the horror of Nazi atrocities was piling up for all to see. Here was massive and blatant evil staring the modern European in the face. Questions of collective guilt were in the air, and even the Swiss, neutral though they were in the war, felt tinges of anxiety about their possible conscious and unconscious complicity. Now Jung looks back over his own earlier views of what was brewing in Germany and at the psychopathological character, Hitler, who led the German people into this quagmire of evil and destruction, and he tries to understand. Again, his recommendation is to "open our eyes to the shadow who looms behind contemporary man" (para. 440), a cry for self-awareness and more accurate judgment of the evil within and around all of us.

1   A letter to Freud

From: The Freud/Jung Letters (293–4, letter 178J)

Dear Professor Freud,   Küsnach-Zürich, 11 February 1910[1]

I am a lazy correspondent. But this time I have (as always) excellent excuses. Preparing the *Jahrbuch* has taken me an incredible amount of time, as I had to work mightily with the blue pencil. The bulk of the manuscripts goes off today. It will be an impressive affair.

Enclosed is the list of addresses. Please let me know if I have forgotten anyone from abroad. You will see that I am setting about it on a rather large scale – I hope with your subsequent approval. Our cause is forging ahead. Only today I heard from a doctor in Munich that the medical students there are taking a massive interest in the new psychology, some of them poking fun at the gentlemen at the Clinic because they understand nothing about it.

Meanwhile I too have received an invitation from the apothecary Knapp in Bern to join the I.F.[2] I have asked for time to think about it and have promised to submit the invitation to the Nuremberg Congress. Knapp wanted to have me also for lectures. The prospect appals me. I am so thoroughly convinced that I would have to read myself the longest ethical lectures that I cannot muster a grain of courage to promote ethics in public, let alone from the psychoanalytical standpoint! At present I am sitting so precariously on the fence between the Dionysian and the Apollinian that I wonder whether it might not be worthwhile to reintroduce a few of the older cultural stupidities such as the monasteries. That is, I really don't know which is the lesser evil. Do you think this Fraternity could have any practical use? Isn't it one of Forel's coalitions against stupidity and evil, and must we not love evil if we are to break away from the obsession with virtue that makes us sick and forbids us the joys of life? If a coalition is to have any ethical significance it should never be an artificial one but must be nourished by the deep instincts of the race. Somewhat like Christian Science, Islam, Buddhism. Religion can be replaced only by religion. Is there perchance a new saviour in the I.F.? What sort of new myth does it hand out for us to live by? Only the wise are ethical from sheer intellectual presumption, the rest of us need the eternal truth of myth.

You will see from this string of associations that the problem does not leave me simply apathetic and cold. The ethical problem of sexual freedom really is enormous and worth the sweat of all noble souls.[3] But 2000 years of Christianity can only be replaced by something equivalent. An ethical fraternity, with its mythical Nothing, not infused by any archaic-infantile driving force, is a pure vacuum and can never evoke in man the slightest trace of that age-old animal power which drives the migrating bird across the sea and without which no irresistible mass movement can come into being. I imagine a far finer and more comprehensive task for ΨA than alliance with an ethical fraternity. I think we must give it time to infiltrate into people from many centres, to revivify among intellectuals a feeling for symbol and myth, ever so gently to transform Christ back into the soothsaying god of the vine, which he was, and in this way absorb those ecstatic instinctual forces of Christianity for the *one* purpose of making the cult and the sacred myth what they once were – a drunken feast of joy where man regained the ethos and holiness of an animal. That was the beauty and purpose of classical religion, which from God knows what temporary biological needs has turned into a Misery Institute. Yet what infinite rapture and wantonness lie dormant in our religion, waiting to be led back to their true destination! A genuine and proper ethical development cannot abandon Christianity but must grow up within it, must bring to fruition its hymn of love, the agony and ecstasy over the dying and resurgent god,[4] the mystic power of the wine, the awesome anthropophagy of the Last Supper – only *this* ethical development can serve the vital forces of religion. But a syndicate of interests dies out after 10 years.[5]

ΨA makes me "proud and discontent,"[6] I don't want to attach it to Forel, that hair-shirted John of the Locusts, but would like to affiliate it with everything that was ever dynamic and alive. One can only let this kind of thing grow. To be practical: I shall submit this crucial question for ΨA to the Nuremberg Congress. I have abreacted enough for today – my heart was bursting with it. Please don't mind all this storming.

With many kind regards,

Most sincerely yours, JUNG

NOTES

1 Published in *Letters*, ed. G. Adler, vol. 1.
2 Holograph: *I.O.* = Knapp's Internationaler Orden für Ethik und Kultur.
3 See above, 51 J n. 2.
4 A reference to Dionysus-Zagreus; cf. *Symbols of Transformation*, CW 5, para. 527. (Also in 1911/12 edn.)
5 For a 1959 comment, see *Letters*, ed. G. Adler, vol. 1, p. 19, n. 8.
6 Holograph: *stolz und unzufrieden* – Goethe, *Faust* I, 2178.

2 Introduction to the religious and psychological problems of alchemy

From: 'Introduction to the religious and psychological problems of alchemy' (from *CW* 12, paras 22–43)

22   The Christ-symbol is of the greatest importance for psychology in so far as it is perhaps the most highly developed and differentiated symbol of the self, apart from the figure of Buddha. We can see this from the scope and substance of all the pronouncements that have been made about Christ: they agree with the psychological phenomenology of the self in unusually high degree, although they do not include all aspects of this archetype. The almost limitless range of the self might be deemed a disadvantage as compared with the definiteness of a religious figure, but it is by no means the task of science to pass value judgments. Not only is the self indefinite but – paradoxically enough – it also includes the quality of definiteness and even of uniqueness. This is probably one of the reasons why precisely those religions founded by historical personages have become world religions, such as Christianity, Buddhism, and Islam. The inclusion in a religion of a unique human personality – especially when conjoined to an indeterminable divine nature – is consistent with the absolute individuality of the self, which combines uniqueness with eternity and the individual with the universal. The self is a union of opposites *par excellence*, and this is where it differs essentially from the Christ-symbol. The androgyny of Christ is the utmost concession the Church has made to the problem of opposites. The opposition between light and good on the one hand and darkness and evil on the other is left in a state of open conflict, since Christ simply represents good, and his counterpart the devil, evil. This opposition is the real world problem, which at present is still unsolved. The self, however, is absolutely paradoxical in that it represents in every respect thesis and antithesis, and at the same time synthesis. (Psychological proofs of this assertion abound, though it is impossible for me to quote them here *in extenso.* I would refer the knowledgeable reader to the symbolism of the mandala.)

23   Once the exploration of the unconscious has led the conscious mind to an experience of the archetype, the individual is confronted with the abysmal contradictions of human nature, and this confrontation in turn leads to the possibility of a direct experience of light and darkness, of Christ and the devil. For better or worse there is only a bare possibility of

this, and not a guarantee; for experiences of this kind cannot of necessity be induced by any human means. There are factors to be considered which are not under our control. Experience of the opposites has nothing whatever to do with intellectual insight or with empathy. It is more what we would call fate. Such an experience can convince one person of the truth of Christ, another of the truth of the Buddha, to the exclusion of all other evidence.

24   Without the experience of the opposites there is no experience of wholeness and hence no inner approach to the sacred figures. For this reason Christianity rightly insists on sinfulness and original sin, with the obvious intent of opening up the abyss of universal opposition in every individual – at least from the outside. But this method is bound to break down in the case of a moderately alert intellect: dogma is then simply no longer believed and on top of that is thought absurd. Such an intellect is merely one-sided and sticks at the *ineptia mysterii*. It is miles from Tertullian's antinomies; in fact, it is quite incapable of enduring the suffering such a tension involves. Cases are not unknown where the rigorous exercises and proselytizings of the Catholics, and a certain type of Protestant education that is always sniffing out sin, have brought about psychic damage that leads not to the Kingdom of Heaven but to the consulting room of the doctor. Although insight into the problem of opposites is absolutely imperative, there are very few people who can stand it in practice – a fact which has not escaped the notice of the confessional. By way of a reaction to this we have the palliative of "moral probabilism," a doctrine that has suffered frequent attack from all quarters because it tries to mitigate the crushing effect of sin.[1] Whatever one may think of this phenomenon one thing is certain: that apart from anything else it holds within it a large humanity and an understanding of human weakness which compensate for the world's unbearable antinomies. The tremendous paradox implicit in the insistence on original sin on the one hand and the concession made by probabilism on the other is, for the psychologist, a necessary consequence of the Christian problem of opposites outlined above – for in the self good and evil are indeed closer than identical twins! The reality of evil and its incompatibility with good cleave the opposites asunder and lead inexorably to the crucifixion and suspension of everything that lives. Since "the soul is by nature Christian" this result is bound to come as infallibly as it did in the life of Jesus: we all have to be "crucified with Christ," i.e. suspended in a moral suffering equivalent to veritable crucifixion. In practice this is only possible up to a point, and apart from that is so unbearable and inimical to life that the ordinary human being can afford to get into such a state only occasionally, in fact as seldom as possible. For how could he remain ordinary in face of such suffering! A more or less probabilistic attitude to the problem of evil is therefore unavoidable. Hence the truth about the self – the unfathomable union of good and evil – comes out concretely in the paradox that although

sin is the gravest and most pernicious thing there is, it is still not so serious that it cannot be disposed of with "probabilist" arguments. Nor is this necessarily a lax or frivolous proceeding but simply a practical necessity of life. The confessional proceeds like life itself, which successfully struggles against being engulfed in an irreconcilable contradiction. Note that at the same time the conflict remains in full force, as is once more consistent with the antinomial character of the self, which is itself both conflict and unity.

25   Christianity has made the antinomy of good and evil into a world problem and, by formulating the conflict dogmatically, raised it to an absolute principle. Into this as yet unresolved conflict the Christian is cast as a protagonist of good, a fellow player in the world drama. Understood in its deepest sense, being Christ's follower involves a suffering that is unendurable to the great majority of mankind. Consequently the example of Christ is in reality followed either with reservation or not at all, and the pastoral practice of the Church even finds itself obliged to "lighten the yoke of Christ." This means a pretty considerable reduction in the severity and harshness of the conflict and hence, in practice, a relativism of good and evil. Good is equivalent to the unconditional imitation of Christ and evil is its hindrance. Man's moral weakness and sloth are what chiefly hinder the imitation, and it is to these that probabilism extends a practical understanding which may sometimes, perhaps, come nearer to Christian tolerance, mildness, and love of one's neighbour than the attitude of those who see in probabilism a mere laxity. Although one must concede a number of cardinal Christian virtues to the probabilist endeavour, one must still not overlook the fact that it obviates much of the suffering involved in the imitation of Christ and that the conflict of good and evil is thus robbed of its harshness and toned down to tolerable proportions. This brings about an approach to the psychic archetype of the self, where even these opposites seem to be united – though, as I say, it differs from the Christian symbolism, which leaves the conflict open. For the latter there is a rift running through the world: light wars against night and the upper against the lower. The two are not one, as they are in the psychic archetype. But, even though religious dogma may condemn the idea of two being one, religious practice does, as we have seen, allow the natural psychological symbol of the self at one with itself an approximate means of expression. On the other hand, dogma insists that three are one, while denying that four are one. Since olden times, not only in the West but also in China, uneven numbers have been regarded as masculine and even numbers as feminine. The Trinity is therefore a decidedly masculine deity, of which the androgyny of Christ and the special position and veneration accorded to the Mother of God are not the real equivalent.

26   With this statement, which may strike the reader as peculiar, we come to one of the central axioms of alchemy, namely the saying of Maria Prophetissa: "One becomes two, two becomes three, and out of the third

comes the one as the fourth." As the reader has already seen from its title, this book is concerned with the psychological significance of alchemy and thus with a problem which, with very few exceptions, has so far eluded scientific research. Until quite recently science was interested only in the part that alchemy played in the history of chemistry, concerning itself very little with the part it played in the history of philosophy and religion. The importance of alchemy for the historical development of chemistry is obvious, but its cultural importance is still so little known that it seems almost impossible to say in a few words wherein that consisted. In this introduction, therefore, I have attempted to outline the religious and psychological problems which are germane to the theme of alchemy. The point is that alchemy is rather like an undercurrent to the Christianity that ruled on the surface. It is to this surface as the dream is to consciousness, and just as the dream compensates the conflicts of the conscious mind, so alchemy endeavours to fill in the gaps left open by the Christian tension of opposites. Perhaps the most pregnant expression of this is the axiom of Maria Prophetissa quoted above, which runs like a *leitmotiv* throughout almost the whole of the lifetime of alchemy, extending over more than seventeen centuries. In this aphorism the even numbers which signify the feminine principle, earth, the regions under the earth, and evil itself are interpolated between the uneven numbers of the Christian dogma. They are personified by the *serpens mercurii*, the dragon that creates and destroys itself and represents the *prima materia*. This fundamental idea of alchemy points back to the תְּהוֹם (Tehom),[2] to Tiamat with her dragon attribute, and thus to the primordial matriarchal world which, in the theomachy of the Marduk myth,[3] was overthrown by the masculine world of the father. The historical shift in the world's consciousness towards the masculine is compensated at first by the chthonic femininity of the unconscious. In certain pre-Christian religions the differentiation of the masculine principle had taken the form of the father–son specification, a change which was to be of the utmost importance for Christianity. Were the unconscious merely complementary, this shift of consciousness would have been accompanied by the production of a mother and daughter, for which the necessary material lay ready to hand in the myth of Demeter and Persephone. But, as alchemy shows, the unconscious chose rather the Cybele-Attis type in the form of the *prima materia* and the *filius macrocosmi*, thus proving that it is not complementary but compensatory. This goes to show that the unconscious does not simply act *contrary* to the conscious mind but *modifies* it more in the manner of an opponent or partner. The son type does not call up a daughter as a complementary image from the depths of the "chthonic" unconscious – it calls up another son. This remarkable fact would seem to be connected with the incarnation in our earthly human nature of a purely spiritual God, brought about by the Holy Ghost impregnating the womb of the Blessed Virgin. Thus the higher, the spiritual, the masculine inclines to the lower, the earthly, the feminine; and accordingly, the mother, who was anterior to the world of the father, accommodates herself to the masculine principle and, with the aid of the human spirit (alchemy or "the philosophy"), produces a son – not the antithesis of Christ but rather his chthonic counterpart, not a divine man but a fabulous being conforming to the nature of the primordial mother. And just as the redemption of man the microcosm is the task of the "upper" son, so the "lower" son has the function of a *salvator macrocosmi*.

27   This, in brief, is the drama that was played out in the obscurities of alchemy. It is superfluous to remark that these two sons were never united, except perhaps in the mind and innermost experience of a few particularly gifted alchemists. But it is not very difficult to see the "purpose" of this drama: in the Incarnation it looked as though the masculine principle of the father-world were approximating to the feminine principle of the mother-world, with the result that the latter felt impelled to approximate in turn to the father-world. What it evidently amounted to was an attempt to bridge the gulf separating the two worlds as compensation for the open conflict between them.

28   I hope the reader will not be offended if my exposition sounds like a Gnostic myth. We are moving in those psychological regions where, as a matter of fact, Gnosis is rooted. The message of the Christian symbol is Gnosis, and the compensation effected by the unconscious is Gnosis in even higher degree. Myth is the primordial language natural to these psychic processes, and no intellectual formulation comes anywhere near the richness and expressiveness of mythical imagery. Such processes are concerned with the primordial images, and these are best and most succinctly reproduced by figurative language.

29   The process described above displays all the characteristic features of psychological compensation. We know that the mask of the unconscious is not rigid – it reflects the face we turn towards it. Hostility lends it a threatening aspect, friendliness softens its features. It is not a question of mere optical reflection but of an autonomous answer which reveals the self-sufficing nature of that which answers. Thus the *filius philosophorum* is not just the reflected image, in unsuitable material, of the son of God; on the contrary, this son of Tiamat reflects the features of the primordial maternal figure. Although he is decidedly hermaphroditic he has a masculine name – a sign that the chthonic underworld, having been rejected by the spirit and identified with evil, has a tendency to compromise. There is no mistaking the fact that he is a concession to the spiritual and masculine principle, even though he carries in himself the weight of the earth and the whole fabulous nature of primordial animality.

30   This answer of the mother-world shows that the gulf between it and the father-world is not unbridgeable, seeing that the unconscious holds the seed of the unity of both. The essence of the conscious mind is discrimination; it must, if it is to be aware of things, separate the opposites,

and it does this *contra naturam*. In nature the opposites seek one another –
les extrêmes se touchent – and so it is in the unconscious, and particularly
in the archetype of unity, the self. Here, as in the deity, the opposites cancel
out. But as soon as the unconscious begins to manifest itself they split
asunder, as at the Creation; for every act of dawning consciousness is a
creative act, and it is from this psychological experience that all our
cosmogonic symbols are derived.

31   Alchemy is pre-eminently concerned with the seed of unity which lies
hidden in the chaos of Tiamat and forms the counterpart to the divine unity.
Like this, the seed of unity has a trinitarian character in Christian alchemy
and a triadic character in pagan alchemy. According to other authorities it
corresponds to the unity of the four elements and is therefore a quaternity.
The overwhelming majority of modern psychological findings speaks in
favour of the latter view. The few cases I have observed which produced
the number three were marked by a systematic deficiency in consciousness,
that is to say, by an unconsciousness of the "inferior function." The
number three is not a natural expression of wholeness, since four represents the minimum number of determinants in a whole judgment. It must
nevertheless be stressed that side by side with the distinct leanings of
alchemy (and of the unconscious) towards quaternity there is always a
vacillation between three and four which comes out over and over again.
Even in the axiom of Maria Prophetissa the quaternity is muffled and
alembicated. In alchemy there are three as well as four *regimina* or
procedures, three as well as four colours. There are always four elements,
but often three of them are grouped together, with the fourth in a special
position – sometimes earth, sometimes fire. Mercurius[4] is of course
quadratus, but he is also a three-headed snake or simply a triunity. This
uncertainty has a duplex character – in other words, the central ideas are
ternary as well as quaternary. The psychologist cannot but mention the
fact that a similar puzzle exists in the psychology of the unconscious: the
least differentiated or "inferior" function is so much contaminated with
the collective unconscious that, on becoming conscious, it brings up
among others the archetype of the self as well – τὸ ἕν τέταρτον, as Maria
Prophetissa says. Four signifies the feminine, motherly, physical; three the
masculine, fatherly, spiritual. Thus the uncertainty as to three or four
amounts to a wavering between the spiritual and the physical – a striking
example of how every human truth is a last truth but one.

32   I began my introduction with human wholeness as the goal to which the
psychotherapeutic process ultimately leads. This question is inextricably
bound up with one's philosophical or religious assumptions. Even when,
as frequently happens, the patient believes himself to be quite un-
prejudiced in this respect, the assumptions underlying his thought, mode
of life, morale, and language are historically conditioned down to the last
detail, a fact of which he is often kept unconscious by lack of education
combined with lack of self-criticism. The analysis of his situation will

therefore lead sooner or later to a clarification of his general spiritual background going far beyond his personal determinants, and this brings up the problems I have attempted to sketch in the preceding pages. This phase of the process is marked by the production of symbols of unity, the so-called mandalas, which occur either in dreams or in the form of concrete visual impressions, often as the most obvious compensation of the contradictions and conflicts of the conscious situation. It would hardly be correct to say that the gaping "rift"[5] in the Christian order of things is responsible for this, since it is easy to show that Christian symbolism is particularly concerned with healing, or attempting to heal, this very wound. It would be more correct to take the open conflict as a symptom of the psychic situation of Western man, and to deplore his inability to assimilate the whole range of the Christian symbol. As a doctor I cannot demand anything of my patients in this respect, also I lack the Church's means of grace. Consequently I am faced with the task of taking the only path open to me: the archetypal images – which in a certain sense correspond to the dogmatic images – must be brought into consciousness. At the same time I must leave my patient to decide in accordance with his assumptions, his spiritual maturity, his education, origins, and temperament, so far as this is possible without serious conflicts. As a doctor it is my task to help the patient to cope with life. I cannot presume to pass judgment on his final decisions, because I know from experience that all coercion – be it suggestion, insinuation, or any other method of persuasion – ultimately proves to be nothing but an obstacle to the highest and most decisive experience of all, which is to be alone with his own self, or whatever else one chooses to call the objectivity of the psyche. The patient must be alone if he is to find out what it is that supports him when he can no longer support himself. Only this experience can give him an indestructible foundation.

33   I would be only too delighted to leave this anything but easy task to the theologian, were it not that it is just from the theologian that many of my patients come. They ought to have hung on to the community of the Church, but they were shed like dry leaves from the great tree and now find themselves "hanging on" to the treatment. Something in them clings, often with the strength of despair, as if they or the thing they cling to would drop off into the void the moment they relaxed their hold. They are seeking firm ground on which to stand. Since no outward support is of any use to them they must finally discover it in themselves – admittedly the most unlikely place from the rational point of view, but an altogether possible one from the point of view of the unconscious. We can see this from the archetype of the "lowly origin of the redeemer."

34   The way to the goal seems chaotic and interminable at first, and only gradually do the signs increase that it is leading anywhere. The way is not straight but appears to go round in circles. More accurate knowledge has proved it to go in spirals: the dream-motifs always return after certain

intervals to definite forms, whose characteristic it is to define a centre. And as a matter of fact the whole process revolves about a central point or some arrangement round a centre, which may in certain circumstances appear even in the initial dreams. As manifestations of unconscious processes the dreams rotate or circumambulate round the centre, drawing closer to it as the amplifications increase in distinctness and in scope. Owing to the diversity of the symbolical material it is difficult at first to perceive any kind of order at all. Nor should it be taken for granted that dream sequences are subject to any governing principle. But, as I say, the process of development proves on closer inspection to be cyclic or spiral. We might draw a parallel between such spiral courses and the processes of growth in plants; in fact the plant motif (tree, flower, etc.) frequently recurs in these dreams and fantasies and is also spontaneously drawn or painted.[6] In alchemy the tree is the symbol of Hermetic philosophy.

35   The first of the following two studies – that which composes Part II – deals with a series of dreams which contain numerous symbols of the centre or goal. The development of these symbols is almost the equivalent of a healing process. The centre or goal thus signifies *salvation* in the proper sense of the word. The justification for such a terminology comes from the dreams themselves, for these contain so many references to religious phenomena that I was able to use some of them as the subject of my book *Psychology and Religion*. It seems to me beyond all doubt that these processes are concerned with the religion-creating archetypes. Whatever else religion may be, those psychic ingredients of it which are empirically verifiable undoubtedly consist of unconscious manifestations of this kind. People have dwelt far too long on the fundamentally sterile question of whether the assertions of faith are true or not. Quite apart from the impossibility of ever proving or refuting the truth of a metaphysical assertion, the very existence of the assertion is a self-evident fact that needs no further proof, and when a *consensus gentium* allies itself thereto the validity of the statement is proved to just that extent. The only thing about it that we can verify is the psychological phenomenon, which is incommensurable with the category of objective rightness or truth. No phenomenon can ever be disposed of by rational criticism, and in religious life we have to deal with phenomena and facts and not with arguable hypotheses.

36   During the process of treatment the dialectical discussion leads logically to a meeting between the patient and his shadow, that dark half of the psyche which we invariably get rid of by means of projection: either by burdening our neighbours – in a wider or narrower sense – with all the faults which we obviously have ourselves, or by casting our sins upon a divine mediator with the aid of *contritio* or the milder *attritio*.[7] We know of course that without sin there is no repentance and without repentance no redeeming grace, also that without original sin the redemption of the world could never have come about; but we assiduously avoid investig-

ating whether in this very power of evil God might not have placed some special purpose which it is most important for us to know. One often feels driven to some such view when, like the psychotherapist, one has to deal with people who are confronted with their blackest shadow.[8] At any rate the doctor cannot afford to point, with a gesture of facile moral superiority, to the tablets of the law and say, "Thou shalt not." He has to examine things objectively and weigh up possibilities, for he knows, less from religious training and education than from instinct and experience, that there is something very like a *felix culpa*. He knows that one can miss not only one's happiness but also one's final guilt, without which a man will never reach his wholeness. Wholeness is in fact a charisma which one can manufacture neither by art nor by cunning; one can only grow into it and endure whatever its advent may bring. No doubt it is a great nuisance that mankind is not uniform but compounded of individuals whose psychic structure spreads them over a span of at least ten thousand years. Hence there is absolutely no truth that does not spell salvation to one person and damnation to another. All universalisms get stuck in this terrible dilemma. Earlier on I spoke of Jesuit probabilism: this gives a better idea than anything else of the tremendous catholic task of the Church. Even the best-intentioned people have been horrified by probabilism, but, when brought face to face with the realities of life, many of them have found their horror evaporating or their laughter dying on their lips. The doctor too must weigh and ponder, not whether a thing is for or against the Church but whether it is for or against life and health. On paper the moral code looks clear and neat enough; but the same document written on the "living tables of the heart" is often a sorry tatter, particularly in the mouths of those who talk the loudest. We are told on every side that evil is evil and that there can be no hesitation in condemning it, but that does not prevent evil from being the most problematical thing in the individual's life and the one which demands the deepest reflection. What above all deserves our keenest attention is the question "Exactly *who* is the doer?" For the answer to this question ultimately decides the value of the deed. It is true that society attaches greater importance at first to what is done, because it is immediately obvious; but in the long run the right deed in the hands of the wrong man will also have a disastrous effect. No one who is far-sighted will allow himself to be hoodwinked by the right deed of the wrong man, any more than by the wrong deed of the right man. Hence the psychotherapist must fix his eye not on what is done but on how it is done, because therein is decided the whole character of the doer. Evil needs to be pondered just as much as good, for good and evil are ultimately nothing but ideal extensions and abstractions of doing, and both belong to the chiaroscuro of life. In the last resort there is no good that cannot produce evil and no evil that cannot produce good.

37   The encounter with the dark half of the personality, or "shadow," comes about of its own accord in any moderately thorough treatment. This

problem is as important as that of sin in the Church. The open conflict is unavoidable and painful. I have often been asked, "And what do you *do* about it?" I do nothing; there is nothing I can do except wait, with a certain trust in God, until, out of a conflict borne with patience and fortitude, there emerges the solution destined – although I cannot foresee it – for that particular person. Not that I am passive or inactive meanwhile: I help the patient to understand all the things that the unconscious produces during the conflict. The reader may believe me that these are no ordinary products. On the contrary, they are among the most significant things that have ever engaged my attention. Nor is the patient inactive; he must do the right thing, and do it with all his might, in order to prevent the pressure of evil from becoming too powerful in him. He needs "justification by works," for "justification by faith" alone has remained an empty sound for him as for so many others. Faith can sometimes be a substitute for lack of experience. In these cases what is needed is real work. Christ espoused the sinner and did not condemn him. The true follower of Christ will do the same, and, since one should do unto others as one would do unto oneself, one will also take the part of the sinner who is oneself. And as little as we would accuse Christ of fraternizing with evil, so little should we reproach ourselves that to love the sinner who is oneself is to make a pact with the devil. Love makes a man better, hate makes him worse – even when that man is oneself. The danger in this point of view is the same as in the imitation of Christ; but the Pharisee in us will never allow himself to be caught talking to publicans and whores. I must emphasize of course that psychology invented neither Christianity nor the imitation of Christ. I wish everybody could be freed from the burden of their sins by the Church. But he to whom she cannot render this service must bend very low in the imitation of Christ in order to take the burden of his cross upon him. The ancients could get along with the Greek wisdom of the ages: Μηδὲν ἄγαν, τῷ καιρῷ πάντα πρόσεστι καλά (Exaggerate nothing, all good lies in right measure). But what an abyss still separates us from reason!

38   Apart from the moral difficulty there is another danger which is not inconsiderable and may lead to complications, particularly with individuals who are pathologically inclined. This is the fact that the contents of the personal unconscious (i.e. the shadow) are indistinguishably merged with the archetypal contents of the collective unconscious and drag the latter with them when the shadow is brought into consciousness. This may exert an uncanny influence on the conscious mind; for activated archetypes have a disagreeable effect even – or I should perhaps say, particularly – on the most cold-blooded rationalist. He is afraid that the lowest form of conviction, namely superstition, is, as he thinks, forcing itself on him. But superstition in the truest sense only appears in such people if they are pathological, not if they can keep their balance. It then takes the form of the fear of "going mad" – for everything that the modern mind cannot define it regards as insane. It must be admitted that the archetypal contents

of the collective unconscious can often assume grotesque and horrible forms in dreams and fantasies, so that even the most hard-boiled rationalist is not immune from shattering nightmares and haunting fears. The psychological elucidation of these images, which cannot be passed over in silence or blindly ignored, leads logically into the depths of religious phenomenology. The history of religion in its widest sense (including therefore mythology, folklore, and primitive psychology) is a treasure-house of archetypal forms from which the doctor can draw helpful parallels and enlightening comparisons for the purpose of calming and clarifying a consciousness that is all at sea. It is absolutely necessary to supply these fantastic images that rise up so strange and threatening before the mind's eye with some kind of context so as to make them more intelligible. Experience has shown that the best way to do this is by means of comparative mythological material.

39   Part II of this volume gives a large number of such examples. The reader will be particularly struck by the numerous connections between individual dream symbolism and medieval alchemy. This is not, as one might suppose, a prerogative of the case in question, but a general fact which only struck me some ten years ago when first I began to come to grips with the ideas and symbolism of alchemy.

40   Part III contains an introduction to the symbolism of alchemy in relation to Christianity and Gnosticism. As a bare introduction it is naturally far from being a complete exposition of this complicated and obscure subject – indeed, most of it is concerned only with the *lapis*-Christ parallel. True, this parallel gives rise to a comparison between the aims of the *opus alchymicum* and the central ideas of Christianity, for both are of the utmost importance in understanding and interpreting the images that appear in dreams and in assessing their psychological effect. This has considerable bearing on the practice of psychotherapy, because more often than not it is precisely the more intelligent and cultured patients who, finding a return to the Church impossible, come up against archetypal material and thus set the doctor problems which can no longer be mastered by a narrowly personalistic psychology. Nor is a mere knowledge of the psychic structure of a neurosis by any means sufficient; for once the process has reached the sphere of the collective unconscious we are dealing with healthy material, i.e. with the universal basis of the individually varied psyche. Our understanding of these deeper layers of the psyche is helped not only by a knowledge of primitive psychology and mythology, but to an even greater extent by some familiarity with the history of our modern consciousness and the stages immediately preceding it. On the one hand it is a child of the Church; on the other, of science, in whose beginnings very much lies hid that which the Church was unable to accept – that is to say, remnants of the classical spirit and the classical feeling for nature which could not be exterminated and eventually found refuge in the natural philosophy of the Middle Ages. As the "spiritus metallorum" and the

astrological components of destiny the old gods of the planet lasted out many a Christian century.[9] Whereas in the Church the increasing differentiation of ritual and dogma alienated consciousness from its natural roots in the unconscious, alchemy and astrology were ceaselessly engaged in preserving the bridge to nature, i.e. to the unconscious psyche, from decay. Astrology led the conscious mind back again and again to the knowledge of Heimarmene, that is, the dependence of character and destiny on certain moments of time; and alchemy afforded numerous "hooks" for the projection of those archetypes which could not be fitted smoothly into the Christian process. It is true that alchemy always stood on the verge of heresy and that certain decrees leave no doubt as to the Church's attitude towards it,[10] but on the other hand it was effectively protected by the obscurity of its symbolism, which could always be explained as harmless allegory. For many alchemists the allegorical aspect undoubtedly occupied the foreground to such an extent that they were firmly convinced that their sole concern was with chemical substances. But there were always a few for whom laboratory work was primarily a matter of symbols and their psychic effect. As the texts show, they were quite conscious of this, to the point of condemning the naïve goldmakers as liars, frauds, and dupes. Their own standpoint they proclaimed with propositions like "Aurum nostrum non est aurum vulgi." Although their labours over the retort were a serious effort to elicit the secrets of chemical transformation, it was at the same time – and often in overwhelming degree – the reflection of a parallel psychic process which could be projected all the more easily into the unknown chemistry of matter since that process is an unconscious phenomenon of nature, just like the mysterious alteration of substances. What the symbolism of alchemy expresses is the whole problem of the evolution of personality described above, the so-called individuation process.

41   Whereas the Church's great buttress is the imitation of Christ, the alchemist, without realizing it and certainly without wanting it, easily fell victim, in the loneliness and obscure problems of his work, to the promptings and unconscious assumptions of his own mind, since, unlike the Christians, he had no clear and unmistakable models on which to rely. The authors he studied provided him with symbols whose meaning he thought he understood in his own way; but in reality they touched and stimulated his unconscious. Ironical towards themselves, the alchemists coined the phrase "obscurum per obscurius." But with this method of explaining the obscure by the more obscure they only sank themselves deeper in the very process from which the Church was struggling to redeem them. While the dogmas of the Church offered analogies to the alchemical process, these analogies, in strict contrast to alchemy, had become detached from the world of nature through their connection with the historical figure of the Redeemer. The alchemical four in one, the philosophical gold, the *lapis angularis*, the *aqua divina*, became, in the

Church, the four-armed cross on which the Only-Begotten had sacrificed himself once in history and at the same time for all eternity. The alchemists ran counter to the Church in preferring to seek through knowledge rather than to find through faith, though as medieval people they never thought of themselves as anything but good Christians. Paracelsus is a classical example in this respect. But in reality they were in much the same position as modern man, who prefers immediate personal experience to belief in traditional ideas, or rather has it forced upon him. Dogma is not arbitrarily invented nor is it a unique miracle, although it is often described as miraculous with the obvious intent of lifting it out of its natural context. The central ideas of Christianity are rooted in Gnostic philosophy, which, in accordance with psychological laws, simply *had* to grow up at a time when the classical religions had become obsolete. It was founded on the perception of symbols thrown up by the unconscious individuation process which always sets in when the collective dominants of human life fall into decay. At such a time there is bound to be a considerable number of individuals who are possessed by archetypes of a numinous nature that force their way to the surface in order to form new dominants. This state of possession shows itself almost without exception in the fact that the possessed identify themselves with the archetypal contents of their un-conscious, and, because they do not realize that the role which is being thrust upon them is the effect of new contents still to be understood, they exemplify these concretely in their own lives, thus becoming prophets and reformers. In so far as the archetypal content of the Christian drama was able to give satisfying expression to the uneasy and clamorous unconscious of the many, the *consensus omnium* raised this drama to a universally binding truth – not of course by an act of judgment, but by the irrational fact of possession, which is far more effective. Thus Jesus became the tutelary image or amulet against the archetypal powers that threatened to possess everyone. The glad tidings announced: "It has happened, but it will not happen to you inasmuch as you believe in Jesus Christ, the Son of God!" Yet it could and it can and it will happen to everyone in whom the Christian dominant has decayed. For this reason there have always been people who, not satisfied with the dominants of conscious life, set forth – under cover and by devious paths, to their destruction or salvation – to seek direct experience of the eternal roots, and, following the lure of the restless unconscious psyche, find themselves in the wilderness where, like Jesus, they come up against the son of darkness, the ἀντίμιμον πνεῦμα. Thus an old alchemist – and he a cleric! – prays: "Horridas nostrae mentis purga tenebras, accende lumen sensibus!" (Purge the horrible darknesses of our mind, light a light for our senses!) The author of this sentence must have been undergoing the experience of the *nigredo*, the first stage of the work, which was felt as "melancholia" in alchemy and corresponds to the encounter with the shadow in psychology.

42   When, therefore, modern psychotherapy once more meets with the

activated archetypes of the collective unconscious, it is merely the repetition of a phenomenon that has often been observed in moments of great religious crisis, although it can also occur in individuals for whom the ruling ideas have lost their meaning. An example of this is the *descensus ad inferos* depicted in *Faust*, which, consciously or unconsciously, is an *opus alchymicum*.

43   The problem of opposites called up by the shadow plays a great – indeed, the decisive – role in alchemy, since it leads in the ultimate phase of the work to the union of opposites in the archetypal form of the *hierosgamos* or "chymical wedding." Here the supreme opposites, male and female (as in the Chinese *yang* and *yin*), are melted into a unity purified of all opposition and therefore incorruptible. The prerequisite for this, of course, is that the artifex should not identify himself with the figures in the work but should leave them in their objective, impersonal state. So long as the alchemist was working in his laboratory he was in a favourable position, psychologically speaking, for he had no opportunity to identify himself with the archetypes as they appeared, since they were all projected immediately into the chemical substances. The disadvantage of this situation was that the alchemist was forced to represent the incorruptible substance as a chemical product – an impossible undertaking which led to the downfall of alchemy, its place in the laboratory being taken by chemistry. But the psychic part of the work did not disappear. It captured new interpreters, as we can see from the example of *Faust*, and also from the signal connection between our modern psychology of the unconscious and alchemical symbolism.

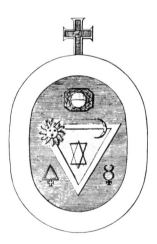

Symbol of the alchemical work.
Hermaphroditisches Sonn- und Mondskind (1752)

NOTES

1 Zöckler ("Probabilismus," p. 67) defines it as follows: "Probabilism is the name generally given to that way of thinking which is content to answer scientific questions with a greater or lesser degree of probability. The moral probabilism with which alone we are concerned here consists in the principle that acts of ethical self-determination are to be guided not by conscious but according to what is probably right, i.e. according to whatever has been recommended by any representative or doctrinal authority." The Jesuit probabilist Escobar (d. 1669) was, for instance, of the opinion that if the penitent should plead a probable opinion as the motive of his action, the father-confessor would be obliged to absolve him even if he were not of the same opinion. Escobar quotes a number of Jesuit authorities on the question of how often one is bound to love God in a lifetime. According to one opinion, loving God once shortly before death is sufficient; another says once a year or once every three or four years. He himself comes to the conclusion that it is sufficient to love God once at the first awakening of reason, then once every five years, and finally once in the hour of death. In his opinion the large number of different moral doctrines forms one of the main proofs of God's kindly providence, "because they make the yoke of Christ so light" (Zöckler, p. 68). Cf. also Harnack, *History of Dogma*, VII, pp. 101ff.

2 Cf. Genesis 1 : 2.

3 The reader will find a collection of these myth motifs in Lang, *Hat ein Gott die Welt erschaffen?* Unfortunately philological criticism will have much to take exception to in this book, interesting though it is for its Gnostic trend.

4 In alchemical writings the word "Mercurius" is used with a very wide range of meaning, to denote not only the chemical element mercury or quicksilver, Mercury (Hermes) the god, and Mercury the planet, but also – and primarily – the secret "transforming substance" which is at the same time the "spirit" indwelling in all living creatures. These different connotations will become apparent in the course of the book. It would be misleading to use the English "Mercury" and "mercury," because there are innumerable passages where neither word does justice to the wealth of implications. It has therefore been decided to retain the Latin "Mercurius" as in the German text, and to use the personal pronoun (since "Mercurius" is personified), the word "quicksilver" being employed only where the chemical element (Hg) is plainly meant. [*Author's note for the English edn*]

5 Przywara, *Deus semper maior*, I, pp. 71ff.

6 See the illustrations in Jung, "Concerning Mandala Symbolism."

7 *Contritio* is "perfect" repentance; *attritio* "imperfect" repentance (*contritio imperfecta*, to which category *contritio naturalis* belongs). The former regards sin as the opposite of the highest good; the latter reprehends it not only on account of its wicked and hideous nature but also from fear of punishment.

8 A religious terminology comes naturally, as the only adequate one in the circumstances, when we are faced with the tragic fate that is the unavoidable concomitant of wholeness. "My fate" means a daemonic will to precisely that fate – a will not necessarily coincident with my own (the ego will). When it is opposed to the ego, it is difficult not to feel a certain "power" in it, whether divine or infernal. The man who submits to his fate calls it the will of God; the man who puts up a hopeless and exhausting fight is more apt to see the devil in it. In either event this terminology is not only universally understood but meaningful as well.

9 Paracelsus still speaks of the "gods" enthroned in the *mysterium magnum* (*Philosophia ad Athenienses*, p. 403), and so does the 18th-cent. treatise of Abraham Eleazar, *Uraltes chymisches Werk*, which was influenced by Paracelsus.

10 Cf. Sanchez, *Opus morale*, Decalog. 2, 49n., 51; and Pignatelli, *Consultationes canonicae*, canon ix.

3   The spirit Mercurius

From: *CW* 13, paras 247–72

5. THE DUAL NATURE OF MERCURIUS

267   Mercurius, following the tradition of Hermes, is many-sided, change-
able, and deceitful. Dorn speaks of "that inconstant Mercurius,"[1] and
another calls him *versipellis* (changing his skin, shifty).[2] He is *duplex*[3] and
his main characteristic is duplicity. It is said of him that he "runs round
the earth and enjoys equally the company of the good and the wicked."[4]
He is "two dragons,"[5] the "twin,"[6] made of "two natures"[7] or "two
substances."[8] He is the "giant of twofold substance," in explanation of
which the text[9] cites the twenty-sixth chapter of Matthew, where the
sacrament of the Last Supper is instituted. The Christ analogy is thus made
plain. The two substances of Mercurius are thought of as dissimilar,
sometimes opposed; as the dragon he is "winged and wingless."[10] A
parable says: "On this mountain lies an ever-waking dragon, who is called
Pantophthalmos, for he is covered with eyes on both sides of his body,
before and behind, and he sleeps with some open and some closed."[11]
There is the "common and the philosophic" Mercurius;[12] he consists of
"the dry and earthy, the moist and viscous."[13] Two of his elements are
passive, earth and water, and two active, air and fire.[14] He is both good
and evil.[15] The "Aurelia occulta" gives a graphic description of him:[16]

> I am the poison-dripping dragon, who is everywhere and can be cheaply
> had. That upon which I rest, and that which rests upon me, will be found
> within me by those who pursue their investigations in accordance with
> the rules of the Art. My water and fire destroy and put together; from
> my body you may extract the green lion and the red. But if you do not
> have exact knowledge of me, you will destroy your five senses with my
> fire. From my snout there comes a spreading poison that has brought
> death to many. Therefore you should skilfully separate the coarse from
> the fine, if you do not wish to suffer utter poverty. I bestow on you the
> powers of the male and the female, and also those of heaven and earth.
> The mysteries of my art must be handled with courage and greatness of
> mind if you would conquer me by the power[17] of fire, for already very
> many have come to grief, their riches and labour lost. I am the egg of

nature, known only to the wise, who in piety and modesty bring forth from me the microcosm, which was prepared for mankind by Almighty God, but given only to the few, while the many long for it in vain, that they may do good to the poor with my treasure and not fasten their souls to the perishable gold. By the philosophers I am named Mercurius; my spouse is the [philosophic] gold; I am the old dragon, found everywhere on the globe of the earth, father and mother, young and old, very strong and very weak, death and resurrection, visible and invisible, hard and soft; I descend into the earth and ascend to the heavens, I am the highest and the lowest, the lightest and the heaviest; often the order of nature is reversed in me, as regards colour, number, weight, and measure; I contain the light of nature; I am dark and light; I come forth from heaven and earth; I am known and yet do not exist at all;[18] by virtue of the sun's rays all colours shine in me, and all metals. I am the carbuncle of the sun, the most noble purified earth, through which you may change copper, iron, tin, and lead into gold.

268   Because of his united double nature Mercurius is described as hermaphroditic. Sometimes his body is said to be masculine and his soul feminine, sometimes the reverse. The *Rosarium philosophorum*, for example, has both versions.[19] As *vulgaris* he is the dead masculine body, but as "our" Mercurius he is feminine, spiritual, alive and life-giving.[20] He is also called husband and wife,[21] bridegroom and bride, or lover and beloved.[22] His contrary natures are often called *Mercurius sensu strictiori* and sulphur, the former being feminine, earth, and Eve, and the latter masculine, water, and Adam.[23] In Dorn he is the "true hermaphroditic Adam,"[24] and in Khunrath he is "begotten of the hermaphroditic seed of the Macrocosm" as "an immaculate birth from the hermaphroditic matter" (i.e. the *prima materia*).[25] Mylius calls him the "hermaphroditic monster."[26] As Adam he is also the microcosm, or even "the heart of the microcosm,"[27] or he has the microcosm "in himself, where are also the four elements and the *quinta essentia* which they call Heaven."[28] The term *coelum* for Mercurius does not, as one might think, derive from the *firmamentum* of Paracelsus, but occurs earlier in Johannes de Rupescissa (fourteenth century).[29] The term *homo* is used as a synonym for "microcosm," as when Mercurius is named the "Philosophic ambisexual Man."[30] In the very old "Dicta Belini" (Belinus or Balinus is a corruption of Apollonius of Tyana), he is the "man rising from the river,"[31] probably a reference to the vision of Ezra.[32] In Trismosin's *Splendor solis* (sixteenth century) there is an illustration of this.[33] The idea itself may go back to the Babylonian teacher of wisdom, Oannes. The designation of Mercurius as the "high man"[34] does not fit in badly with such a pedigree. The terms Adam and microcosm occur frequently in the texts,[35] but the Abraham le Juif forgery unblushingly calls Mercurius Adam Kadmon.[36] As I have discussed this unmistakable continuation of the Gnostic doctrine of the

Anthropos elsewhere,[37] there is no need for me to go more closely now into this aspect of Mercurius.[38] Nevertheless, I would like to emphasize once again that the Anthropos idea coincides with the psychological concept of the self. The atman and purusha doctrine as well as alchemy give clear proofs of this.

269   Another aspect of the dual nature of Mercurius is his characterization as *senex*[39] and *puer*.[40] The figure of Hermes as an old man, attested by archaeology, brings him into direct relation with Saturn – a relationship which plays a considerable role in alchemy (see infra, pars. 274ff.). Mercurius truly consists of the most extreme opposites; on the one hand he is undoubtedly akin to the godhead, on the other he is found in sewers. Rosinus (Zosimos) even calls him the *terminus ani*.[41] In the Bundahish,[42] the anus of Garotman is "like hell on earth."

6. THE UNITY AND TRINITY OF MERCURIUS

270   In spite of his obvious duality the unity of Mercurius is also emphasized, especially in his form as the lapis. "In all the world he is One."[43] The unity of Mercurius is at the same time a trinity, with clear reference to the Holy Trinity, although his triadic nature does not derive from Christian dogma but is of earlier date. Triads occur as early as the treatise of Zosimos, περὶ ἀρετῆς (Concerning the Art).[44] Martial calls Hermes *omnia solus et ter unus* (All and Thrice One).[45] In Monakris (Arcadia), a three-headed Hermes was worshipped, and in Gaul there was a three-headed Mercurius.[46] This Gallic god was also a psychopomp. The triadic character is an attribute of the gods of the underworld, as for instance the three-bodied Typhon, three-bodied and three-faced Hecate,[47] and the "ancestors" (τριτοπάτορες) with their serpent bodies. According to Cicero,[48] these latter are the three sons of Zeus the King, the *rex antiquissimus*.[49] They are called the "forefathers" and are wind-gods;[50] obviously by the same logic the Hopi Indians believe that snakes are at the same time flashes of lightning auguring rain. Khunrath calls Mercurius *triunus*[51] and *ternarius*.[52] Mylius represents him as a three-headed snake.[53] The "Aquarium sapientum" says that he is a "triune, universal essence which is named Jehova.[54] He is divine and at the same time human."[55]

271   From all this one must conclude that Mercurius corresponds not only to Christ, but to the triune divinity in general. The "Aurelia occulta" calls him "Azoth," and explains the term as follows: "For he is the A and O that is everywhere present. The philosophers have adorned [him] with the name Azoth, which is compounded of the A and Z of the Latins, the alpha and omega of the Greeks, and the aleph and tau of the Hebrews:

$$A \left\{ \begin{array}{c} Z \\ \omega \\ \hbar \end{array} \right\} \text{Azoth."}^{56}$$

The parallel with the Trinity could not be more clearly indicated. The anonymous commentator of the "Tractatus aureus" puts the parallel with Christ as Logos just as unmistakably. All things proceed from the "philosophic heaven adorned with an infinite multitude of stars,"[57] from the creative Word incarnate, the Johannine Logos, without which "was not any thing made that was made." The commentator says: "Thus the Word of renewal is invisibly inherent in all things, but it is not evident in elementary solid bodies unless they have been brought back to the fifth, or heavenly and astral essence. Hence this Word of renewal is the seed of promise, or the philosophic heaven refulgent with the infinite lights of the stars."[58] Mercurius is the Logos become world. The description given here may point to his basic identity with the collective unconscious, for as I tried to show in my essay "On the Nature of the Psyche,"[59] the image of the starry heaven seems to be a visualization of the peculiar nature of the unconscious. Since Mercurius is often called *filius*, his sonship is beyond question.[60] He is therefore like a brother to Christ and a second son of God, though in point of time he must be accounted the elder and the first-born. This idea goes back to the conceptions of the Euchites reported in Michael Psellus,[61] who believed that God's first son was Satanaël[62] and that Christ was the second.[63] However, Mercurius is not only the counterpart of Christ in so far as he is the "son"; he is also the counterpart of the Trinity as a whole in so far as he is conceived to be a chthonic triad. According to this view he would be equal to one half of the Christian Godhead. He is indeed the dark chthonic half, but he is not simply evil as such, for he is called "good *and* evil," or a "system of the higher powers in the lower." He calls to mind that double figure which seems to stand behind both Christ and the devil – that enigmatic Lucifer whose attributes are shared by both. In Rev. 22 : 16 Christ says of himself: "I am the root and the offspring of David, the bright and the morning star."

272   One peculiarity of Mercurius which undoubtedly relates him to the Godhead and to the primitive creator god is his ability to beget himself. In the "Allegoriae super librum Turbae" he says: "The mother bore me and is herself begotten of me."[64] As the uroboros dragon, he impregnates, begets, bears, devours, and slays himself, and "himself lifts himself on high," as the *Rosarium* says,[65] so paraphrasing the mystery of God's sacrificial death. Here, as in many similar instances, it would be rash to assume that the alchemists were as conscious of their reasoning processes as perhaps we are. But man, and through him the unconscious, expresses a great deal that is not necessarily conscious in all its implications. Nevertheless I should like to avoid giving the impression that the alchemists were absolutely unconscious of their thought-processes. How little this was so is proved by the above quotations. But although Mercurius, in many texts, is stated to be *trinus et unus*, this does not prevent him from sharing very strongly the *quaternity* of the lapis, with which he is essentially identical. He thus exemplifies that strange dilemma

which is posed by the problem of three and four – the well-known axiom of Maria Prophetissa. There is a classical *Hermes tetracephalus* as well as the *Hermes tricephalus*.[66] The groundplan of the Sabaean temple of Mercurius was a triangle inside a square.[67] In the scholia to the "Tractatus aureus" the sign for Mercurius is a square inside a triangle surrounded by a circle (symbol of totality).[68]

NOTES

1 *Theatr. chem.*, I (1659), p. 470.
2 Aegidius de Vadis, ibid., II (1659), p. 105.
3 "Aquarium sap.," *Mus. herm.*, p. 84; Trevisanus, in *Theatr. chem.*, I (1659), p. 695; Mylius, *Phil. ref.*, p. 176.
4 "Aurelia occulta," *Theatr. chem.*, IV (1659), p. 506.
5 "Brevis manuductio," *Mus. herm.*, p. 788.
6 Valentinus, "Practica," ibid., p. 425.
7 Mylius, *Phil. ref.*, p. 18; "Exercitationes in Turbam," *Art aurif.*, I, pp. 159, 161.
8 Dorn, in *Theatr. chem.*, I (1659), p. 420.
9 "Aquarium sap.," *Mus. herm.*, p. 111. [Cf. infra, par. 384. n. 5.]
10 "Summarium philosophicum," ibid., pp. 172f.
11 Cf. the snake vision of Ignatius Loyola and the polyophthalmia motif discussed in "On the Nature of the Psyche," pp. 198f.
12 "Tractatus aureus," *Mus. herm.*, p. 25.
13 "Consilium coniugii," *Ars chemica* (1566), p. 59.
14 *Rosarium*, in *Art. aurif.*, II, p. 208.
15 Khunrath, *Hyl. Chaos*, p. 218.
16 *Theatr. chem.*, IV (1659), pp. 501ff.
17 I read *vi* instead of *vim*.
18 This paradox recalls the Indian *asat* (non-existing). Cf. Chhāndogya Upanishad, VI, ii, 1 (Sacred Books of the East, II, p. 93).
19 *Art. aurif.*, II, pp. 239, 249.
20 "Introit. apert.," *Mus. herm.*, p. 653.
21 "Gloria mundi," ibid., p. 250.
22 *Aurora consurgens* I, Parable VII.
23 Ruland, *Lexicon alchemiae*, p. 47.
24 *Theatr. chem.*, I (1659), p. 510.
25 *Hyl. Chaos*, p. 62.
26 *Phil. ref.*, p. 19.
27 Happelius in *Theatr. chem.*, IV (1659), p. 327.
28 *Phil. ref.*, p. 5.
29 *La Vertu et propriété de la quinte essence*, p. 15. The "metal of the philosophers" will become like "heaven," says the "Tractatus Micreris," *Theatr. chem.*, V (1660), p. 100.
30 Khunrath, *Hyl. Chaos*, p. 195.
31 Manget, *Bibliotheca chemica*, I, p. 478b.
32 IV Ezra 13 : 25–53. Cf. Charles, *Apocrypha and Pseudepigrapha*, II, pp. 618f.
33 In *Aureum vellus* (1598), Tract 3: *Splendor Solis* (1920 facsimile), p. 23, Pl. VIII.
34 Ruland, *Lexicon alchemiae*, p. 47.
35 John Dee in *Theatr. chem.*, II (1659), p. 195; *Rosarium*, in *Art aurif.*, II, p. 309.
36 Eleazar, *Uraltes Chymisches Werck*, p. 51. Adam Kadmon is the Primordial Man; cf. *Mysterium Coniunctionis*, ch. V.

37 "Paracelsus as a Spiritual Phenomenon," supra. pars. 165ff., and *Psychology and Alchemy*, index, s.v.

38 Gayomart also is a kind of vegetation numen like Mercurius, and like him fertilizes his mother, the earth. At the place where his life came to an end the earth turned to gold, and where his limbs disintegrated various metals appeared. Cf. Christensen, *Les Types du premier homme et du premier roi dans l'histoire légendaire des Iraniens*, pp. 26, 29.

39 *Senex draco* in Valentinus, "Practica," *Mus. herm.*, p. 425. In *Verus Hermes* (1620),. pp. 15, 16, Mercurius is also designated with the Gnostic name "Father-Mother."

40 "De arte chimica," *Art. aurif.*, I, p. 581. *Regis puellus* in "Introit. apert.," *Mus. herm.*, pp. 678, 655.

41 *Art. aurif.*, I, p. 310. Here it is the stone identical with Mercurius that is so called. The context disallows the reading "anni." The passage which follows soon after, "nascitur in duobus montibus," refers to the "Tractatus Aristotelis" (*Theatr. chem.*, V, 1660, pp. 787ff.), where the act of defecation is described. (Cf. supra, "Paracelsus as a Spiritual Phenomenon," par. 182, n. 61.) Corresponding illustrations for *Aurora consurgens* may be found in the Codex Rhenoviensis.

42 Ch. XXVIII. Cf. Reitzenstein and Schaeder, *Studien zum antiken Synkretismus aus Iran und Griechenland*, p. 119.

43 *Rosarium*, in *Art. aurif.*, II, p. 253.

44 Berthelot, *Alch. grecs*, III, vi, 18: "The unity of the composition [produces] the indivisible triad, and thus an undivided triad composed of separate elements creates the cosmos, through the forethought [προνολα] of the First Author, the cause and demiurge of creation; wherefore he is called Trismegistos, having beheld triadically that which is created and that which creates."

45 *Epigrammata*, V, 24.

46 Reinach, *Cultes, mythes et religions*, III, pp. 160f.

47 Schweitzer, *Herakles*, pp. 84ff.

48 *De natura deorum*, 3, 21, 53.

49 There is also a *Zeus triops*.

50 Roscher, *Lexicon*, V, col. 1208.

51 *Hyl. Chaos*, pp. 6 and 199.

52 Ibid., p. 203.

53 *Phil. ref.*, p. 96.

54 This peculiar designation refers to the demiurge, the saturnine Ialdabaoth, who was connected with the "God of the Jews."

55 *Mus. herm.*, p. 112.

56 *Theatr. chem.*, IV (1659), p. 507.

57 Ibid., p. 614.

58 Ibid., p. 615.

59 Pp. 198f.

60 Cf. *Rosarium*, in *Art. aurif.*, II, p. 248: "filius ... coloris coelici" (cited from Haly's "Secretum"); Khunrath, *Hyl. Chaos*, passim: "filius macrocosmi," p. 59: "unigenitus"; Penotus in *Theatr chem.*, I (1659), p. 601: "filius hominis, fructus virginis."

61 *De daemonibus* (trans. Marcilio Ficino), fol. N. V^v.

62 Cf. the report on the Bogomils in Euthymios Zigabenos, "Panoplia dogmatica" (Migne, *P.G.*, vol. 130, cols. 129ff.).

63 The duality of the sonship appears to date back to the Ebionites in Epiphanius: "Two, they assert, were raised up by God, the one (is) Christ, the other the devil" (*Panarium*, XXX, 16, 2).

64 *Art. aurif.*, I, p. 151. The same is said of God in the *Contes del Graal* of Chrétien de Troyes:

> "Ce doint icil glorïeus pere
> Qui de sa fille fist sa mere."

(Hilka, *Der Percevalroman*, p. 372.)

65 *Art. aurif.*, II, p. 339.
66 Schweitzer, *Herakles*, p. 84.
67 Chwolsohn, *Die Ssabier und der Ssabismus*, II, p. 367.
68 *Bibl. chem.*, I, p. 409.

4   The problem of the fourth

From: *CW* 11, paras 243–85

I. THE CONCEPT OF QUATERNITY

243   The *Timaeus*, which was the first to propound a triadic formula for the God-image in philosophical terms, starts off with the ominous question: "One, two, three – but . . . where is the fourth?" This question is, as we know, taken up again in the Cabiri scene in *Faust*:

> Three we brought with us,
>   The fourth would not come.
> He was the right one
>   Who thought for them all.

244   When Goethe says that the fourth was the one "who thought for them all," we rather suspect that the fourth was Goethe's own thinking function.[1] The Cabiri are, in fact, the mysterious creative powers, the gnomes who work under the earth, i.e. below the threshold of consciousness, in order to supply us with lucky ideas. As imps and hobgoblins, however, they also play all sorts of nasty tricks, keeping back names and dates that were "on the tip of the tongue," making us say the wrong thing, etc. They give an eye to everything that has not already been anticipated by the conscious mind and the functions at its disposal. As these functions can be used consciously only because they are adapted, it follows that the unconscious, autonomous function is not or cannot be used consciously because it is unadapted. The differentiated and differentiable functions are much easier to cope with, and, for understandable reasons, we prefer to leave the "inferior" function round the corner, or to repress it altogether, because it is such an awkward customer. And it is a fact that it has the strongest tendency to be infantile, banal, primitive, and archaic. Anybody who has a high opinion of himself will do well to guard against letting it make a fool of him. On the other hand, deeper insight will show that the primitive and archaic qualities of the inferior function conceal all sorts of significant relationships and symbolical meanings, and instead of laughing off the Cabiri as ridiculous Tom Thumbs he may begin to suspect that they are a treasure-house of hidden wisdom. Just as, in *Faust*, the fourth thinks

for them all, so the whereabouts of the eighth should be asked "on Olympus." Goethe showed great insight in not underestimating his inferior function, thinking, although it was in the hands of the Cabiri and was undoubtedly mythological and archaic. He characterizes it perfectly in the line: "The fourth would not come." Exactly! It wanted for some reason to stay behind or below.[2]

245   Three of the four orienting functions are available to consciousness. This is confirmed by the psychological experience that a rational type, for instance, whose superior function is thinking, has at his disposal one, or possibly two, auxiliary functions of an irrational nature, namely sensation (the "fonction du réel") and intuition (perception via the unconscious). His inferior function will be feeling (valuation), which remains in a retarded state and is contaminated with the unconscious. It refuses to come along with the others and often goes wildly off on its own. This peculiar dissociation is, it seems, a product of civilization, and it denotes a freeing of consciousness from any excessive attachment to the "spirit of gravity." If that function, which is still bound indissolubly to the past and whose roots reach back as far as the animal kingdom,[3] can be left behind and even forgotten, then consciousness has won for itself a new and not entirely illusory freedom. It can leap over abysses on winged feet; it can free itself from bondage to sense-impressions, emotions, fascinating thoughts, and presentiments by soaring into abstraction. Certain primitive initiations stress the idea of transformation into ghosts and invisible spirits and thereby testify to the relative emancipation of consciousness from the fetters of non-differentiation. Although there is a tendency, characteristic not only of primitive religions, to speak rather exaggeratedly of complete transformation, complete renewal and rebirth, it is, of course, only a relative change, continuity with the earlier state being in large measure preserved. Were it otherwise, every religious transformation would bring about a complete splitting of the personality or loss of memory, which is obviously not so. The connection with the earlier attitude is maintained because part of the personality remains behind in the previous situation; that is to say it lapses into unconsciousness and starts building up the shadow.[4] The loss makes itself felt in consciousness through the absence of at least one of the four orienting functions, and the missing function is always the opposite of the superior function. The loss need not necessarily take the form of complete absence; in other words, the inferior function may be either unconscious or conscious, but in both cases it is autonomous and obsessive and not influenceable by the will. It has the "all-or-none" character of an instinct. Although emancipation from the instincts brings a differentiation and enhancement of consciousness, it can only come about at the expense of the unconscious function, so that conscious orientation lacks that element which the inferior function could have supplied. Thus it often happens that people who have an amazing range of consciousness know less about themselves than the veriest infant, and all

because "the fourth would not come" – it remained down below – or up above – in the unconscious realm.

246   As compared with the trinitarian thinking of Plato, ancient Greek philosophy favoured thinking of a quaternary type. In Pythagoras the great role was played not by three but by four; the Pythagorean oath, for instance, says that the tetraktys "contains the roots of eternal nature."[5] The Pythagorean school was dominated by the idea that the soul was a square and not a triangle. The origin of these ideas lies far back in the dark pre-history of Greek thought. The quaternity is an archetype of almost universal occurrence. It forms the logical basis for any whole judgment. If one wishes to pass such a judgment, it must have this fourfold aspect. For instance, if you want to describe the horizon as a whole, you name the four quarters of heaven. Three is not a natural coefficient of order, but an artificial one. There are four elements, four prime qualities, four colours, four castes, four ways of spiritual development in Buddhism, etc. So, too, there are four aspects of psychological orientation, beyond which nothing fundamental remains to be said. In order to orient ourselves, we must have a function which ascertains that something is there (sensation); a second function which establishes *what* it is (thinking); a third function which states whether it suits us or not, whether we wish to accept it or not (feeling); and a fourth function which indicates where it came from and where it is going (intuition). When this has been done, there is nothing more to say. Schopenhauer proves that the "Principle of Sufficient Reason" has a fourfold root.[6] This is so because the fourfold aspect is the minimum requirement for a complete judgment. The ideal of completeness is the circle or sphere, but its natural minimal division is a quaternity.

247   Now if Plato had had the idea of the Christian Trinity [7] – which of course he did not – and had on that account placed his triad above everything, one would be bound to object that this cannot be a whole judgment. A necessary fourth would be left out; or, if Plato took the three-sided figure as symbolic of the Beautiful and the Good and endowed it with all positive qualities, he would have had to deny evil and imperfection to it. In that case, what has become of them? The Christian answer is that evil is a *privatio boni*. This classic formula robs evil of absolute existence and makes it a shadow that has only a relative existence dependent on light. Good, on the other hand, is credited with a positive substantiality. But, as psychological experience shows, "good" and "evil" are opposite poles of a moral judgment which, as such, originates in man. A judgment can be made about a thing only if its opposite is equally real and possible. The opposite of a seeming evil can only be a seeming good, and an evil that lacks substance can only be contrasted with a good that is equally non-substantial. Although the opposite of "existence" is "non-existence," the opposite of an existing good can never be a non-existing evil, for the latter is a contradiction in terms and opposes to an existing good something incommensurable with it; the opposite of a non-existing (negative) evil

can only be a non-existing (negative) good. If, therefore, evil is said to be a mere privation of good, the opposition of good and evil is denied outright. How can one speak of "good" at all if there is no "evil"? Or of "light" if there is no "darkness," or of "above" if there is no "below"? There is no getting round the fact that if you allow substantiality to good, you must also allow it to evil. If evil has no substance, good must remain shadowy, for there is no substantial opponent for it to defend itself against, but only a shadow, a mere privation of good. Such a view can hardly be squared with observed reality. It is difficult to avoid the impression that apotropaic tendencies have had a hand in creating this notion, with the understandable intention of settling the painful problem of evil as optimistically as possible. Often it is just as well that we do not know the danger we escape when we rush in where angels fear to tread.

248   Christianity also deals with the problem in another way, by asserting that evil has substance and personality as the devil, or Lucifer. There is one view which allows the devil a malicious, goblin-like existence only, thus making him the insignificant head of an insignificant tribe of wood-imps and poltergeists. Another view grants him a more dignified status, depending on the degree to which it identifies him with "ills" in general. How far "ills" may be identified with "evil" is a controversial question. The Church distinguishes between physical ills and moral ills. The former may be willed by divine Providence (e.g. for man's improvement), the latter not, because sin cannot be willed by God even as a means to an end. It would be difficult to verify the Church's view in concrete instances, for psychic and somatic disorders are "ills," and, as illnesses, they are moral as well as physical. At all events there is a view which holds that the devil, though created, is autonomous and eternal. In addition, he is the adversary of Christ: by infecting our first parents with original sin he corrupted creation and made the Incarnation necessary for God's work of salvation. In so doing he acted according to his own judgment, as in the Job episode, where he was even able to talk God round. The devil's prowess on these occasions hardly squares with his alleged shadow-existence as the *privatio boni*, which, as we have said, looks very like a euphemism. The devil as an autonomous and eternal personality is much more in keeping with his role as the adversary of Christ and with the psychological reality of evil.

249   But if the devil has the power to put a spoke in God's Creation, or even corrupt it, and God does nothing to stop this nefarious activity and leaves it all to man (who is notoriously stupid, unconscious, and easily led astray), then, despite all assurances to the contrary, the evil spirit must be a factor of quite incalculable potency. In this respect, anyhow, the dualism of the Gnostic systems makes sense, because they at least try to do justice to the real meaning of evil. They have also done us the supreme service of having gone very thoroughly into the question of where evil comes from. Biblical tradition leaves us very much in the dark on this point, and it is only too obvious why the old theologians were in no particular hurry to enlighten

us. In a monotheistic religion everything that goes against God can only be traced back to God himself. This thought is objectionable, to say the least of it, and has therefore to be circumvented. That is the deeper reason why a highly influential personage like the devil cannot be accommodated properly in a trinitarian cosmos. It is difficult to make out in what relation he stands to the Trinity. As the adversary of Christ, he would have to take up an equivalent counterposition and be, like him, a "son of God."[8] But that would lead straight back to certain function views according to which the devil, as Satanaël,[9] is God's first son, Christ being the second.[9a] A further logical inference would be the abolition of the Trinity formula and its replacement by a quaternity.

250   The idea of a quaternity of divine principles was violently attacked by the Church Fathers when an attempt was made to add a fourth – God's "essence" – to the Three Persons of the Trinity. This resistance to the quaternity is very odd, considering that the central Christian symbol, the Cross, is unmistakably a quaternity. The Cross, however, symbolizes God's suffering in his immediate encounter with the world.[10] The "prince of this world," the devil (John 12 : 31, 14 : 30), vanquishes the God-man at this point, although by so doing he is presumably preparing his own defeat and digging his own grave. According to an old view, Christ is the "bait on the hook" (the Cross), with which he catches "Leviathan" (the devil).[11] It is therefore significant that the Cross, set up midway between heaven and hell as a symbol of Christ's struggle with the devil, corresponds to the quaternity.

251   Medieval iconology, embroidering on the old speculations about the Theotokos, evolved a quaternity symbol in its representations of the coronation of the Virgin[12] and surreptitiously put it in place of the Trinity. The Assumption of the Blessed Virgin Mary, i.e. the taking up of Mary's soul into heaven *with her body*, is admitted as ecclesiastical doctrine but has not yet become dogma.[13] Although Christ, too, rose up with his body, this has a rather different meaning, since Christ was a divinity in the first place and Mary was not. In her case the body would have been a much more material one than Christ's, much more an element of space-time reality.[14] Ever since the *Timaeus* the "fourth" has signified "realization," i.e. entry into an essentially different condition, that of worldly materiality, which, it is authoritatively stated, is ruled by the Prince of this world – for matter is the diametrical opposite of spirit. It is the true abode of the devil, whose hellish hearth-fire burns deep in the interior of the earth, while the shining spirit soars in the aether, freed from the shackles of gravity.

252   The *Assumptio Mariae* paves the way not only for the divinity of the Theotokos (i.e. her ultimate recognition as a goddess),[15] but also for the quaternity. At the same time, matter is included in the metaphysical realm, together with the corrupting principle of the cosmos, evil. One can explain that matter was originally pure, or at least capable of purity, but this does not do away with the fact that matter represents the *concreteness* of God's

thoughts and is, therefore, the very thing that makes individuation possible, with all its consequences. The adversary is, quite logically, conceived to be the soul of matter, because they both constitute a point of resistance without which the relative autonomy of individual existence would be simply unthinkable. The will to be different and contrary is characteristic of the devil, just as disobedience was the hallmark of original sin. These, as we have said, are the necessary conditions for the Creation and ought, therefore, to be included in the divine plan and – ultimately – in the divine realm.[16] But the Christian definition of God as the *summum bonum* excludes the Evil One right from the start, despite the fact that in the Old Testament he was still one of the "sons of God." Hence the devil remained outside the Trinity as the "ape of God" and in opposition to it. Medieval representations of the triune God as having three heads are based on the three-headedness of Satan, as we find it, for instance, in Dante. This would point to an infernal Anti-trinity, a true "umbra trinitatis" analogous to the Antichrist.[17] The devil is, undoubtedly, an awkward figure: he is the "odd man out" in the Christian cosmos. That is why people would like to minimize his importance by euphemistic ridicule or by ignoring his existence altogether; or, better still, to lay the blame for him at man's door. This is in fact done by the very people who would protest mightily if sinful man should credit himself, equally, with the origin of all good. A glance at the Scriptures, however, is enough to show us the importance of the devil in the divine drama of redemption.[18] If the power of the Evil One had been as feeble as certain persons would wish it to appear, either the world would not have needed God himself to come down to it or it would have lain within the power of man to set the world to rights, which has certainly not happened so far.

253   Whatever the metaphysical position of the devil may be, in psychological reality evil is an effective, not to say menacing, limitation of goodness, so that it is no exaggeration to assume that in this world good and evil more or less balance each other, like day and night, and that this is the reason why the victory of the good is always a special act of grace.

254   If we disregard the specifically Persian system of dualism, it appears that no real devil is to be found anywhere in the early period of man's spiritual development. In the Old Testament, he is vaguely foreshadowed in the figure of Satan. But the real devil first appears as the adversary of Christ,[19] and with him we gaze for the first time into the luminous realm of divinity on the one hand and into the abyss of hell on the other. The devil is autonomous; he cannot be brought under God's rule, for if he could he would not have the power to be the adversary of Christ, but would only be God's instrument. Once the indefinable One unfolds into two, it becomes something definite: the man Jesus, the Son and Logos. This statement is possible only by virtue of something else that is *not* Jesus, not Son or Logos. The act of love embodied in the Son is counterbalanced by Lucifer's denial.

255   Inasmuch as the devil was an angel created by God and "fell like lightning from heaven," he too is a divine "procession" that became Lord of this world. It is significant that the Gnostics thought of him sometimes as the imperfect demiurge and sometimes as the Saturnine archon, Ialdabaoth. Pictorial representations of this archon correspond in every detail with those of a diabolical demon. He symbolized the power of darkness from which Christ came to rescue humanity. The archons issued from the womb of the unfathomable abyss, i.e. from the same source that produced the Gnostic Christ.

256   A medieval thinker observed that when God separated the upper waters from the lower on the second day of Creation, he did not say in the evening, as he did on all the other days, that it was good. And he did not say it because on that day he had created the *binarius*, the origin of all evil.[20] We come across a similar idea in Persian literature, where the origin of Ahriman is attributed to a *doubting thought* in Ahura-Mazda's mind. If we think in non-trinitarian terms, the logic of the following schema seems inescapable:

257   So it is not strange that we should meet the idea of Antichrist so early. It was probably connected on the one hand with the astrological synchronicity of the dawning aeon of Pisces,[21] and on the other hand with the increasing realization of the duality postulated by the Son, which in turn is prefigured in the fish symbol:)(, showing two fishes, joined by a commissure, moving in opposite directions.[22] It would be absurd to put any kind of causal construction on these events. Rather, it is a question of preconscious, prefigurative connections between the archetypes themselves, suggestions of which can be traced in other constellations as well and above all in the formation of myths.

258   In our diagram, Christ and the devil appear as equal and opposite, thus conforming to the idea of the "adversary." This opposition means conflict to the last, and it is the task of humanity to endure this conflict until the time or turning-point is reached where good and evil begin to relativize themselves, to doubt themselves, and the cry is raised for a morality "beyond good and evil." In the age of Christianity and in the domain of trinitarian thinking such an idea is simply out of the question, because the conflict is too violent for evil to be assigned any other logical relation to the Trinity than that of an absolute opposite. In an emotional opposition, i.e. in a conflict situation, thesis and antithesis cannot be viewed together at the same time. This only becomes possible with cooler assessment of the relative value of good and the relative non-value of evil. Then it can

no longer be doubted, either, that a common life unites not only the Father and the "light" son, but the Father and his *dark* emanation. The unspeakable conflict posited by duality resolves itself in a fourth principle, which restores the unity of the first in its full development. The rhythm is built up in three steps, but the resultant symbol is a quaternity.

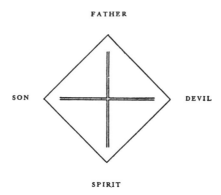

259   The dual aspect of the Father is by no means unknown to religious speculation.[23] This is proved by the allegory of the monoceros, or unicorn, who symbolizes Yahweh's angry moodiness. Like this irritable beast, he reduced the world to chaos and could only be moved to love in the lap of a pure virgin.[24] Luther was familiar with a *deus absconditus*. Murder, sudden death, war, sickness, crime, and every kind of abomination fall in with the unity of God. If God reveals his nature and takes on definite form as a man, then the opposites in him must fly apart: here good, there evil. So it was that the opposites latent in the Deity flew apart when the Son was begotten and manifested themselves in the struggle between Christ and the devil, with the Persian Ormuzd-Ahriman antithesis, perhaps, as the underlying model. The world of the Son is the world of moral discord, without which human consciousness could hardly have progressed so far as it has towards mental and spiritual differentiation. That we are not unreservedly enthusiastic about this progress is shown by the fits of doubt to which our modern consciousness is subject.

260   Despite the fact that he is potentially redeemed, the Christian is given over to moral suffering, and in his suffering he needs the Comforter, the Paraclete. He cannot overcome the conflict on his own resources; after all, he didn't invent it. He has to rely on divine comfort and mediation, that is to say on the spontaneous revelation of the spirit, which does not obey man's will but comes and goes as *it* wills. This spirit is an autonomous psychic happening, a hush that follows the storm, a reconciling light in the darknesses of man's mind, secretly bringing order into the chaos of his soul. The Holy Ghost is a comforter like the Father, a mute, eternal, unfathomable One in whom God's love and God's terribleness come together in wordless union. And through this union the original meaning

of the still-unconscious Father-world is restored and brought within the scope of human experience and reflection. Looked at from a quaternary standpoint, the Holy Ghost is a reconciliation of opposites and hence the answer to the suffering in the Godhead which Christ personifies.

261 The Pythagorean quaternity was a natural phenomenon, an archetypal image, but it was not yet a moral problem, let alone a divine drama. Therefore it "went underground." It was a purely naturalistic, intuitive idea born of the nature-bound mind. The gulf that Christianity opened out between nature and spirit enabled the human mind to think not only beyond nature but in opposition to it, thus demonstrating its divine freedom, so to speak. This flight from the darkness of nature's depths culminates in trinitarian thinking, which moves in a Platonic, "supracelestial" realm. But the question of the fourth, rightly or wrongly, remained. It stayed down "below," and from there threw up the heretical notion of the quaternity and the speculations of Hermetic philosophy.

262 In this connection I would like to call attention to Gerhard Dorn, a physician and alchemist, and a native of Frankfurt. He took great exception to the traditional quaternity of the basic principles of his art, and also to the fourfold nature of its goal, the *lapis philosophorum.* It seemed to him that this was a heresy, since the principle that ruled the world was a Trinity. The quaternity must therefore be of the devil.[25] Four, he maintained, was a doubling of two, and two was made on the second day of Creation, but God was obviously not altogether pleased with the result of his handiwork that evening. The *binarius* is the devil of discord and, what is worse, of feminine nature. (In East and West alike even numbers are feminine.) The cause of dissatisfaction was that, on this ominous second day of Creation, just as with Ahura-Mazda, a split was revealed in God's nature. Out of it crept the "four-horned serpent," who promptly succeeded in seducing Eve, because she was related to him by reason of her binary nature. ("Man was created by God, woman by the ape of God.")

263 The devil is the aping shadow of God, the ἀντίμιμον πνεῦμα, in Gnosticism and also in Greek alchemy. He is "Lord of this world," in whose shadow man was born, fatally tainted with the original sin brought about by the devil. Christ, according to the Gnostic view, cast off the shadow he was born with and remained without sin. His sinlessness proves his essential lack of contamination with the dark world of nature-bound man, who tries in vain to shake off this darkness. ("Uns bleibt ein Erdenrest / zu tragen peinlich."[26]) Man's connection with physis, with the material world and its demands, is the cause of his anomalous position: on the one hand he has the capacity for enlightenment, on the other he is in thrall to the Lord of this world. ("Who will deliver me from the body of this death?") On account of his sinlessness, Christ on the contrary lives in the Platonic realm of pure ideas whither only man's thought can reach, but not he himself in his totality. Man is, in truth, the bridge spanning the gulf between "this world" – the realm of the dark Tricephalus – and the

heavenly Trinity. That is why, even in the days of unqualified belief in the Trinity, there was always a quest for a lost fourth, from the time of the Neopythagoreans down to Goethe's *Faust*. Although these seekers thought of themselves as Christians, they were really Christians only on the side, devoting their lives to a work whose purpose it was to redeem the "four-horned serpent," the fallen Lucifer, and to free the *anima mundi* imprisoned in matter. What in their view lay hidden in matter was the *lumen luminum*, the *Sapientia Dei*, and their work was a "gift of the Holy Spirit." Our quaternity formula confirms the rightness of their claims; for the Holy Ghost, as the synthesis of the original One which then became split, issues from a source that is both light and dark. "For the powers of the right and the left unite in the harmony of wisdom," we are told in the Acts of John.[27]

264   It will have struck the reader that two corresponding elements cross one another in our quaternity schema. On the one hand we have the polaristic identity of Christ and his adversary, and on the other the unity of the Father unfolded in the multiplicity of the Holy Ghost. The resultant cross is the symbol of the suffering Godhead that redeems mankind. This suffering could not have occurred, nor could it have had any effect at all, had it not been for the existence of a power opposed to God, namely "this world" and its Lord. The quaternity schema recognizes the existence of this power as an undeniable fact by fettering trinitarian thinking to the reality of this world. The Platonic freedom of the spirit does not make a whole judgment possible: it wrenches the light half of the picture away from the dark half. This freedom is to a large extent a phenomenon of civilization, the lofty preoccupation of that fortunate Athenian whose lot it was not to be born a slave. We can only rise above nature if somebody else carries the weight of the earth for us. What sort of philosophy would Plato have produced had he been his own house-slave? What would the Rabbi Jesus have taught if he had had to support a wife and children? If he had had to till the soil in which the bread he broke had grown, and weed the vineyard in which the wine he dispensed had ripened? The dark weight of the earth must enter into the picture of the whole. In "this world" there is no good without its bad, no day without its night, no summer without its winter. But civilized man can live without the winter, for he can protect himself against the cold; without dirt, for he can wash; without sin, for he can prudently cut himself off from his fellows and thereby avoid many an occasion for evil. He can deem himself good and pure because hard necessity does not teach him anything better. The natural man, on the other hand, has a wholeness that astonishes one, though there is nothing particularly admirable about it. It is the same old unconsciousness, apathy, and filth.

265   If, however, God is born as a man and wants to unite mankind in the fellowship of the Holy Ghost, he must suffer the terrible torture of having to endure the world in all its reality. This is the cross he has to bear, and he himself is a cross. The whole world is God's suffering, and every

individual man who wants to get anywhere near his own wholeness knows that this is the way of the cross.

266   These thoughts are expressed with touching simplicity and beauty in the Negro film *The Green Pastures*.[28] For many years God ruled the world with curses, thunder, lightning, and floods, but it never prospered. Finally he realized that he would have to become a man himself in order to get at the root of the trouble.

267   After he had experienced the world's suffering, this God who became man left behind him a Comforter, the Third Person of the Trinity, who would make his dwelling in many individuals still to come, none of whom would enjoy the privilege or even the possibility of being born without sin. In the Paraclete, therefore, God is closer to the real man and his darkness than he is in the Son. The light God bestrides the bridge – Man – from the day side; God's shadow, from the night side. What will be the outcome of this fearful dilemma, which threatens to shatter the frail human vessel with unknown storms and intoxications? It may well be the revelation of the Holy Ghost out of man himself. Just as man was once revealed out of God, so, when the circle closes, God may be revealed out of man. But since, in this world, an evil is joined to every good, the ἀντιμιμον πνεῦμα will twist the indwelling of the Paraclete into a self-deification of man, thereby causing an inflation of self-importance of which we had a foretaste in the case of Nietzsche. The more unconscious we are of the religious problem in the future, the greater the danger of our putting the divine germ within us to some ridiculous or demoniacal use, puffing ourselves up with it instead of remaining conscious that we are no more than the stable in which the Lord is born. Even on the highest peak we shall never be "beyond good and evil," and the more we experience of their inextricable entanglement the more uncertain and confused will our moral judgment be. In this conflict, it will not help us in the least to throw the moral criterion on the rubbish heap and to set up new tablets after known patterns; for, as in the past, so in the future the wrong we have done, thought, or intended will wreak its vengeance on our souls, no matter whether we turn the world upside down or not. Our knowledge of good and evil has dwindled with our mounting knowledge and experience, and will dwindle still more in the future, without our being able to escape the demands of ethics. In this utmost uncertainty we need the illumination of a holy and whole-making spirit – a spirit that can be anything rather than our reason.

II. THE PSYCHOLOGY OF THE QUATERNITY

268   As I have shown in the previous chapter [in *CW*], one can think out the problem of the fourth without having to discard a religious terminology. The development of the Trinity into a quaternity can be represented in

projection on metaphysical figures, and at the same time the exposition gains in plasticity. But any statements of this kind can – and for scientific reasons, must – be reduced to man and his psychology, since they are mental products which cannot be presumed to have any metaphysical validity. They are, in the first place, projections of psychic processes, and nobody really knows what they are "in themselves," i.e. if they exist in an unconscious sphere inaccessible to man. At any rate, science ought not to treat them as anything other than projections. If it acts otherwise, it loses its independence. And since it is not a question of individual fantasies but – at least so far as the Trinity is concerned – of a collective phenomenon, we must assume that the development of the idea of the Trinity is a collective process, representing a differentiation of consciousness that has been going on for several thousand years.

269   In order to interpret the Trinity-symbol psychologically, we have to start with the individual and regard the symbol as an expression of his psyche, rather as if it were a dream-image. It is possible to do this because even collective ideas once sprang from single individuals and, moreover, can only be "had" by individuals. We can treat the Trinity the more easily as a dream in that its life is a drama, as is also the case with every dream that is moderately well developed.

270   Generally speaking, the father denotes the earlier state of consciousness when one was still a child, still dependent on a definite, ready-made pattern of existence which is habitual and has the character of law. It is a passive, unreflecting condition, a mere awareness of what is given, without intellectual or moral judgment.[29] This is true both individually and collectively.

271   The picture changes when the accent shifts to the son. On the individual level the change usually sets in when the son starts to put himself in his father's place. According to the archaic pattern, this takes the form of quasi-father-murder – in other words, violent identification with the father followed by his liquidation. This, however, is not an advance; it is simply a retention of the old habits and customs with no subsequent differentiation of consciousness. No detachment from the father has been effected. Legitimate detachment consists in conscious differentiation from the father and from the habitus represented by him. This requires a certain amount of knowledge of one's own individuality, which cannot be acquired without moral discrimination and cannot be held on to unless one has understood its meaning.[30] Habit can only be replaced by a mode of life consciously chosen and acquired. The Christianity symbolized by the "Son" therefore forces the individual to discriminate and to reflect, as was noticeably the case with those Church Fathers[31] who laid such emphasis on ἐπιστήμη (knowledge) as opposed to ἀνάγκη (necessity) and ἄγνοια (ignorance). The same tendency is apparent in the New Testament controversies over the Jews' righteousness in the eyes of the law, which stands exclusively for the old habitus.

272   The third step, finally, points beyond the "Son" into the future, to a continuing realization of the "spirit," i.e. a living activity proceeding from "Father" and "Son" which raises the subsequent stages of consciousness to the same level of independence as that of "Father" and "Son." This extension of the *filiatio*, whereby men are made children of God, is a metaphysical projection of the psychic change that has taken place. The "Son" represents a transition stage, an intermediate state, part child, part adult. He is a transitory phenomenon, and it is thanks to this fact that the "Son"-gods die an early death. "Son" means the transition from a permanent initial stage called "Father" and "auctor rerum" to the stage of being a father oneself. And this means that the son will transmit to his children the procreative spirit of life which he himself has received and from which he himself was begotten. Brought down to the level of the individual, this symbolism can be interpreted as follows: the state of unreflecting awareness known as "Father" changes into the reflective and rational state of consciousness known as "Son." This state is not only in opposition to the still-existing earlier state, but, by virtue of its consciousness and rational nature, it also contains many latent possibilities of dissociation. Increased discrimination begets conflicts that were unconscious before but must now be faced, because, unless they are clearly recognized, no moral decisions can be taken. The stage of the "Son" is therefore a conflict situation *par excellence*: the choice of possible ways is menaced by just as many possibilities of error. "Freedom from the law" brings a sharpening of opposites, in particular of the moral opposites. Christ crucified between two thieves is an eloquent symbol of this fact. The exemplary life of Christ is in itself a "transitus" and amounts therefore to a bridge leading over to the third stage, where the initial stage of the Father is, as it were, recovered. If it were no more than a repetition of the first stage, everything that had been won in the second stage – reason and reflection – would be lost, only to make room for a renewed state of semiconsciousness, of an irrational and unreflecting nature. To avoid this, the values of the second stage must be held fast; in other words, reason and reflection must be preserved intact. Though the new level of consciousness acquired through the emancipation of the son continues in the third stage, it must recognize that *it* is not the source of the ultimate decisions and flashes of insight which rightly go by the name of "gnosis," but that these are inspired by a higher authority which, in projected form, is known as the "Holy Ghost." Psychologically speaking, "inspiration" comes from an unconscious function. To the naïve-minded person the agent of inspiration appears as an "intelligence" correlated with, or even superior to, consciousness, for it often happens that an idea drops in on one like a saving *deus ex machina*.

273   Accordingly, the advance to the third stage means something like a recognition of the unconscious, if not actual subordination to it.[32] Adulthood is reached when the son reproduces his own childhood state by

voluntarily submitting to a paternal authority, either in psychological form, or factually in projected form, as when he recognizes the authority of the Church's teachings. This authority can, of course, be replaced by all manner of substitutes, which only proves that the transition to the third stage is attended by unusual spiritual dangers, consisting chiefly in rationalistic deviations that run counter to the instincts.[33] Spiritual transformation does not mean that one should remain a child, but that the adult should summon up enough honest self-criticism admixed with humility to see where, and in relation to what, he must behave as a child – irrationally, and with unreflecting receptivity. Just as the transition from the first stage to the second demands the sacrifice of childish dependence, so, at the transition to the third stage, an exclusive independence has to be relinquished.

274   It is clear that these changes are not everyday occurrences, but are very fateful transformations indeed. Usually they have a numinous character, and can take the form of conversions, illuminations, emotional shocks, blows of fate, religious or mystical experiences, or their equivalents. Modern man has such hopelessly muddled ideas about anything "mystical," or else such a rationalistic fear of it, that, if ever a mystical experience should befall him, he is sure to misunderstand its true character and will deny or repress its numinosity. It will then be evaluated as an inexplicable, irrational, and even pathological phenomenon. This sort of misinterpretation is always due to lack of insight and inadequate understanding of the complex relationships in the background, which as a rule can only be clarified when the conscious data are supplemented by material derived from the unconscious. Without this, too many gaps remain unfilled in a man's experience of life, and each gap is an opportunity for futile rationalizations. If there is even the slightest tendency to neurotic dissociation, or an indolence verging upon habitual unconsciousness, then false causalities will be preferred to truth every time.

275   The numinous character of these experiences is proved by the fact that they are *overwhelming* – an admission that goes against not only our pride, but against our deep-rooted fear that consciousness may perhaps lose its ascendancy, for pride is often only a reaction covering up a secret fear. How thin these protective walls are can be seen from the positively terrifying suggestibility that lies behind all psychic mass movements, beginning with the simple folk who call themselves "Jehovah's Witnesses," the "Oxford Groups" (so named for reasons of prestige[34]) among the upper classes, and ending with the National Socialism of a whole nation – all in search of the unifying mystical experience!

276   Anyone who does not understand the events that befall him is always in danger of getting stuck in the transitional stage of the Son. The criterion of adulthood does not consist in being a member of certain sects, groups, or nations, but in submitting to the spirit of one's own independence. Just as the "Son" proceeds from the "Father," so the "Father" proceeds from

the stage of the "Son," yet this Father is not a mere repetition of the original Father or an identification with him, but one in whom the vitality of the "Father" continues its procreative work. This third stage, as we have seen, means articulating one's ego-consciousness with a supra-ordinate totality, of which one cannot say that it is "I," but which is best visualized as a more comprehensive being, though one should of course keep oneself conscious all the time of the anthropomorphism of such a conception. Hard as it is to define, this unknown quantity can be experienced by the psyche and is known in Christian parlance as the "Holy Ghost," the breath that heals and makes whole. Christianity claims that this breath also has personality, which in the circumstances could hardly be otherwise. For close on two thousand years history has been familiar with the figure of the Cosmic Man, the Anthropos, whose image has merged with that of Yahweh and also of Christ. Similarly, the saints who received the stigmata became Christ-figures in a visible and concrete sense, and thus carriers of the Anthropos-image. They symbolize the working of the Holy Ghost among men. The Anthropos is a symbol that argues in favour of the personal nature of the "totality," i.e. the self. If, however, you review the numerous symbols of the self, you will discover not a few among them that have no characteristics of human personality at all. I won't back up this statement with psychological case histories, which are *terra incognita* to the layman anyway, but will only refer to the historical material, which fully confirms the findings of modern scientific research. Alchemical symbolism has produced, aside from the personal figures, a whole series of non-human forms, geometrical configurations like the sphere, circle, square, and octagon, or chemical symbols like the Philosophers' Stone, the ruby, diamond, quicksilver, gold, water, fire, and spirit (in the sense of a volatile substance). This choice of symbols tallies more or less with the modern products of the unconscious.[35] I might mention in this connection that there are numerous theriomorphic spirit symbols, the most important Christian ones being the lamb, the dove, and the snake (Satan). The snake symbolizing the Gnostic Nous and the Agathodaimon has a pneumatic significance (the devil, too, is a spirit). These symbols express the non-human character of the totality or self, as was reported long ago when, at Pentecost, the spirit descended on the disciples in tongues of fire. From this point of view we can share something of Origen's perplexity as to the nature of the Holy Ghost. It also explains why the Third Person of the Trinity, unlike Father and Son, has no personal quality.[36] "Spirit" is not a personal designation but the qualitative definition of a substance of aeriform nature.

277   Whenever, as in the present instance, the unconscious makes such sweepingly contradictory statements, experience tells us that the situation is far from simple. The unconscious is trying to express certain facts for which there are no conceptual categories in the conscious mind. The contents in question need not be "metaphysical," as in the case of the

Holy Ghost. Any content that transcends consciousness, and for which the apperceptive apparatus does not exist, can call forth the same kind of paradoxical or antinomial symbolism. For a naïve consciousness that sees everything in terms of black and white, even the unavoidable dual aspect of "man and his shadow" can be transcendent in this sense and will consequently evoke pardoxical symbols. We shall hardly be wrong, therefore, if we conjecture that the striking contradictions we find in our spirit symbolism are proof that the Holy Ghost is a *complexio oppositorum* (union of opposites). Consciousness certainly possesses no conceptual category for anything of this kind, for such a union is simply inconceivable except as a violent collision in which the two sides cancel each other out. This would mean their mutual annihilation.

278   But the spontaneous symbolism of the *complexio oppositorum* points to the exact opposite of annihilation, since it ascribes to the product of their union either everlasting duration, that is to say incorruptibility and adamantine stability, or supreme and inexhaustible efficacy.[37]

279   Thus the spirit as a *complexio oppositorum* has the same formula as the "Father," the *auctor rerum*, who is also, according to Nicholas of Cusa, a union of opposites.[38] The "Father," in fact, contains the opposite qualities which appear in his son and his son's adversary. Riwkah Schärf[39] has shown just how far the monotheism of the Old Testament was obliged to make concessions to the idea of the "relativity" of God. The Book of Job comes within a hair's breadth of the dualism which flowered in Persia for some centuries before and after Christ, and which also gave rise to various heretical movements within Christianity itself. It was only to be expected, therefore, that, as we said above, the dual aspect of the "Father" should reappear in the Holy Ghost, who in this way effects an apocatastasis of the Father. To use an analogy from physics, the Holy Ghost could be likened to the stream of photons arising out of the destruction of matter, while the "Father" would be the primordial energy that promotes the formation of protons and electrons with their positive and negative charges. This, as the reader will understand, is not an explanation, but an analogy which is possible because the physicist's models ultimately rest on the same archetypal foundations that also underlie the speculations of the theologian. Both are psychology, and it too has no other foundation.

III. GENERAL REMARKS ON SYMBOLISM

280   Although it is extremely improbable that the Christian Trinity is derived directly from the triadic World-Soul in the *Timaeus*, it is nevertheless rooted in the same archetype. If we wish to describe the phenomenology of this archetype, we shall have to consider all the aspects which go to make up the total picture. For instance, in our analysis of the *Timaeus*, we found that the number three represents an intellectual schema only, and that the second mixture reveals the resistance of the "recalcitrant fourth"

ingredient, which we meet again as the "adversary" of the Christian Trinity. Without the fourth the three have no reality as we understand it; they even lack meaning, for a "thought" has meaning only if it refers to a possible or actual reality. This relationship to reality is completely lacking in the idea of the Trinity, so much so that people nowadays tend to lose sight of it altogether, without even noticing the loss. But we can see what this loss means when we are faced with the problem of reconstruction – that is to say in all those cases where the conscious part of the psyche is cut off from the unconscious part by a dissociation. This split can only be mended if consciousness is able to formulate conceptions which give adequate expression to the contents of the unconscious. It seems as if the Trinity plus the incommensurable "fourth" were a conception of this kind. As part of the doctrine of salvation it must, indeed, have a saving, healing, wholesome effect. During the process of integrating the unconscious contents into consciousness, undoubted importance attaches to the business of seeing how the dream-symbols relate to trivial everyday realities. But, in a deeper sense and on a long-term view, this procedure is not sufficient, as it fails to bring out the significance of the archetypal contents. These reach down, or up, to quite other levels than so-called common sense would suspect. As *a priori* conditions of all psychic events, they are endued with a dignity which has found immemorial expression in godlike figures. No other formulation will satisfy the needs of the unconscious. The unconscious is the unwritten history of mankind from time unrecorded. Rational formulae may satisfy the present and the immediate past, but not the experience of mankind as a whole. This calls for the all-embracing vision of the myth, as expressed in symbols. If the symbol is lacking, man's wholeness is not represented in consciousness. He remains a more or less accidental fragment, a suggestible wisp of consciousness, at the mercy of all the utopian fantasies that rush in to fill the gap left by the totality symbols. A symbol cannot be made to order as the rationalist would like to believe. It is a legitimate symbol only if it gives expression to the immutable structure of the unconscious and can therefore command general acceptance. So long as it evokes belief spontaneously, it does not require to be understood in any other way. But if, from sheer lack of understanding, belief in it begins to wane, then, for better or worse, one must use understanding as a tool if the incalculable consequences of a loss are to be avoided. What should we then put in place of the symbol? Is there anybody who knows a better way of expressing something that has never yet been understood?

281   As I have shown in *Psychology and Alchemy* and elsewhere, trinity and quaternity symbols occur fairly frequently in dreams, and from this I have learnt that the idea of the Trinity is based on something that can be experienced and must, therefore, have a meaning. This insight was not won by a study of the traditional sources. If I have succeeded in forming an intelligible conception of the Trinity that is in any way based on empirical

reality, I have been helped by dreams, folklore, and the myths in which these number motifs occur. As a rule they appear spontaneously in dreams, and such dreams look very banal from the outside. There is nothing at all of the myth or fairytale about them, much less anything religious. Mostly it is three men and a woman, either sitting at a table or driving in a car, or three men and a dog, a huntsman with three hounds, three chickens in a coop from which the fourth has escaped, and suchlike. These things are indeed so banal that one is apt to overlook them. Nor do they wish to say anything more specific, at first, than that they refer to functions and aspects of the dreamer's personality, as can easily be ascertained when they appear as three or four known persons with well-marked characteristics, or as the four principal colours, red, blue, green, and yellow. It happens with some regularity that these colours are correlated with the four orienting functions of consciousness. Only when the dreamer begins to reflect that the four are an allusion to his total personality does he realize that these banal dream-motifs are like shadow pictures of more important things. The fourth figure is, as a rule, particularly instructive: it soon becomes incompatible, disagreeable, frightening, or in some way odd, with a different sense of good and bad, rather like a Tom Thumb beside his three normal brothers. Naturally the situation can be reversed, with three odd figures and one normal one. Anybody with a little knowledge of fairytales will know that the seemingly enormous gulf that separates the Trinity from these trivial happenings is by no means unbridgeable. But this is not to say that the Trinity can be reduced to this level. On the contrary, the Trinity represents the most perfect form of the archetype in question. The empirical material merely shows, in the smallest and most insignificant psychic detail, how the archetype works. This is what makes the archetype so important, firstly as an organizing schema and a criterion for judging the quality of an individual psychic structure, and secondly as a vehicle of the synthesis in which the individuation process culminates. This goal is symbolized by the putting together of the four; hence the quaternity is a symbol of the self, which is of central importance in Indian philosophy and takes the place of the Deity. In the West, any amount of quaternities were developed during the Middle Ages; here I would mention only the *Rex gloriae* with the four symbols of the evangelists (three theriomorphic, one anthropomorphic). In Gnosticism there is the figure of Barbelo ("God is four"). These examples and many others like them bring the quaternity into closest relationship with the Deity, so that, as I said earlier, it is impossible to distinguish the self from a God-image. At any rate, I personally have found it impossible to discover a criterion of distinction. Here faith or philosophy alone can decide, neither of which has anything to do with the empiricism of the scientist.

282   One can, then, explain the God-image aspect of the quaternity as a reflection of the self, or, conversely, explain the self as an *imago Dei* in man. Both propositions are psychologically true, since the self, which can

only be perceived subjectively as a most intimate and unique thing, requires universality as a background, for without this it could not manifest itself in its absolute separateness. Strictly speaking, the self must be regarded as the extreme opposite of God. Nevertheless we must say with Angelus Silesius: "He cannot live without me, nor I without him." So although the empirical symbol requires two diametrically opposite interpretations, neither of them can be proved valid. The symbol means both and is therefore a paradox. This is not the place to say anything more about the role these number symbols play in practice; for this I must refer the reader to the dream material in *Psychology and Alchemy*, Part II.

283   In view of the special importance of quaternity symbolism one is driven to ask how it came about that a highly differentiated form of religion like Christianity reverted to the archaic triad in order to construct its trinitarian God-image.[40] With equal justification one could also ask (as has, in fact, been done) with what right Christ is presumed to be a symbol of the self, since the self is by definition a *complexio oppositorum*, whereas the Christ figure wholly lacks a dark side? (In dogma, Christ is *sine macula peccati* – 'unspotted by sin.')

284   Both questions touch on the same problem. I always seek the answer to such questions on empirical territory, for which reason I must now cite the concrete facts. It is a general rule that most geometrical or numerical symbols have a quaternary character. There are also ternary or trinitarian symbols, but in my experience they are rather rare. On investigating such cases carefully, I have found that they were distinguished by something that can only be called a "medieval psychology." This does not imply any backwardness and is not meant as a value judgment, but only as denoting a special problem. That is to say, in all these cases there is so much unconsciousness, and such a large degree of primitivity to match it, that a spiritualization appears necessary as a compensation. The saving symbol is then a triad in which the fourth is lacking because it has to be unconditionally rejected.

285   In my experience it is of considerable practical importance that the symbols aiming at wholeness should be correctly understood by the doctor. They are the remedy with whose help neurotic dissociations can be repaired, by restoring to the conscious mind a spirit and an attitude which from time immemorial have been felt as solving and healing in their effects. They are " représentations collectives" which facilitate the much-needed union of conscious and unconscious. This union cannot be accomplished either intellectually or in a purely practical sense, because in the former case the instincts rebel and in the latter case reason and morality. Every dissociation that falls within the category of the psychogenic neuroses is due to a conflict of this kind, and the conflict can only be resolved through the symbol. For this purpose the dreams produce symbols which in the last analysis coincide with those recorded throughout history.

But the dream-images can be taken up into the dreamer's consciousness, and grasped by his reason and feeling, only if his conscious mind possesses the intellectual categories and moral feelings necessary for their assimilation. And this is where the psychotherapist often has to perform feats that tax his patience to the utmost. The synthesis of conscious and unconscious can only be implemented by a conscious confrontation with the latter, and this is not possible unless one understands what the unconscious is saying. During this process we come upon the symbols investigated in the present study, and in coming to terms with them we re-establish the lost connection with ideas and feelings which make a synthesis of the personality possible. The loss of gnosis, i.e. knowledge of the ultimate things, weighs much more heavily than is generally admitted. Faith alone would suffice too, did it not happen to be a charisma whose true possession is something of a rarity, except in spasmodic form. Were it otherwise, we doctors could spare ourselves much thankless work. Theology regards our efforts in this respect with mistrustful mien, while pointedly declining to tackle this very necessary task itself. It proclaims doctrines which nobody understands, and demands a faith which nobody can manufacture. This is how things stand in the Protestant camp. The situation in the Catholic camp is more subtle. Of especial importance here is the ritual with its sacral action, which dramatizes the living occurrence of archetypal meaning and thus makes a direct impact on the unconscious. Can any one, for instance, deny the impression made upon him by the sacrament of the Mass, if he has followed it with even a minimum of understanding? Then again, the Catholic Church has the institution of confession and the director of conscience, which are of the greatest practical value when these activities devolve upon suitable persons. The fact that this is not always so proves, unfortunately, to be an equally great disadvantage. Thirdly, the Catholic Church possesses a richly developed and undamaged world of dogmatic ideas, which provide a worthy receptacle for the plethora of figures in the unconscious and in this way give visible expression to certain vitally important truths with which the conscious mind should keep in touch. The faith of a Catholic is not better or stronger than the faith of a Protestant, but a person's unconscious is gripped by the Catholic form no matter how weak his faith may be. That is why, once he slips out of this form, he may easily fall into a fanatical atheism, of a kind that is particularly to be met with in Latin countries.

NOTES

1 "Feeling is all; / Names are sound and smoke." [This problem of the "fourth" in *Faust* is also discussed in *Psychology and Alchemy*, pars. 201ff. – EDITORS.]
2 Cf. *Psychological Types*, Def. 30.
3 Cf. the Hymn of Valentinus (Mead, *Fragments of a Faith Forgotten*, p. 307): "All things depending in spirit I see; all things supported in spirit I view; flesh from soul depending; soul by air supported; air from aether hanging; fruits born of the

deep; babe born of the womb." Cf. also the προσφυὴς ψυχή of Isodorus, who supposed that all manner of animal qualities attached to the human soul in the form of "outgrowths." [Cf. *Aion*, par. 370.]

4 Cf. the alchemical symbol of the *umbra solis* and the Gnostic idea that Christ was born "not without some shadow."

5 The four ῥιζώματα of Empedocles.

6 "On the Fourfold Root of the Principle of Sufficient Reason," in *Two Essays by Arthur Schopenhauer.*

7 In Plato the quaternity takes the form of a cube, which he correlates with earth. Lü Pu-wei (*Frühling und Herbst*, trans. into German by Wilhelm, p. 38) says: "Heaven's way is round, earth's way is square."

8 In her "Die Gestalt des Satans im Alten Testament" (*Symbolik des Geistes*, pp. 153ff.), Riwkah Schärf shows that Satan is in fact one of God's sons, at any rate in the Old Testament sense.

9 The suffix *-el* means god, so Satanaël = Satan-God.

9a Michael Psellus, "De Daemonibus," 1497, fol. NVᵛ, ed. M. Ficino. Cf. also Epiphanius, *Panarium*, Haer. XXX, in Migne, *P.G.*, vol. 41, cols. 406ff.

10 Cf. Przywara's meditations on the Cross and its relation to God in *Deus Semper Major* I. Also the early Christian interpretation of the Cross in the Acts of John, trans. by James, pp. 228ff.

11 See *Psychology and Alchemy*, fig. 28.

12 Cf. *Psychology and Alchemy*, pars. 315ff., and the first paper in this volume, pars. 122ff.

13 As this doctrine has already got beyond the stage of "conclusio probabilis" and has reached that of "conclusio certa," the "definitio sollemnis" is now only a matter of time. The Assumption is, doctrinally speaking, a "revelatum implicitum"; that is to say, it has never been revealed explicitly, but, in the gradual course of development, it became clear as an original content of the Revelation. (Cf. Wiederkehr, *Die leibliche Aufnahme der allerseligsten Jungfrau Maria in den Himmel.*) From the psychological standpoint, however, and in terms of the history of symbols, this view is a consistent and logical restoration of the archetypal situation, in which the exalted status of Mary is revealed implicitly and must therefore become a "conclusio certa" in the course of time.

   [This note was written in 1948, two years before the promulgation of the dogma. The bodily assumption of Mary into heaven was defined as a dogma of the Catholic faith by Pope Pius XII in November 1950 by the Apostolic Constitution *Munificentissimus Deus (Acta Apostolicae Sedis*, Rome, XLII, pp. 753ff.), and in an Encyclical Letter, *Ad Caeli Reginam*, of October 11, 1954, the same Pope instituted a feast to be observed yearly in honour of Mary's "regalis dignitas" as Queen of Heaven and Earth (*Acta Apostolicae Sedis*, XLVI, pp. 625ff.). – EDITORS.]

14 Although the assumption of Mary is of fundamental significance, it was not the first case of this kind. Enoch and Elijah were taken up to heaven with their bodies, and many holy men rose from their graves when Christ died.

15 Her divinity may be regarded as a tacit *conclusio probabilis*, and so too may the worship or adoration (προσκύνησις) to which she is entitled.

16 Koepgen (p. 185) expresses himself in similar terms: "The essence of the devil is his hatred for God; and God allows this hatred. There are two things which Divine Omnipotence alone makes possible: Satan's hatred and the existence of the human individual. Both are by nature completely inexplicable. But so, too, is their relationship to God."

17 Just how alive and ingrained such conceptions are can be seen from the title of a modern book by Sosnosky, *Die rote Dreifaltigkeit: Jakobiner und Bolscheviken* ["The Red Trinity: Jacobins and Bolsheviks"].

18 Koepgen's views are not so far from my own in certain respects. For instance, he says that "Satan acts, in a sense, as God's power. . . . The mystery of one God in Three Persons opens out a new freedom in the depths of God's being, and this even makes possible the thought of a personal devil existing alongside God and in opposition to him" (p. 186).

19 Since Satan, like Christ, is a son of God, it is evident that we have here the archetype of the hostile brothers. The Old Testament prefiguration would therefore be Cain and Abel and their sacrifice. Cain has a Luciferian nature because of his rebellious progressiveness, but Abel is the pious shepherd. At all events, the vegetarian trend got no encouragement from Yahweh [Gen. 4:5].

20 See the first paper in this volume, par. 104.

21 In antiquity, regard for astrology was nothing at all extraordinary. [Cf. "Synchronicity: An Acausal Connecting Principle," pars. 827ff., and *Aion*, pars. 127ff. – EDITORS.]

22 This applies to the zodion of the Fishes. In the astronomical constellation itself, the fish that corresponds approximately to the first 1,000 years of our era is vertical, but the other fish is horizontal.

23 God's antithetical nature is also expressed in his androgyny. Priscillian therefore calls him "masculofoemina," on the basis of Genesis 1:27: "So God created man in his own image . . . male and female created he them."

24 Cf. *Psychology and Alchemy*, pars. 520ff.

25 Cf. above, pars. 104ff.

26 *Faust* Part II, Act 5. ("Earth's residue to bear / Hath sorely pressed us." Trans. by Bayard Taylor.)

27 Cf. James, *The Apocryphal New Testament*, p. 255.

28 [From a play by Marc Connelly, adapted from stories by Roark Bradford based on American Negro folk-themes. – EDITORS.]

29 Yahweh approaches the moral problem comparatively late – only in Job. Cf. "Answer to Job," in this volume.

30 Koepgen (p. 231) therefore calls Jesus, quite rightly, the first "autonomous" personality.

31 Justin Martyr, *Apologia* II: "that we may not remain children of necessity and ignorance, but of choice and knowledge." Clement of Alexandria, *Stromata*, I, 9: "And how necessary it is for him who desires to be partaker of the power of God, to treat of intellectual subjects by philosophizing!" II, 4: "Knowledge accordingly is characterized by faith; and faith, by a kind of divine mutual and reciprocal correspondence, becomes characterized by knowledge." VII, 10: "For by it (Gnosis) faith is perfected, inasmuch as it is solely by it that the believer becomes perfect." "And knowledge is the strong and sure demonstration of what is received by faith." (Trans. by Wilson, I, p. 380; II, pp. 10, 446–7.)

32 Submission to any metaphysical authority is, from the psychological standpoint, submission to the unconscious. There are no scientific criteria for distinguishing so-called metaphysical factors from psychic ones. But this does not mean that psychology denies the existence of metaphysical factors.

33 The Church knows that the "discernment of spirits" is no simple matter. It knows the dangers of subjective submission to God and therefore reserves the right to act as a director of conscience.

34 The "Oxford Movement" was originally the name of the Catholicizing trend started by the Anglican clergy in Oxford, 1833. [Whereas the "Oxford Groups," or "Moral Rearmament Movement," were founded in 1921, also at Oxford, by Frank Buchanan as "a Christian revolution . . . the aim of which is a new social order under the dictatorship of the Spirit of God, and which issues in personal, social, racial, national, and supernatural renaissance" (Buchanan, cited in *Webster's International Dictionary*, 2nd edn, 1950) – EDITORS.]

35 Cf. *Psychology and Alchemy*, Part II.
36 Thomas Aquinas (*Summa theologica*, I, xxxvi, art. 1): "Non habet nomen proprium" (he has no proper name). I owe this reference to the kindness of F. Victor White, O.P.
37 Both these categories are, as we know, attributes of the *lapis philosophorum* and of the symbols of the self.
38 It should not be forgotten, however, that the opposites which Nicholas had in mind were very different from the psychological ones.
39 Cf. "Die Gestalt des Satans im Alten Testament," in *Symbolik des Geistes*, pp. 153ff.
40 In the Greek Church the Trinity is called τριάς.

5   Two letters to Father Victor White

From: *C.J. Jung: Letters, Vol. 2* (58–61, 163–74)

30 April 1952

Dear Victor,

The *privatio boni* seems to be a puzzle.[1] A few days ago I had an interesting interview with a Jesuit father from Munich (Lotz is his name). He is professor of dogmatics (?) or Christian philosophy. He was just in the middle of *Antwort auf Hiob* and under the immediate impact of my argument against the *privatio*. He admitted that it is a puzzle, but that the modern interpretation would explain "Evil" as a "disintegration" or a "decomposition" of "Good." If you hypostatize – as the Church does – the concept or idea of Good and give to it metaphysical substance (i.e. *bonum* = *esse* or having *esse*), then "decomposition" would be indeed a very suitable formula, also satisfactory from the psychological standpoint, as Good is always an effort and a composite achievement while Evil is easily sliding down or falling asunder. But if you take your simile of the good egg,[2] it would become a bad egg by decomposition. A bad egg is not characterized by a mere decrease of goodness however, since it produces qualities of its own that did not belong to the good egg. It develops among other things H_2S, which is a particularly unpleasant substance in its own right. It derives very definitely from the highly complex albumen of the good egg and thus forms a most obvious evidence for the thesis: Evil derives from Good.

Thus the formula of "decomposition" is rather satisfactory in so far as it acknowledges that Evil is as substantial as Good, because H_2S is as tangibly real as the albumen. In this interpretation Evil is far from being a μὴ ὄν. Pater Lotz therefore had my applause. But what about the *privatio boni?* Good, by definition, must be good throughout, even in its smallest particles. You cannot say that a small good is bad. If then a good thing disintegrates into minute fragments, each of them remains good and therefore eatable like a loaf of bread divided into small particles. But when the bread rots, it oxidizes and changes its original substance. There are no more nourishing carbohydrates, but acids, i.e. from a good substance has come a bad thing. The "decomposition" theory would lead to the ultimate conclusion that the Summum Bonum can disintegrate and produce H_2S, the characteristic smell of Hell. Good then would be corruptible, i.e. it would possess an inherent possibility of decay. This possibility of corruption means nothing less than a tendency inherent in the Good to decay and to change into Evil. That obviously confirms my heretical views. But I don't even go as far as Pater Lotz: I am quite satisfied with nonhypostatizing Good and Evil. I consider them not as substances but as a merely psychological judgment since I have no means of establishing them as metaphysical substances. I don't deny the possibility of a belief that they are substances and that Good prevails against Evil. I even take into consideration that there is a large consensus in that respect, for which there must be important reasons (as I have pointed out in *Aion*).[3] But if you try to make something logical or rationalistic out of that belief, you get into a remarkable mess, as the argument with Pater Lotz clearly shows.

You know, I am not only empirical but also practical. In practice you say nothing when you hold that in an evil deed is a small Good: there is big Evil and a little bit of Good. In practice you just can't deny the ὀυσία of Evil. On the metaphysical plane you are free to declare that what we call "substantially evil" is in metaphysical reality a small Good. But such a statement does not make much sense to me. You call God the Lord over Evil, but if the latter is μὴ ὄν, He is Lord over nothing, not even over the Good, because He is it Himself as the Summum Bonum that has created only good things which have however a marked tendency to go wrong. Nor does evil or corruption derive from man, since the serpent is prior to him, so πόθεν τὸ κακόν???[4]

The necessary answer is: Metaphysically there is no Evil at all; it is only in man's world and it stems from man. This statement however contradicts the fact that paradise was not made by man. He came last into it, nor did he make the serpent. If even God's most beautiful angel, Lucifer, has such a desire to get corrupt, his nature must show a considerable defect of moral qualities – like Yahweh, who insists jealously on morality and is himself unjust. No wonder that His creation has a yellow streak.

Does the doctrine of the Church admit Yahweh's moral defects? If so, Lucifer merely portrays his creator; if not, what about the 89th Psalm,[5] etc.? *Yahweh's immoral behaviour rests on biblical facts. A morally dubious creator cannot be expected to produce a perfectly good world*, not even perfectly good angels.

I know theologians always say: one should not overlook the Lord's greatness, majesty, and kindness and one shouldn't ask questions anyhow. I don't overlook God's fearful greatness, but I should consider myself a coward and immoral if I allowed myself to be deterred from asking questions.

On the practical level the *privatio boni* doctrine is morally dangerous, because it belittles and irrealizes Evil and thereby weakens the Good, because it deprives it of its necessary opposite: there is no white without black, no right without left, no above without below, no warm without cold, no truth without error, no light without darkness, etc. If Evil is an illusion, Good is necessarily illusory too. That is the reason why I hold that the *privatio boni* is illogical, irrational and even a nonsense. The moral opposites are an epistemological necessity and, when hypostatized, they produce an amoral Yahweh and a Lucifer and a Serpent and sinful Man and a suffering Creation.

I hope we can continue worrying this bone in the summer!

Cordially yours, C. G.

P.S. Unfortunately I have no copy of the letter to the Prot. theologian.[6] But I will send you an offprint of my answer to Buber,[7] who has called me a Gnostic. He does not understand psychic reality.

[ORIGINAL IN ENGLISH]

Dear Victor,   Bollingen, 10 April 1954

Your letter[8] has been lying on my desk waiting for a suitable time to be answered. In the meantime I was still busy with a preface I had promised to P. Radin and K. Kerényi. They are going to bring out a book together about the figure of the *trickster*.[9] He is the collective shadow. I finished my preface yesterday. I suppose you know the Greek-Orthodox priest, Dr. Zacharias?[10] He has finished his book representing a reception, or better – an attempt – to integrate Jungian psychology into Christianity as he sees it. Dr Rudin S.J. from the Institute of Apologetics did not like it. Professor Gebhard Frei on the other hand was very positive about it.

I am puzzled about your conception of Christ and I try to understand it. It looks to me as if you were mixing up the idea of Christ being human and being divine. Inasmuch as he is divine he knows, of course, everything, because all things macrocosmic are supposed to be microcosmic as well and can therefore be said to be known by the self. (Things moreover behave as if they were known.) It is an astonishing fact, indeed, that the collective unconscious seems to be in contact with nearly everything. There is of course no empirical evidence for such a generalization, but plenty of it for its indefinite extension. The *sententia*, therefore: *animam Christi nihil ignoravisse*[11] etc. is not contradicted by psychological experience. *Rebus sic stantibus*, Christ as the self can be said *ab initio cognovisse omnia* etc. I should say that Christ knew his shadow – Satan – whom he cut off from himself right in the beginning of his career. The self is a unit, consisting however of two, i.e. of opposites, otherwise it would not be a totality. Christ has consciously divorced himself from his shadow. Inasmuch as he is divine, he is the self, yet only its white half. Inasmuch as he is human, he has never lost his shadow completely, but seems to have been conscious of it. How could he say otherwise: "Do not call me good . . . "?[12] It is also reasonable to believe that as a human he was not wholly conscious of it, and inasmuch as he was unconscious he projected it indubitably. The split through his self made him as a human being as good as possible, although he was unable to reach the degree of perfection his white self already possessed. The Catholic doctrine cannot but declare that *Christ even as a human being knew everything*. This is the logical consequence of the perfect union of the *duae naturae.* Christ as understood by the Church is to me a spiritual, i.e. mythological being; even his humanity is divine as it is generated by the celestial Father and exempt from original sin. When I speak of him as a human being, I mean its few traces we can gather from the gospels. It is not enough for the reconstruction of an empirical character. Moreover, even if we could reconstruct an individual personality, it would not fulfil the role of redeemer and God-man who is identical with the "all-knowing" self. Since the individual human being is characterized by a selection of tendencies and qualities, it is a specification and not a wholeness, i.e. it cannot be individual without incompleteness and restriction, whereas the Christ of the doctrine is perfect, complete, whole and therefore not individual at all, but a collective mythologem, viz. an archetype. He is far more divine than human and far more universal than individual.

Concerning the omniscience it is important to know that *Adam* already was equipped with supernatural knowledge according to Jewish and Christian tradition,[13] all the more so Christ.

I think that the great split[14] in those days was by no means a mistake but a very important collective fact of synchronistic correspondence with the then new aeon of Pisces. Archetypes, in spite of their conservative nature, are not static but *in a continuous dramatic flux.* Thus the self as a monad or continuous unit would be dead. But it lives inasmuch as it splits and unites again. There is no energy without opposites!

All conservatives and institutionalists are Pharisees, if you apply this name without prejudice. Thus it was to be expected that just the better part of Jewry would be hurt most by the revelation of an exclusively good God and loving Father. This novelty emphasized with disagreeable clearness that the Yahweh hitherto worshipped had some additional, less decorous propensities. For obvious reasons the orthodox Pharisees could not defend their creed by insisting on the bad qualities of their God. Christ with his teaching of an exclusively good God must have been most awkward for them. They probably believed him to be hypocritical, since this was his main objection against them. One gets that way when one has to hold on to something which once has been good and had meant considerable progress or improvement at the time. It was an enormous step forward when Yahweh revealed himself as a *jealous* God, letting his chosen people feel that he was after them with blessings and with punishments, and that God's goal was man. Not knowing better, they cheated him by obeying his Law literally. But as Job discovered Yahweh's primitive amorality, God found out about the trick of observing the Law and swallowing camels.[15]

The old popes and bishops succeeded in getting so much heathendom, barbarism and real evil out of the Church that it became much better than some centuries before: there were no Alexander VI,[16] no auto-da-fés, no thumbscrews and racks any more, so that the compensatory drastic virtues (asceticism etc.) lost their meaning to a certain extent. The great split, having been a merely spiritual fact for a long time, has at last got into the world, as a rule in its coarsest and least recognizable form, viz. as the iron curtain, the completion of the second Fish.[17]

Now a new synthesis must begin. But how can absolute evil be connected and identified with absolute good? It seems to be impossible. When Christ withstood Satan's temptation, that was the fatal moment when the shadow was cut off. Yet it had to be cut off in order to enable man to become morally conscious. If the moral opposites could be united at all, they would be suspended altogether and there could be no morality at all. That is certainly not what synthesis aims at. In such a case of irreconcilability the opposites are united by a neutral or ambivalent bridge, a symbol expressing either side in such a way that they can function together.[18] This symbol is the *cross* as interpreted of old, viz. as the tree of life or simply as the tree to which Christ is inescapably affixed. This particular feature points to the compensatory significance of the tree: the tree symbolizes that entity from which Christ had been separated and with which he ought to be connected again to make his life or his being complete. In other words, the *Crucifixus* is the symbol uniting the absolute moral opposites. Christ represents the light; the tree, the darkness; he the son, it the mother. Both are *androgynous* (tree = phallus).[19] Christ is so much identical with the cross that both terms have become almost interchangeable in ecclesiastical language (f.i. "redeemed through Christ or through the cross" etc.). The tree brings back all that has been lost through Christ's extreme spiritualization, namely the elements of nature. Through its branches and leaves the tree gathers the powers of light and air, and through its roots those of the earth and the water. Christ was suffering on account of his split and he recovers his perfect life at Easter, when he is buried again in the womb of the virginal mother. (Represented also in the myth of Attis by the tree, to which an image of Attis was nailed, then cut down and carried into the cave of the mother Kybele.[20] The Nativity Church of Bethlehem is erected over an Attis sanctuary!)[21] This mythical complex seems to represent a further development of the old drama, existence becoming real through reflection in consciousness, Job's tragedy.[22] But now it is the problem of dealing with the results of conscious discrimination. The first attempt is moral appreciation and decision for the Good. Although this decision is indispensable, it is not too good in the long run. You must not get stuck with it, otherwise you grow out of life and die slowly. Then the one-sided emphasis on the Good becomes doubtful, but there is apparently no possibility of reconciling Good and Evil. That is where we are now.

The symbolic history of Christ's life shows, as the essential teleological tendency, the crucifixion, vis. the union of Christ with the symbol of the tree. It is no longer a matter of an impossible reconciliation of Good and Evil, but of man with his vegetative (= unconscious) life. In the case of the Christian symbol the tree, however, is dead and man upon the Cross is going to die, i.e. the solution of the problem takes place after death. That is so far as Christian truth goes. But it is possible that the Christian symbolism expresses man's mental condition in the aeon of Pisces, as the ram and the bull gods do for the ages of Aries and Taurus. In this case the post-mortal solution would be symbolic of an entirely new psychological status, viz. that of Aquarius, which is certainly a oneness, presumably that of the Anthropos, the realization of Christ's allusion: *"Dii estis."*[23] This is a formidable secret and difficult to understand, because it means that man will be essentially God and God man. The signs pointing in this direction consist in the fact that the cosmic power of self-destruction is given into the hands of man and that man inherits the dual nature of the Father. He will [mis]understand it and he will be tempted to ruin the universal life of the earth by radioactivity. Materialism and atheism, the negation of God, are indirect means to attain this goal. Through the negation of God one becomes deified, i.e. god-almighty-like, and then one knows what is good for mankind. That is how destruction begins. The intellectual schoolmasters in the Kremlin are a classic example. The danger of following the same path is very great indeed. It begins with the lie, i.e. the projection of the shadow.

There is need of people knowing about their shadow, because there must be somebody who does not project. They ought to be in a visible position where they would be expected to project and unexpectedly they do not project! They can thus set a visible example which would not be seen if they were invisible.

There is certainly Pharisaism, law consciousness, power drive, sex obsession, and the wrong kind of formalism in the Church. But these things are symptoms that the old showy and easily understandable ways and methods have lost their significance and should be slowly replaced by more meaningful principles. This indeed means trouble with the Christian vices. Since you cannot overthrow a whole world because it harbours also some evil, it will be a more individual or "local" fight with what you rightly call *avidya*. As "tout passe," even theological books are not true forever, and even if they expect to be believed one has to tell them in a loving and fatherly way that they make some mistakes. A true and honest introverted thinking is a grace and possesses for at least a time divine authority, particularly if it is modest, simple and straight. The people who write such books are not the voice of God. They are only human. It is true that the right kind of thinking isolates oneself. But did you become a monk for the sake of congenial society? Or do you assume that it isolates only a theologian? It has done the same to me and will do so to everybody that is blessed with it.

That is the reason why there are compensatory functions. The introverted thinker is very much in need of a developed feeling, i.e. of a less autoerotic, sentimental, melodramatic and emotional relatedness to people and things. The compensation will be a hell of a conflict to begin with, but later on, by understanding what *nirdvandva*[24] means, they[25] become the pillars at the gate of the transcendent function, i.e. the *transitus* to the self.

We should recognize that life is a *transitus*. There is an old covered bridge near Schmerikon[26] with an inscription: "Alles ist Uebergang."[27] Even the Church and her *sententiae* are only alive inasmuch as they change. All old truths want a new interpretation, so that they can live on in a new form. They can't be substituted or replaced by something else without losing their functional value altogether. The Church certainly expects of you that you assimilate its doctrine. But in assimilating it, you change it imperceptibly and sometimes even noticeably. Introverted thinking is aware of such subtle alterations, while other minds swallow them wholesale. If you try to be literal about the doctrine, you are putting yourself aside until there is nobody left that would represent it but corpses. If, on the other hand, you truly assimilate the doctrine, you will alter it creatively by your individual understanding and thus give life to it. The life of most ideas consists in their controversial nature, i.e., you can disagree with them even if you recognize their importance for a majority. If you fully agreed with them you could replace yourself just as well by a gramophone record. Moreover, if you don't disagree, you are no good as a *directeur de conscience*, since there are many other people suffering from the same difficulty and being badly in need of your understanding.

I appreciate the particular moral problem you are confronted with. But I should rather try to understand why you were put into your actual situation of profound conflict before you think it is a fundamental mistake. I remember vividly your *charga geomantica*[28] that depicts so drastically the way you became a monk. I admit there are people with the peculiar gift of getting inevitably and always into the wrong place. With such people nothing can be done except get them out of the wrong hole into another equally dubious one. But if I find an intelligent man in an apparently wrong situation, I am inclined to think it makes sense somehow. There may be some work for him to do. Much work is needed where much has gone wrong or where much should be improved. That is one of the reasons why the Church attracts quite a number of intelligent and responsible men in the secret (or unconscious?) hope that they will be strong enough to carry its meaning and not its words into the future. The old trick of law obedience is still going strong, but the original Christian teaching is a reminder. The man who allows the institution to swallow him is not a good servant.

It is quite understandable that the ecclesiastical authorities must protect the Church against subversive influences. But it would be sabotage if this principle were carried to the extreme, because it would kill the attempts at improvement also. The Church is a "Durchgang" [passage] and bridge between representatives of higher and lower consciousness and as such she quite definitely makes sense. Since the world is largely *sub principatu diaboli*, it is unavoidable that there is just as much evil in the Church as everywhere else, and as everywhere else you have got to be careful. What would you do if you were a bank-clerk or a medical assistant at a big clinic? You are always and everywhere in a moral conflict unless you are blissfully unconscious. I think it is not only honest but even highly moral and altruistic to be what one professes to be as completely as possible, with the full consciousness that you are making this effort for the weak and the unintelligent who cannot live without a reliable support. He is a good physician who does not bother the patient with his own doubts and feelings of inferiority. Even if he knows little or is quite inefficient the right *persona medici* might carry the day if seriously and truly performed for the patient. The grace of God may step in when you don't lose your head in a clearly desperate situation. If it has been done, even with a lie, in favour of the patient, it has been well done, and you are justified, although you never get out of the awkward feeling that you are a dubious number. I wonder whether there is any true servant of God who can rid himself of this profound insecurity balancing his obvious rightness. I cannot forget that crazy old Negro Mammy[29] who told me: "God is working in me like a clock – funny and serious." By "clock" seems to be meant something precise and regular, even monotonous; by "funny and serious" compensating irrational events and aspects – a humorous seriousness expressing the playful and formidable nature of fateful experiences.

If I find myself in a critical or doubtful situation, I always ask myself whether there is not something in it, explaining the need of my presence, before I make a plan of how to escape. If I should find nothing hopeful or meaningful in it, I think I would not hesitate to jump out of it as quick as possible. Well, I may be all wrong, but the fact that you find yourself in the Church does not impress me as being wholly nonsensical. Of course huge sacrifices are expected of you, but I wonder whether there is any vocation or any kind of meaningful life that does not demand sacrifices of a sort. There is no place where those striving after consciousness could find absolute safety. Doubt and insecurity are indispensable components of a complete life. Only those who can lose this life *really*, can gain it. A "complete" life does not consist in a theoretical completeness, but in the fact that one accepts, without reservation, the particular fatal tissue in which one finds oneself embedded, and that one tries to make sense of it or to create a cosmos from the chaotic mess into which one is born. If one lives properly and completely, time and again one will be confronted with a situation of which one will say: "This is too much. I cannot bear it any more." Then the question must be answered: "Can one really not bear it?"

Fidem non esse caecum sensum religionis e latebris subconscientiae erumpentem,[30] etc., indeed not! *Fides* in its ecclesiastical meaning is a construction expressed by the wholly artificial credo, but no spontaneous product of the unconscious. You can swear to it in all innocence, as well as I could, if asked. Also you can *teach*, if asked, the *solid* doctrine of St. Thomas Aquinas, as I could if I knew it. You can and will and must criticize it, yet with a certain discrimination, as there are people incapable of understanding your argument. *Quieta movere*[31] is not necessarily a good principle. Being an analyst, you know how little you can say, and sometimes it is quite enough when only the analyst knows. Certain things transmit themselves by air when they are really needed.

I don't share at all X.'s idea that one should not be so finicky about conscience. It is definitely dishonest and – sorry – a bit too Catholic. One must be finicky when it comes to a moral question, and what a question! You are asked to decide whether you can deal with ambiguity, deception, "doublecrossing" and other damnable things for the love of your neighbour's soul. If it is a case of "the end justifying the means," you had better buy a through ticket to hell. It is a devilish hybris even to think that one could be in such an exalted position to decide about the means one is going to apply. There is no such thing, not even in psychotherapy. If you don't want to go to the dogs morally, there is only one question, namely "Which is the necessity you find yourself burdened with when you take to heart your brother's predicament?" The question is *how you are applied* in the process of the cure, and not at all what the means are you could offer to buy yourself off. It depends very much indeed upon the way you envisage your position with reference to the Church. I should advocate an analytical attitude, which is permissible as well as honest, viz. take the Church as your ailing employer and your colleagues as the unconscious inmates of a hospital.

Is the LSD-drug mescalin?[32] It has indeed very curious effects – *vide* Aldous Huxley![33] – of which I know far too little. I don't know either what its psychotherapeutic value with neurotic or psychotic patients is. I only know there is no point in wishing to *know* more of the collective unconscious than one gets through dreams and intuition. The more you know of it, the greater and heavier becomes your moral burden, because the unconscious contents transform themselves into your individual tasks and duties as soon as they begin to become conscious. Do you want to increase loneliness and mis-understanding? Do you want to find more and more complications and increasing responsibilities? You get enough of it. If I once could say that I had done everything I know I had to do, then perhaps I should realize a legitimate need to take mescalin. But if I should take it now, I would not be sure at all that I had not taken it out of idle curiosity. I should hate the thought that I had touched on the sphere where the paint is made that colours the world, where the light is created that makes shine the splendour of the dawn, the lines and shapes of all form, the sound that fills the orbit, the thought that illuminates the darkness of the void. There are some poor impoverished creatures, perhaps, for whom mescalin would be a heavensent gift without a counterpoison, but I am profoundly mistrustful of the "pure gifts of the Gods." You pay very dearly for them. *Quidquid id est, timeo Danaos et dona ferentes.*[34]

This is not the point at all, to know of or about the unconscious, nor does the story end here; on the contrary it is how and where you begin the real quest. If you are too unconscious it is a great relief to know a bit of the collective unconscious. But it soon becomes dangerous to know more, because one does not learn at the same time how to balance it through a conscious equivalent. That is the mistake Aldous Huxley makes: he does not know that he is in the role of the "Zauberlehrling," who learned from his master how to call the ghosts but did not know how to get rid of them again:

Die ich rief, die Geister,
Werd ich nun nicht los![35]

It is really the mistake of our age. We think it is enough to discover new things, but we don't realize that knowing more demands a corresponding development of morality. Radioactive clouds over Japan, Calcutta, and Saskatchewan point to progressive poisoning of the universal atmosphere.

I should indeed be obliged to you if you could let me see the material they get with LSD. It is quite awful that the alienists have caught hold of a new poison to play with, without the faintest knowledge or feeling of responsibility. It is just as if a surgeon had never learned further than to cut open his patient's belly and to leave things there. When one gets to know unconscious contents one should know how to deal with them. I can only hope that the doctors will feed themselves thoroughly with mescalin, the *alkaloid of divine grace*, so that they learn for themselves its marvellous effect. You have not finished with the conscious side yet. Why should you expect more from the unconscious? For 35 years I have known enough of the collective unconscious and my whole effort is concentrated upon preparing the ways and means to deal with it.

Now to end this very long epistle I must say how much I have appreciated your confidence, frankness, courage and honesty. This is so rare and so precious an event that it is a pleasure to answer at length. I hope you will find a way out to Switzerland.

. . .

The winter, though very cold, has dealt leniently with me. Both my wife and myself are tired, though still active, but in a very restricted way.

I am spending the month of April in Bollingen *procul negotiis*[36] and the worst weather we have known for years.

Cordially yours, C. G.

NOTES

1 Cf. White, 9 Apr. 52, to which he sent a short reply on 20 Apr., complaining of "the deadlock of assertion and counter-assertion" in spite of good will. "We move in different circles, and our minds have been formed in different philosophical climates."

2 In his letter of 20 Apr. W. wrote: "The validity of any particular judgment of value is surely quite another question from the meaning of the terms [good and evil] employed. There is surely nothing religious or archetypal in my motivation, nor anything illogical or transcendental, when I call an egg 'bad' because it *lacks* what I think an egg ought to have."

3 Cf. pars. 81ff., 100f.

4 = whence evil?

5 In *Aion*, par. 169, Jung mentions a story told by Abraham ben Meier ibn Ezra (Jewish scholar and poet, 1092–1167) of "a great sage who was reputed to be unable to read the 89th Psalm because it saddened him too much." The story occurs in Ibn Ezra's Commentary on the Psalms. Psalm 89 deals with Yahweh's lack of loyalty toward King David; to Jung this was a parallel to the tragedy of Job.

6 Cf. White, Spring 52, n. 7.

7 Cf. Neumann, 28 Feb. 52, n. 9.

8 W. wrote a long letter on 3 Mar. 54 in answer to Jung's of 24 Nov. 53, expressing agreement with most of what he said. It deals largely with Jung's views on the problem of "Christ's shadow," which contradict the Catholic doctrine that Christ knew everything (and therefore could not have a shadow).

9 Jung's commentary "On the Psychology of the Trickster Figure" (*CW* 9/1) for Paul Radin, *The Trickster* (1956; orig. *Der göttliche Schelm*, 1954). Kerényi wrote the other commentary.

10 Cf. Zacharias, 24 Aug. 53.

11 "Christ's soul was not ignorant of anything." This and the following *ab initio cognovisse omnia* ("from the beginning he knew everything") are two statements of the Holy Roman Office (one of the eleven departments of the Roman Curia) laid down in 1918 and quoted by W.

12 Cf. Matthew 19 : 17, Mark 10 : 18, Luke 18 : 19.

13 *Mysterium*, *CW* 14, pars. 570ff.

14 The separation of Christ, the epitome of good, from his shadow, the devil.

15 Matthew 23 : 24: "Ye blind guides, which strain at a gnat, and swallow a camel."

16 Rodrigo Borgia (1431–1503), the most notorious of the corrupt and venal popes of the Renaissance.

17 The astrological sign of Pisces consists of two fishes which were frequently regarded as moving in opposite directions. Traditionally, the reign of Christ corresponds to the first fish and ended with the first millennium, whereas the second fish coincides with the reign of Antichrist, now nearing its end with the entry of the vernal equinox into the sign of Aquarius. Cf. *Aion*, *CW* 9/2, pars. 148f., and "Answer to Job," *CW* 11, par. 725.

18 The bridge is the "uniting symbol," which represents psychic totality, the self. Cf. *Psychological Types*, *CW* 6, par. 828.

19 The tree often symbolizes the mother and appears as such in the numerous tree-birth myths (cf. *Symbols of Transformation*, *CW* 5, Part II, ch. V). But it is also a phallic symbol and thus has an androgynous character. (For Christ's androgyny cf. *Mysterium*, pars. 526, 565 & n. 63.)

20 Attis was one of the young dying gods, the lover of Kybele, the Great Mother goddess of Anatolia. In her rites, taking place in March, a pine tree, symbol of Attis, was carried into her sanctuary. Cf. White, 25 Nov. 50, n. 5.

21 A sanctuary of Adonis, another young dying god closely related to Attis, existed since ancient times in a cave at Bethlehem. It is supposed to be identical with Christ's birthplace, over which Constantine the Great (*ca.* 288–337) had a basilica built.

22 Cf. *Memories*, pp. 338f./312, and Neumann, 10 Mar. 59.

23 "Ye are gods." John 10 : 34.

24 *Nirdvandva* (Skt.), "free from the opposites (love and hate, joy and sorrow, etc.). Cf. *Psychological Types*, pars. 327ff.

25 Here "they" refers to the compensatory (or inferior) functions. Cf. ibid., Def. 30.

26 A village in Canton St. Gallen, on the Upper Lake of Zurich, near the Tower at Bollingen.

27 = "All is transition."

28 In geomancy, an ancient method of divination still widely practised in the Orient, especially the Far East, earth or pebbles are thrown on the ground and the resultant pattern is interpreted. In Europe the pattern was known as the *charta geomantica*. A later development was to make dots at random on a piece of paper: the "Art of Punctuation." (Cf. "Synchronicity," *CW* 8, par. 866.) Jung was fond of experimenting with all such mantic methods in order to test synchronistic events. He became acquainted with the *Ars Geomantica* through "De animae intell-

ectualis scientia seu geomantica," *Fasciculus geomanticus* (Verona, 1687), by the English physician and mystical philospher Robert Fludd (1574–1637), who is discussed in Pauli's "The Influence of Archetypal Ideas on the Scientific Theories of Kepler," *The Interpretation of Nature and the Psyche* (tr., 1955).

29 Possibly a patient Jung interviewed during his work with mentally deranged Negroes at St. Elizabeth's Hospital in Washington, D.C., in 1912. Cf. *The Freud/ Jung Letters*, 323J, n. 3. And cf. Loeb, 26 Aug. 41, n.

30 On 1 Sept. 1910 Pius X edited a *motu proprio* (a document issued by the Pontiff on his own initiative) in which the sentence occurs: "Certissime teneo ac sincere profiteor fidem non esse caecum sensum religionis e latebris subconscientiae . . . erumpentem" (I maintain as quite certain and sincerely avow that faith is not a blind religious feeling which breaks out of the darkness of the subconscious).

31 Lit. "to move what is at rest"; more colloquially, "rousing sleeping dogs."

32 W. mentioned that he had been invited to a lunatic asylum "to talk to the staff, and (as I found) try to lend a hand with religious-archetypal material which patients were producing under the L.S.D. drug." – Jung wrote "mescal."

33 Aldous Huxley, *The Doors of Perception* (1954).

34 "[Men of Troy, trust not the horse!] Be it what it may, I fear the Danaans, though their hands proffer gifts" (Virgil, *Aeneid*, I, 48).

35 Goethe's poem "The Magician's Apprentice": "I cannot get rid / Of the spirits I bid."

36 = away from work.

6 Good and evil in analytical psychology[1]

From: *CW* 10, paras 858–86

858   I would like to express my warmest thanks to Professor Seifert[2] for all he has said to us concerning the problem of the shadow. If I comply with your wish to add a few words, it will be about the purely empirical aspect of good and evil which the therapist has to deal with as a concrete fact. I must confess that I always experience difficulties when discussing the problem of good and evil with philosophers or theologians. I have the impression that they are not talking about the thing itself, but only about words, about the concepts which denote or refer to it. We allow ourselves so easily to be deluded by words, we substitute words for the whole of reality. People talk to me about evil, or about good, and presume that I know what it is. But I don't. When someone speaks of good or evil, it is of what *he* calls good or evil, or what *he* feels as good or evil. Then he speaks about it with great assurance, not knowing whether it really is so or whether what he calls good or evil really corresponds to the facts. Perhaps the speaker's view of the world is not in keeping with the real facts at all, so that an inner, subjective picture is substituted for objectivity.

859   If we wish to come to an understanding about so complex a question as good and evil, we must start with the following proposition: good and evil are in themselves *principles*, and we must bear in mind that a principle exists long before us and extends far beyond us.

860   When we speak of good and evil we are speaking concretely of something whose deepest qualities are in reality unknown to us. Whether it is experienced as evil and sinful depends, furthermore, on our subjective judgment, as also does the extent and gravity of the sin.

861   You probably know the joke about the father confessor in Texas, to whom a young man comes with an awfully long face. "What's the matter?" he inquires. "Something terrible has happened." "But what has happened?" "I've committed murder." "How many?" This shows how differently two people can experience the same fact, the same reality. I call a certain fact bad, often without being sure that it really is so. Some things seem to me bad, though in reality they are not. For instance, after dismissing a patient I have often wanted to kick myself because I thought I had done him an injustice. Perhaps I had been too brutal or did not tell

him the right thing. Next time he comes he tells me: "That was a wonderful session – just what I needed to be told." The exact opposite can also happen: I think what an excellent session it has been, what a successful dream-interpretation – and then it turns out to be all wrong.

862   Where do we get this belief, this apparent certainty, that we know what is good and what is bad? "Ye shall be as gods, knowing good and evil." Only the gods know, not us. This is profoundly true in psychology. If you take the attitude: "This thing may be very bad – but on the other hand it may not," then you have a chance of doing the right thing. But if you already know in advance you are behaving as if you were a god. We are all only limited human beings and we do not know in any fundamental sense what is good and bad in a given case. We know it only abstractly. To see through a concrete situation to the bottom is God's affair alone. We may perhaps form an opinion about it but we do not know whether it is finally valid. At most we can say cautiously: judged by such and such a standard such and such a thing is good or evil. Something that appears evil to one nation may be regarded as good by another nation. This relativity of values applies also in the realm of aesthetics: a modern work of art is for one person of supreme value, for which he is ready to lay out a large sum of money, whereas another person can make neither head nor tail of it.

863   In spite of all this we cannot simply abstain from judgment. If we call good something that seems to us bad, we have in effect told a lie. If I tell someone, "What you have written is a masterpiece," thinking on the quiet that it is worth nothing, that is a lie. Maybe the lie has a positive effect on him for the moment, so that he feels flattered. But a really constructive effect is produced only when I give him the best, a positive recognition that springs from conviction, and give it moreover at the right moment. When we pass emphatic judgments we are in an emotional state of mind and are then least able to apply valid criteria.

864   My attitude to this problem is empirical, not theoretical or aprioristic. When a patient comes to the therapist he has a conflict, and the question is then how to uncover this conflict situation, which very often is unconscious, and above all to find a way out of the conflict. Probably the only thing I can do is to tell myself cautiously: we don't know exactly what's up. It seems to be such and such – but may not another interpretation be given with equal right? The situation may seem rather negative at first, but then one comes to see that this is just what the patient was fated to run into. So I say at most: I hope to God I'm doing the right thing. It may perhaps be an emotionally excessive situation, when the patient, as Albertus Magnus says, is "in an excess of affect." If we look closely we shall see that good and evil are, as I said, *principles*. The word "principle" comes from *prius*, that which is "first" or "in the beginning." The ultimate principle we can conceive of is God. Principles, when reduced to their ultimates, are simply aspects of God. Good and evil are principles of

our ethical judgment, but, reduced to their ontological roots, they are "beginnings," aspects of God, names for God. Whenever, therefore, in an excess of affect, in an emotionally excessive situation, I come up against a paradoxical fact or happening, I am in the last resort encountering an aspect of God, which I cannot judge logically and cannot conquer because it is stronger than me – because, in other words, it has a numinous quality and I am face to face with what Rudolf Otto calls the *tremendum* and *fascinosum*. I cannot "conquer" a *numinosum*, I can only open myself to it, let myself be overpowered by it, trusting in its meaning. A principle is always a supraordinate thing, mightier than I am. I cannot even "conquer" the ultimate principles of physics, they simply confront me, loom over me, as sheer facts, as laws that "prevail." Here there is something that we cannot conquer.

865   If I say in an excess of affect, "This is a rotten wine" or "This fellow is a dirty dog," I shall hardly be in a position to know whether these judgments are right. Another person might judge the same wine and the same man quite differently. We know only the surfaces of things, only how they appear to us – and so we must be very modest. How often have I wished to get rid – so it seemed to me – of some absolutely harmful tendency in a patient, and yet in a deeper sense he was perfectly right to follow it. I want, for instance, to warn somebody of the deadly danger he is running into. If I am successful I think it was a fine therapeutic achievement. Afterwards I see – if he did not take my advice – that it was just the right thing for him to run into this danger. And this raises the question: did he not *have* to be in danger of death? If he had dared nothing, if he had not risked his life, perhaps he would have been poorer by a supremely important experience. He would never have risked his life and therefore would never have gained it.

866   So in the matter of good and evil, one can, as a therapist, only hope that one is getting the facts straight, though one can never be sure. As a therapist I cannot, in any given case, deal with the problem of good and evil philosophically but can only approach it empirically. *But because I take an empirical attitude it does not mean that I relativize good and evil as such.* I see very clearly: this is evil, but the paradox is just that for this particular person in this particular situation at this particular stage of development it may be good. Contrariwise, good at the wrong moment in the wrong place may be the worst thing possible. If it were not like this everything would be so simple – too simple. If I make no *a priori* judgments and listen to the facts as they are, then I do not always know beforehand what is good for the patient and what is bad. So many factors are involved, but we cannot yet see their meaning, they appear to us veiled in the shadow, and only afterwards does light penetrate the veil. What appears "in the shadow" of the Old Testament is revealed in the New Testament in the light of truth.

867   So it is in psychology. It is presumptuous to think we can always

say what is good or bad for the patient. Perhaps he knows something is really bad and does it anyway and then gets a bad conscience. From the therapeutic, that is to say the empirical point of view, this may be very good indeed for him. Perhaps he *has* to experience the power of evil and suffer accordingly, because only in that way can he give up his Pharisaic attitude to other people. Perhaps fate or the unconscious or God – call it what you will – had to give him a hard knock and roll him in the dirt, because only such a drastic experience could strike home, pull him out of his infantilism, and make him more mature. How can anyone find out how much he needs to be saved if he is quite sure that there is nothing he needs saving from? He sees his own shadow, his crookedness, but he turns his eyes away, does not confront himself, does not come to terms with himself, risks nothing – and then boasts before God and his fellows of his spotless white garment, which in reality he owes only to his cowardice, his regression, his super-angelic perfectionism. And instead of being ashamed, he stands in the front row of the temple and thanks God he is not as other men.

868   Such a person thinks he is justified because he knows what wrong is and avoids it. Consequently it never becomes a content of his actual life and he does not know from what he needs to be saved. Even the apocryphal saying: "Man, if thou knowest what thou dost, thou art blessed, but if thou knowest not, thou art accursed and a transgressor of the law," only gives us half a chance. A man who knows what he is doing when he commits evil may have a chance of being blessed, but in the meantime he is in hell. For the evil you do, even when you do it knowingly, is still evil and works accordingly. Yet if you had not taken this step, if you had not trodden this path, perhaps it would have been a psychic regression, a retrograde step in your inner development, a piece of infantile cowardice. Whoever thinks that by "knowing what you do" you guard against sin or save yourself from sin is wrong; on the contrary, you have steeped yourself in sin. But this saying is so paradoxical that it is terribly shocking to our ordinary feelings. The Church, however, knows of this paradox when she speaks of the *felix culpa* of our first parents (in the Liturgy for Easter Eve). If they had not sinned there would have been no *felix culpa* to bring after it the still greater miracle of the redemption. Nevertheless, evil remains evil. There is nothing for it but to accustom ourselves to thinking in paradoxes.

869   Without wishing it, we human beings are placed in situations in which the great "principles" entangle us in something, and God leaves it to us to find a way out. Sometimes a clear path is opened with his help, but when it really comes to the point one has the feeling of having been abandoned by every good spirit. In critical situations the hero always mislays his weapon, and at such moments, as before death, we are confronted with the nakedness of this fact. And one does not know how one got there. A thousand twists of fate all of a sudden land you in such a situation. This

is symbolically represented by Jacob's fight with the angel at the ford. Here a man can do nothing but stand his ground. It is a situation that challenges him to react as a whole man. Then it may turn out that he can no longer keep to the letter of the moral law. That is where his most personal ethics begin: in grim confrontation with the Absolute, in striking out on a path condemned by current morality and the guardians of the law. And yet he may feel that he has never been truer to his innermost nature and vocation, and hence never nearer to the Absolute, because he alone and the Omniscient have seen the actual situation as it were from inside, whereas the judges and condemners see it only from outside.

870   There is a well-known story of the young man who attained his majority. His father said to him: "Now you are twenty. Ordinary people stick to the Bible and what the parson says. The more intelligent mind the penal code." In other words: you are caught between "official" religion and civic morality. When your own conscience collides with them your most personal ethical decisions begin, in full consciousness of your creative freedom either to observe the moral code or not. I may, for instance, get into a situation where, in order to keep a professional secret, I have to lie. It would be futile to shrink from this with the excuse that I am a "moral" man. To the devil with such self-respect!

871   I am telling you all this in order to make my attitude in practice clear. I do not see it is my job to discuss these things philosophically. For me they are practical matters. Of course I am also interested in their philo-sophical aspect, but philosophy butters no parsnips. The reality of good and evil consists in things and situations that happen to you, that are too big for you, where you are always as if facing death. Anything that comes upon me with this intensity I experience as numinous, no matter whether I call it divine or devilish or just "fate." Something stronger than oneself, invincible, is at work and one is up against it. The trouble is that we are so accustomed to thinking these problems out until everything is as clear as twice two makes four. But in practice it does not work like that, we do not reach a solution in principle as to how we should always act. To want one is wrong. It is the same here as with the laws of nature, which we also think of as valid everywhere. Conventional morality is exactly like classical physics: a statistical truth, a statistical wisdom. The modern physicist knows that causality is a statistical truth, but in practice he will always ask what law is valid in this particular case. So it is in the realm of morality. We should not be misled into thinking we have said something absolutely valid when we pass judgment on a particular case: this is bad, this is good. Often we have to pass judgments, we can't get out of it. Perhaps we may even say the truth, hit the mark. But to regard our judgments as absolutely valid would be nonsensical; it would mean wanting to be like God. Often even the person doing the action does not discern its inner moral quality, the sum of all the conscious and un-conscious motives underlying it, and how much less those who judge the

action but see it only from the outside, only its appearance, not its deepest essence. Kant rightly requires the individual and society to advance from an "ethic of action" to an "ethic of conviction." But to see into the ultimate depths of the conviction behind the action is possible only to God. Our judgment, therefore, as to what is good or evil in practice will have to be very cautious and modest, not so apodictic, as though we could see into all the darkest corners. Ideas of morality are often as widely divergent as are views on what constitutes a delicacy for the Eskimo and for ourselves.

872   My attitude, it may be objected, is empirical in the extreme, but we need such an attitude in order to find a solution. When we observe how people behave when they are faced with a situation that has to be evaluated ethically, we become aware of a strange double effect: suddenly they see both sides. They become aware not only of their moral inferiorities but also, automatically, of their good qualities. They rightly say, "I can't be as bad as all that." To confront a person with his shadow is to show him his light. Once one has experienced a few times what it is like to stand judgingly between the opposites, one begins to understand what is meant by the self. Anyone who perceives his shadow and his light simultaneously sees himself from two sides and thus gets in the middle.

873   That is the secret of the Eastern attitude: observing the opposites teaches the Easterner the character of Maya. It gives reality the glint of illusion. Behind the opposites and in the opposites is true reality, which sees and comprehends the whole. The Indian calls this Atman. Reflecting on ourselves we can say, "I am he who speaks good and evil," or better, "I am he through whom good and evil are spoken. The one who is in me, who voices the principles, uses me as a means of expression. He speaks through me." This corresponds to what the Indian calls Atman – that which, figuratively speaking, "breathes through" me. Not through me alone, but through all; for it is not only the individual Atman but Atman-Purusha, the universal Atman, the pneuma, who breathes through all. We use the word "self" for this, contrasting it with the little ego. From what I have said it will be clear that this self is not just a rather more conscious or intensified ego, as the words "self-conscious," "self-satisfied," etc. might lead one to suppose. What is meant by the self is not only in me but in all beings, like the Atman, like Tao. It is psychic totality.

874   It is a misunderstanding to accuse me of having made out of this an "immanent God" or a "God-substitute." I am an empiricist and as such I can demonstrate empirically the existence of a totality supraordinate to consciousness. Consciousness experiences this supraordinate totality as something numinous, as a *tremendum* or *fascinosum*. As an empiricist I am interested only in the experiential character of this totality, which in itself, ontologically considered, is indescribable. This "self" never at any time takes the place of God, though it may perhaps be a vessel for divine grace. Such misunderstandings arise from the assumption that I am an

irreligious man who does not believe in God and just needs to be shown the way to belief.

875   In the history of Indian philosophy, too, there have been constant attempts not to identify the Atman with the monistically conceived Brahman (the Absolute Ground of all being), for instance in Ramanuja as opposed to Shankara, or in Bhakti-Yoga; and Aurobindo thinks that the Indian of today has advanced so far from the level of unconsciousness to conscious realization that his Absolute can no longer have the character of a merely unconscious, impersonal cosmic force. But these are no longer questions for the pure empiricist. As an empiricist I can at least establish that the Easterner like the Westerner is lifted out of the play of Maya, or the play of the opposites, through the experience of the Atman, the "self," the higher totality. He knows that the world consists of darkness and light. I can master their polarity only by freeing myself from them by contemplating both, and so reaching a middle position. Only there am I no longer at the mercy of the opposites.

[Jung's talk appears to have ended here. Then followed an unrecorded question, evidently concerning the East. – EDITORS.]

876   We have a false picture of the East. From the East comes the humorous question: Who takes longer to be saved, the man who loves God or the man who hates him? Naturally we expect that the man who hates God takes much longer. But the Indian says: If he loves God, it takes seven years, but if he hates him only three. For the man who hates God thinks much more about him. What ruthless subtlety! But the question is absolutely right the way it is meant. It is a sort of quiz question which may be put to the educated public but not to a peasant.

877   This story reminds me of something I saw in Ceylon. Two peasants had got their carts stuck in a narrow street. One can imagine what a flood of vituperation this would have let loose here in Switzerland. But what actually happened there was this: They bowed to each other and said: "Passing disturbance, no soul." That is to say the disturbance takes place only outwardly, in the realm of Maya, and not in the realm of true reality, where it neither happened nor left a mark. One might think this almost unbelievable in such simple people. One stands amazed. But this attitude is so ingrained in them that they take it for granted. Richard Wilhelm witnessed much the same thing. Two rickshaw boys were having a fearful argument. Wilhelm thought they were going to let fly with their fists at any moment, and that blood would flow. Just then one of them rushed at the other – but rushed past him and aimed a mighty kick at the wheel of his rickshaw, and that was the end of the argument. I myself saw two boys quarrelling and fighting with their fists, but the fists always stopped in the air, a few centimetres from the face, and no harm was done. That comes from the way these boys were brought up: it was Ceylon, where the old

Buddhism still rules. It is a moral education that has become a habit, and there is nothing especially meritorious about it.

878   Now, ladies and gentlemen, have you any further questions?

[A question was asked about the devil and his special reality today, since every epoch has its own peculiar devil.]

879   The devil nowadays is something quite frightful! If you look at our situation you just cannot see where it will end. Things will go on like this as if by force. All the divine powers in creation are gradually being placed in man's hands. Through nuclear fission something tremendous has happened, tremendous power has been given to man. When Oppenheimer saw the first test of an atomic bomb the words of the Bhagavad Gita flashed into his mind: "Brighter than a thousand suns." The forces that hold the fabric of the world together have got into the hands of man, so that he even has the idea of making an artificial sun. God's powers have passed into our hands, our fallible human hands. The consequences are inconceivable. The powers themselves are not evil, but in the hands of man they are an appalling danger – in evil hands. Who says that the evil in the world we live in, that is right in front of us, is not real! Evil is terribly real, for each and every individual. If you regard the principle of evil as a reality you can just as well call it the devil. I personally find it hard to believe that the idea of the *privatio boni* still holds water.

[What should the psychotherapist do? Should he give the patient a hint of how to deal with evil, or should he urge the patient to find out for himself?]

880   You are tempting me to lay down a rule. But I would rather advise: do the one thing or do the other according to circumstances, and in your therapeutic work do not act on any *a priori*, but in each case listen to what the concrete situation demands. Let that be your only *a priori*. For instance, a patient is still so unconscious that you simply *cannot* take up an attitude towards his problems. He identifies himself, like a psychotic, with his unconscious and would rather regard the analyst as crazy than understand his own inner situation. Try telling a completely unconscious mother, a sort of Kali Durga, who considers herself the best mother in the world, that she is to blame for the neurosis of her elder daughter and the unhappy marriage of her younger daughter – then you will hear something! And above all: the patient is not helped. Something must grow from inside *her*. Another patient has reached a certain level of consciousness and expects orientation from you. It would then be a great mistake to make your attitude clear. The right thing must be said at the right time in the right place.

881   A patient should not be regarded as an inferior being whom one lays on a couch while one sits behind him like a god, letting a word drop now and then. Everything suggestive of illness should be avoided. The patient is tending in this direction anyway and would like nothing better than to take

refuge in illness: ". . . now I can give up, now I must just lie there, now I am good and sick." Illness too is a solution of sorts, a way of disposing of life's problems: "I am ill, now the doctor must help!" As a therapist I mustn't be naïve. Unless the patient should really be in bed he should be treated like a normal person, indeed like a partner. That provides a sound basis for the treatment. People often come to me expecting me to let loose some medical magic. Then they are disappointed when I treat them as normal people and myself act like a normal man. One patient had experienced only the strong silent god sitting behind the couch. As soon as I began to talk to her she said astonished, almost horrified: "But you're expressing your affects, you're even telling me what you think!" Naturally I have affects and show them. Nothing is more important than this: every human being should be taken as a real human being and treated according to his peculiarities.

882   Therefore I say to the young psychotherapist: Learn the best, know the best – and then forget everything when you face the patient. No one has yet become a good surgeon by learning the text-books off by heart. Yet the danger that faces us today is that the whole of reality will be replaced by words. This accounts for the terrible lack of instinct in modern man, particularly the city-dweller. He lacks all contact with the life and breath of nature. He knows a rabbit or a cow only from the illustrated paper, the dictionary, or the movies, and thinks he knows what it is really like – and is then amazed that cowsheds "smell," because the dictionary didn't say so. It is the same with the danger of making a diagnosis. One knows that this disease is treated by So-and-so in chapter seventeen, and one thinks that this is the important thing. But the poor patient goes on suffering.

883   People speak sometimes of "overcoming" evil. But have we the power to overcome it? It should be remembered, first, that "good" and "evil" are only our judgment in a given situation, or, to put it differently, that certain "principles" have taken possession of our judgment. Secondly, it is often impossible to speak of overcoming evil, because at such times we are in a "closed" situation, in an aporia, where whatever we choose is not good. The important thing is to be aware that we are then in a numinous situation, surrounded on all sides by God, who can bring about either the one or the other and often does. There are plenty of examples of this in the Old Testament. Or think of Teresa of Avila when she had a mishap on a journey: the coach broke down while crossing a small river and she fell into the icy water. "Lord, how can you permit such things?" "Well, that's how I treat my friends." "Aha, that's why you have so few!" Teresa had got into a situation where evil – in this case physical evil – was done to her; she did not know how to integrate it, but nevertheless felt God's immediate presence. That is how the "principles," the "primordial powers," approach a person – they put him in a numinous situation where there is no rational solution, where he does not feel himself the maker and master of the situation, but rather that it is God. No one can then foresee

what will happen. Often we cannot say in such situations how the problem of good and evil will work out. We have to put our trust in the higher powers.

884   If I am faced with this problem in analysis I may say: "Well, let's wait and see what the dreams turn up, or whether higher powers will intervene, perhaps through illness or death. In any case don't decide. You and I are not God."

885   In making the shadow conscious we must be very careful that the unconscious does not play yet another trick and prevent a real confrontation with the shadow. A patient may see the darkness in himself for a moment, but the next moment he tells himself that it is not so bad after all, a mere bagatelle. Or else he exaggerates his remorse, because it is so nice to have such a wonderful remorseful feeling, to enjoy it like a warm eiderdown on a cold winter's morning when one should be getting up. This dishonesty, this refusal to see, ensures that there will be no confrontation with the shadow. Yet if there were a confrontation, then with increasing consciousness the good and the positive features would come to light too. We must therefore beware of the danger of wallowing in affects – remorse, melancholy, etc. – because they are seductive. It is easy enough to pride oneself on being able to feel such beautiful regrets. That is why people love plays, films, or preachers that move them to tears, because they can then enjoy their own emotions.

886   In the course of our discussion we heard the word "esoteric."³ It is said, for instance, that the psychology of the unconscious leads to an esoteric form of ethics. But we have to be careful in using such a word. Esotericism means mystification. Yet we never know the real secrets, even the so-called esotericists do not know them. Esotericists – at least earlier – were supposed not to reveal their secrets. But the real secrets cannot be revealed. Nor is it possible to make an "esoteric" science out of them, for the simple reason that they are not known. What are called esoteric secrets are mostly artificial secrets, not real ones. Man needs to have secrets, and since he has no notion of the real ones he fakes them. But the real ones come to him out of the depths of the unconscious, and then he may reveal things which he ought really to have kept secret. Here again we see the numinous character of the reality in the background. It is not we who have secrets, it is the real secrets that have us.

NOTES

1 [An extemporaneous address to the Stuttgarter Gemeinschaft "Arzt und Seelsorger," whose members travelled to Zurich to conduct the eighth annual meeting, upon which occasion Professor Jung met the group. A transcript prepared by Gebhard Frei was approved, with corrections, by the author and was first published in *Gut und Böse in der Psychotherapie* (ed. by Wilhelm Bitter, Stuttgart, 1959), a report of the meeting. The present translation (here revised) appeared

first in the *Journal of Analytical Psychology* (London), V (1960), 91–9.
– EDITORS.]
2 [Friedrich Seifert, of Munich, a participant in the meeting.]
3 [Presumably in one of the other talks in this symposium. – EDITORS.]

7   The shadow

From: *CW* 9/2, paras 13–19

13   Whereas the contents of the personal unconscious are acquired during the individual's lifetime, the contents of the collective unconscious are invariably archetypes that were present from the beginning. Their relation to the instincts has been discussed elsewhere.[1] The archetypes most clearly characterized from the empirical point of view are those which have the most frequent and the most disturbing influence on the ego. These are the *shadow*, the *anima*, and the *animus*.[2] The most accessible of these, and the easiest to experience, is the shadow, for its nature can in large measure be inferred from the contents of the personal unconscious. The only exceptions to this rule are those rather rare cases where the positive qualities of the personality are repressed, and the ego in consequence plays an essentially negative or unfavourable role.

14   The shadow is a moral problem that challenges the whole ego-personality, for no one can become conscious of the shadow without considerable moral effort. To become conscious of it involves recognizing the dark aspects of the personality as present and real. This act is the essential condition for any kind of self-knowledge, and it therefore, as a rule, meets with considerable resistance. Indeed, self-knowledge as a psychotherapeutic measure frequently requires much painstaking work extending over a long period.

15   Closer examination of the dark characteristics – that is, the inferiorities constituting the shadow – reveals that they have an *emotional* nature, a kind of autonomy, and accordingly an obsessive or, better, possessive quality. Emotion, incidentally, is not an activity of the individual but something that happens to him. Affects occur usually where adaptation is weakest, and at the same time they reveal the reason for its weakness, namely a certain degree of inferiority and the existence of a lower level of personality. On this lower level with its uncontrolled or scarcely controlled emotions one behaves more or less like a primitive, who is not only the passive victim of his affects but also singularly incapable of moral judgment.

16   Although, with insight and good will, the shadow can to some extent be assimilated into the conscious personality, experience shows that there are

certain features which offer the most obstinate resistance to moral control and prove almost impossible to influence. These resistances are usually bound up with *projections*, which are not recognized as such, and their recognition is a moral achievement beyond the ordinary. While some traits peculiar to the shadow can be recognized without too much difficulty as one's own personal qualities, in this case both insight and good will are unavailing because the cause of the emotion appears to lie, beyond all possibility of doubt, in the *other person*. No matter how obvious it may be to the neutral observer that it is a matter of projections, there is little hope that the subject will perceive this himself. He must be convinced that he throws a very long shadow before he is willing to withdraw his emotionally-toned projections from their object.

17   Let us suppose that a certain individual shows no inclination whatever to recognize his projections. The projection-making factor then has a free hand and can realize its object – if it has one – or bring about some other situation characteristic of its power. As we know, it is not the conscious subject but the unconscious which does the projecting. Hence one meets with projections, one does not make them. The effect of projection is to isolate the subject from his environment, since instead of a real relation to it there is now only an illusory one. Projections change the world into the replica of one's own unknown face. In the last analysis, therefore, they lead to an autoerotic or autistic condition in which one dreams a world whose reality remains forever unattainable. The resultant *sentiment d'incomplétude* and the still worse feeling of sterility are in their turn explained by projection as the malevolence of the environment, and by means of this vicious circle the isolation is intensified. The more projections are thrust in between the subject and the environment, the harder it is for the ego to see through its illusions. A forty-five-year-old patient who had suffered from a compulsion neurosis since he was twenty and had become completely cut off from the world once said to me: "But I can never admit to myself that I've wasted the best twenty-five years of my life!"

18   It is often tragic to see how blatantly a man bungles his own life and the lives of others yet remains totally incapable of seeing how much the whole tragedy originates in himself, and how he continually feeds it and keeps it going. Not *consciously*, of course – for consciously he is engaged in bewailing and cursing a faithless world that recedes further and further into the distance. Rather, it is an unconscious factor which spins the illusions that veil his world. And what is being spun is a cocoon, which in the end will completely envelop him.

19   One might assume that projections like these, which are so very difficult if not impossible to dissolve, would belong to the realm of the shadow – that is, to the negative side of the personality. This assumption becomes untenable after a certain point, because the symbols that then appear no longer refer to the same but to the opposite sex, in a man's case to a woman

and vice versa. The source of projections is no longer the shadow – which is always of the same sex as the subject – but a contrasexual figure. Here we meet the animus of a woman and the anima of a man, two corresponding archetypes whose autonomy and unconsciousness explain the stubbornness of their projections. Though the shadow is a motif as well known to mythology as anima and animus, it represents first and foremost the personal unconscious, and its content can therefore be made conscious without too much difficulty. In this it differs from anima and animus, for whereas the shadow can be seen through and recognized fairly easily, the anima and animus are much further away from consciousness and in normal circumstances are seldom if ever realized. With a little self-criticism one can see through the shadow – so far as its nature is personal. But when it appears as an archetype, one encounters the same difficulties as with anima and animus. In other words, it is quite within the bounds of possibility for a man to recognize the relative evil of his nature, but it is a rare and shattering experience for him to gaze into the face of absolute evil.

NOTES

1 "Instinct and the Unconscious" and "On the Nature of the Psyche," pars. 397ff.
2 The contents of this chapter are taken from a lecture delivered to the Swiss Society for Practical Psychology, in Zurich, 1948. The material was first published in the *Wiener Zeitschrift für Nervenheilkunde und deren Grenzgebiete*, I (1948) : 4.

8   North Africa

From: *Memories, Dreams, Reflections* (238–46)

At the beginning of 1920 a friend told me that he had a business trip to make to Tunis, and would I like to accompany him? I said yes immediately. We set out in March, going first to Algiers. Following the coast, we reached Tunis and from there Sousse, where I left my friend to his business affairs.

At last I was where I had longed to be: in a non-European country where no European language was spoken and no Christian conceptions prevailed, where a different race lived and a different historical tradition and philosophy had set its stamp upon the face of the crowd. I had often wished to be able for once to see the European from outside, his image reflected back at him by an altogether foreign milieu. To be sure, there was my ignorance of the Arabic language, which I deeply regretted; but to make up for this I was all the more attentive in observing the people and their behaviour. Frequently I sat for hours in an Arab coffee house, listening to conversations of which I understood not a word. But I studied people's gestures, and especially their expression of emotions; I observed the subtle change in their gestures when they spoke with a European, and thus learned to see to some extent with different eyes and to know the white man outside his own environment.

What the Europeans regard as Oriental calm and apathy seemed to me a mask; behind it I sensed a restlessness, a degree of agitation, which I could not explain. Strangely, in setting foot upon Moorish soil, I found myself haunted by an impression which I myself could not understand: I kept thinking that the land smelled queer. It was the smell of blood, as though the soil were soaked with blood. This strip of land, it occurred to me, had already borne the brunt of three civilisations: Carthaginian, Roman, and Christian. What the technological age will do with Islam remains to be seen.

When I left Sousse, I travelled south to Sfax, and thence into the Sahara, to the oasis city of Tozeur. The city lies on a slight elevation, on the margin of a plateau, at whose foot lukewarm, slightly saline springs well up profusely and irrigate the oasis through a thousand little canals. Towering date palms formed a green, shady roof overhead, under which peach, apricot, and fig trees flourished, and beneath these alfalfa of an unbelievable green. Several kingfishers, shining like jewels, flitted through the foliage. In the comparative coolness of this green shade strolled figures clad in white, among them a great number of affectionate couples holding one another in close embrace – obviously homosexual friendships. I felt suddenly transported to the times of classical Greece, where this inclination formed the cement of a society of men and of the *polis* based on that society. It was clear that men spoke to men and women to women here. Only a few of the latter were to be seen, nunlike, heavily veiled figures. I saw a few without veils. These, my dragoman explained, were prostitutes. On the main streets the scene was dominated by men and children.

My dragoman confirmed my impression of the prevalence of homo-sexuality, and of its being taken for granted, and promptly made me offers. The good fellow could have no notion of the thoughts which had struck me like a flash of lightning, suddenly illuminating my point of observation. I felt cast back many centuries to an infinitely more naïve world of adolescents who were preparing, with the aid of slender knowledge of the Koran, to emerge from their original state of twilight consciousness, in which they had existed from time immemorial, and to become aware of their own existence, in self-defence against the forces threatening them from the North.

While I was still caught up in this dream of a static, age-old existence, I suddenly thought of my pocket watch, the symbol of the European's accelerated tempo. This, no doubt, was the dark cloud that hung threateningly over the heads of these unsuspecting souls. They suddenly seemed to me like the game who do not see the hunter but, vaguely uneasy, scent him – "him" being the god of time who will inevitably chop into the bits and pieces of days, hours, minutes, and seconds that duration which is still the closest thing to eternity.

From Tozeur I went on to the oasis of Nefta. I rode off with my dragoman early in the morning, shortly after sunrise. Our mounts were large, swift-footed mules, on which we made rapid progress. As we approached the oasis, a single rider, wholly swathed in white, came towards us. With proud bearing he rode by without offering us any greeting, mounted on a black mule whose harness was banded and studded with silver. He made an impressive, elegant figure. Here was a man who certainly possessed no pocket watch, let alone a wrist watch; for he was obviously and unselfconsciously the person he had always been. He lacked that faint note of foolishness which clings to the European. The European is, to be sure, convinced that he is no longer what he was ages ago; but he does not know what he has since become. His watch tells him that since the "Middle Ages" time and its synonym, progress, have crept up on him and irrevocably taken something from him. With lightened baggage he continues his journey, with steadily increasing velocity, towards nebulous goals. He compensates for the loss of gravity and the corresponding *sentiment d'incomplétude* by the illusion of his triumphs, such as steamships, railways, aeroplanes, and rockets, that rob him of his duration and transport him into another reality of speeds and explosive accelerations.

The deeper we penetrated into the Sahara, the more time slowed down for me; it even threatened to move backwards. The shimmering heat waves rising up contributed a good deal to my dreamy state, and when we reached the first palms and dwelling of the oasis, it seemed to me that everything here was exactly the way it should be and the way it had always been.

Early the next morning I was awakened by the various unfamiliar noises outside my inn. There was a large open square which had been empty the night before, but which was now crowded with people, camels, mules, and donkeys. The camels groaned and announced in manifold variations of tone their chronic discontent, and the donkeys competed with cacophonous screams. The people ran around in a great state of excitement, shouting and gesticulating. They looked savage and rather alarming. My dragoman explained that a great festival was being celebrated that day. Several desert tribes had come in during the night to do two days of field work for the marabout. The marabout was the administrator of poor relief and owned many fields in the oasis. The people were to lay out a new field and irrigation canals to match.

At the farther end of the square there suddenly rose a cloud of dust; a green flag unfolded, and drums rolled. At the head of a long procession of hundreds of wild-looking men carrying baskets and short, wide hoes appeared a white-bearded, venerable old man. He radiated inimitable natural dignity as though he were a hundred years old. This was the marabout, astride a white mule. The men danced around him, beating small drums. The scene was one of wild excitement, hoarse shouting, dust, and heat. With fanatic purposefulness the procession swarmed by out into the oasis, as if going to battle.

I followed this horde at a cautious distance, and my dragoman made no attempt to encourage me to approach closer until we reached the spot where the "work" was going on. Here, if possible, even greater excitement prevailed; people were beating drums and shouting wildly; the site of the work resembled a disturbed anthill; everything was being done with the utmost haste. Carrying their baskets filled with heavy loads of earth, men danced along to the rhythm of the drums; others hacked into the ground at a furious rate, digging ditches and erecting dams. Through this wild tumult the marabout rode along on his white mule, evidently issuing instructions with the dignified, mild, and weary gestures of advanced age. Wherever he came, the haste, shouting, and rhythm intensified, forming the background against which the calm figure of the holy man stood out with extraordinary effectiveness. Towards evening the crowd was visibly overcome by exhaustion; the men soon dropped down beside their camels into deep sleep. During the night, after the usual stupendous concert of the dogs, utter stillness prevailed, until at the first rays of the rising sun the invocation of the muezzin – which always deeply stirred me – summoned the people to their morning prayer.

This scene taught me something: these people live from their affects, are moved and have their being in emotion. Their consciousness takes care of their orientation in space and transmits impressions from outside, and it is also stirred by inner impulses and affects. But it is not given to reflection; the ego has almost no autonomy. The situation is not so different with the

European; but we are, after all, somewhat more complicated. At any rate the European possesses a certain measure of will and directed intention. What we lack is intensity of life.

Without wishing to fall under the spell of the primitive, I nevertheless had been psychically infected. This manifested itself outwardly in an infectious enteritis which cleared up after a few days, thanks to the local treatment of rice water and calomel.

Overcharged with ideas, I finally went back to Tunis. The night before we embarked for Marseilles I had a dream which, I sensed, summed up the whole experience. This was just as it should be, for I had accustomed myself to living always on two planes simultaneously, one conscious, which attempted to understand and could not, and one unconscious, which wanted to express something and could not formulate it any better than by a dream.

I dreamt that I was in an Arab city, and as in most such cities there was a citadel, a casbah. The city was situated in the broad plain, and had a wall all round it. The shape of the wall was square, and there were four gates.

The casbah in the interior of the city was surrounded by a wide moat (which is not the way it really is in Arab countries). I stood before a wooden bridge leading over the water to a dark, horseshoe-shaped portal, which was open. Eager to see the citadel from the inside also, I stepped out on the bridge. When I was about half-way across it, a handsome, dark Arab of aristocratic, almost royal bearing came towards me from the gate. I knew that this youth in the white burnous was the resident prince of the citadel. When he came up to me, he attacked me and tried to knock me down. We wrestled. In the struggle we crashed against the railing; it gave way and both of us fell into the moat, where he tried to push my head under water to drown me. No, I thought, this is going too far. And in my turn I pushed his head under water. I did so although I felt great admiration for him; but I did not want to let myself be killed. I had no intention of killing him; I wanted only to make him unconscious and incapable of fighting.

Then the scene of the dream changed, and he was with me in a large vaulted octagonal room in the centre of the citadel. The room was all white, very plain and beautiful. Along the light-coloured marble walls stood low divans, and before me on the floor lay an open book with black letters written in magnificent calligraphy on milky-white parchment. It was not Arabic script; rather, it looked to me like the Uigurian script of West Turkestan, which was familiar to me from the Manichean fragments from Turfan. I did not know the contents, but nevertheless I had the feeling that this was "*my* book," that I had written it. The young prince with whom I had just been wrestling sat to the right of me on the floor. I explained to him that now that I had overcome him he must read the book. But he resisted. I placed my arm around his shoulders and forced him, with a sort of paternal kindness and patience, to read the book. I knew that this was absolutely essential, and at last he yielded.

In this dream, the Arab youth was the double of the proud Arab who had ridden past us without a greeting. As an inhabitant of the casbah he was a figuration of the self, or rather, a messenger or emissary of the self. For the casbah from which he came was a perfect mandala: a citadel surrounded by a square wall with four gates. His attempt to kill me was an echo of the motif of Jacob's struggle with the angel; he was – to use the language of the Bible – like an angel of the Lord, a messenger of God who wished to kill men because he did not know them.

Actually, the angel ought to have had his dwelling in me. But he knew only angelic truth and understood nothing about man. Therefore he first came forward as my enemy; however, I held my own against him. In the second part of the dream I was the master of the citadel; he sat at my feet and had to learn to understand my thoughts, or rather, learn to know man.

Obviously, my encounter with Arab culture had struck me with over-whelming force. The emotional nature of these unreflective people who are so much closer to life than we are exerts a strong suggestive influence upon those historical layers in ourselves which we just have overcome and left behind, or which we think we have overcome. It is like the paradise of childhood from which we imagine we have emerged, but which at the slightest provocation imposes fresh defeats upon us. Indeed, our cult of progress is in danger of imposing on us even more childish dreams of the future, the harder it presses us to escape from the past.

On the other hand, a characteristic of childhood is that, thanks to its naïveté and unconsciousness, it sketches a more complete picture of the self, of the whole man in his pure individuality, than adulthood. Consequently, the sight of a child or a primitive will arouse certain longings in adult, civilised persons – longings which relate to the unfulfilled desires and needs of those parts of the personality which have been blotted out of the total picture in favour of the adopted persona.

In travelling to Africa to find a psychic observation post outside the sphere of the European I unconsciously wanted to find that part of my personality which had become invisible under the influence and the pressure of being European. This part stands in unconscious opposition to myself, and indeed I attempt to suppress it. In keeping with its nature, it wishes to make me unconscious (force me under water) so as to kill me; but my aim is, through insight, to make it more conscious, so that we can find a common *modus vivendi*. The Arab's dusky complexion marks him as a "shadow," but not the personal shadow, rather an ethnic one associated not with my persona but with the totality of my personality, that is, with the self. As master of the casbah, he must be regarded as a kind of shadow of the self. The pre-dominantly rationalistic European finds much that is human alien to him, and he prides himself on this without realising that this rationality is won at the expense of his vitality, and that the primitive part of his personality is consequently condemned to a more or less underground existence.

The dream reveals how my encounter with North Africa affected me. First of all there was the danger that my European consciousness would be overwhelmed by an unexpectedly violent assault of the unconscious psyche.

Consciously, I was not a bit aware of any such situation; on the contrary, I could not help feeling superior because I was reminded at every step of my European nature. That was unavoidable: my being European gave me a certain perspective on these people who were so differently constituted from myself, and utterly marked me off from them. But I was not prepared for the existence of unconscious forces within myself which would take the part of these strangers with such intensity, so that a violent conflict ensued. The dream expressed this conflict in the symbol of an attempted murder.

I was not to recognise the real nature of this disturbance until some years later, when I stayed in tropical Africa. It had been, in fact, the first hint of "going black under the skin," a spiritual peril which threatens the uprooted European in Africa to an extent not fully appreciated. "Where danger is, there is salvation also" – these words of Hölderlin often came to my mind in such situations. The salvation lies in our ability to bring the unconscious urges to consciousness with the aid of warning dreams. These dreams show that there is something in us which does not merely submit passively to the influence of the unconscious, but on the contrary rushes eagerly to meet it, identifying itself with the shadow. Just as a childhood memory can suddenly take possession of consciousness with so lively an emotion that we feel wholly transported back to the original situation, so these seemingly alien and wholly different Arab surroundings awaken an archetypal memory of an only too well known prehistoric past which apparently we have entirely forgotten. We are remembering a potentiality of life which has been overgrown by civilisation, but which in certain places is still existent. If we were to relive it naïvely, it would constitute a relapse into barbarism. Therefore we prefer to forget it. But should it appear to us again in the form of a conflict, then we should keep it in our consciousness and test the two possibilities against each other – the life we live and the one we have forgotten. For what has apparently been lost does not come to the fore again without sufficient reason. In the living psychic structure, nothing takes place in a merely mechanical fashion; everything fits into the economy of the whole, relates to the whole. That is to say, it is all purposeful and has meaning. But because consciousness never has a view of the whole, it usually cannot understand this meaning. We must therefore content ourselves for the time being with noting the phenomenon and hoping that the future, or further investigation, will reveal the significance of this clash with the shadow of the self. In any case, I did not at the time have any glimmering of the nature of this archetypal experience, and knew still less about the historical parallels. Yet though I did not then grasp the full meaning of the dream, it lingered in my memory, along with the liveliest wish to go to Africa again at the next opportunity. That wish was not to be fulfilled for another five years.

9 A psychological view of conscience[1]

From: *CW* 10, paras 825–57

825　The etymology of the word "conscience" tells us that it is a special form of "knowledge" or "consciousness."[2] The peculiarity of "con-science" is that it is a knowledge of, or certainty about, the emotional value of the ideas we have concerning the motives of our actions. According to this definition, conscience is a complex phenomenon con-sisting on the one hand in an elementary act of the will, or in an impulse to act for which no conscious reason can be given, and on the other hand in a judgment grounded on rational feeling. This judgment is a value judgment, and it differs from an intellectual judgment in that, besides having an objective, general, and impartial character, it reveals the subjective point of reference. A value judgment always implicates the subject, presupposing that something is good or beautiful *for me*. If, on the other hand, I say that it is good or beautiful for certain other people, this is not necessarily a value judgment but may just as well be an intellectual statement of fact. Conscience, therefore, is made up of two layers, the lower one comprising a particular psychic event, while the upper one is a kind of superstructure representing the positive or negative judgment of the subject.

826　As we might expect from the complexity of the phenomenon, its empirical phenomenology covers a very wide field. Conscience may appear as an act of conscious reflection which anticipates, accompanies, or follows certain psychic events, or as a mere emotional concomitant of them, in which case its moral character is not immediately evident. Thus, an apparently groundless anxiety state may follow a certain action, without the subject being conscious of the least connection between them. Often the moral judgment is displaced into a dream which the subject does not understand. For example, a business man I knew was made what looked like a perfectly serious and honourable offer which, it turned out much later, would have involved him in a disastrous fraud had he accepted it. The following night after he received this offer, which as I say seemed to him quite acceptable, he dreamt that his hands and forearms were covered with black dirt. He could see no connection with the events of the previous day, because he was unable to admit to himself that the offer had touched him on the vulnerable spot: his expectation of a good business deal. I warned him about this, and he was careful enough to take certain precautions which did in fact save him from more serious harm. Had he examined the situation right at the beginning he would undoubtedly have had a bad conscience, for he would have understood that it was a "dirty business" which his morality would not have allowed him to touch. He would, as we say, have made his hands dirty. The dream represented this locution in pictorial form.

827   In this instance the classical characteristic of conscience, the *conscientia peccati* ("consciousness of sin"), is missing. Accordingly the specific fooling-tone of a bad conscience is missing too. Instead, the symbolical image of black hands appeared in a dream, calling his attention to some dirty work. In order to become conscious of his moral reaction, i.e. to feel his conscience, he had to tell the dream to me. This was an act of conscience on his part, in so far as dreams always made him feel rather uncertain. He had got this feeling of uncertainty in the course of an analysis, which showed him that dreams often contribute a great deal to self-knowledge. Without this experience he would probably have overlooked the dream.

828   From this we learn one important fact: the moral evaluation of an action, which expresses itself in the specific feeling-tone of the accompanying ideas, is not always dependent on consciousness but may function without it. Freud put forward the hypothesis that in these cases there is a repression exerted by a psychic factor, the so-called superego. But if the conscious mind is to accomplish the voluntary act of repression, we must presuppose that there is some recognition of the moral obnoxiousness of the content to be repressed, for without this motive the corresponding impulse of the will cannot be released. But it was just this knowledge which the business man lacked, to such an extent that he not only felt no moral reaction but put only a limited trust in my warning. The reason for this was that he in no way recognized the dubious nature of the offer and therefore lacked any motive for repression. Hence the hypothesis of conscious repression cannot apply in this case.

829   What happened was in reality an unconscious act which accomplished itself as though it were conscious and intentional – as though, in other words, it were an act of conscience. It is as if the subject recognized the immorality of the offer and this recognition had released the appropriate emotional reaction. But the entire process took place subliminally, and the only trace it left behind was the dream, which, as a moral reaction, remained unconscious. "Conscience," in the sense in which we defined it above, as a "knowledge" of the ego, a *conscientia*, simply does not exist in this case. If conscience is a kind of knowledge, then it is not the empirical subject who is the knower, but rather an unconscious personality who, to all appearances, behaves like a conscious subject. It knows the dubious nature of the offer, it recognizes the acquisitive greed of the ego, which does not shrink even from illegality, and it causes the appropriate

judgment to be pronounced. This means that the ego has been replaced by an unconscious personality who performs the necessary act of conscience.

830   It was these and similar experiences which led Freud to endow the superego with special significance. The Freudian superego is not, however, a natural and inherited part of the psyche's structure; it is rather the consciously acquired stock of traditional customs, the "moral code" as incorporated, for instance, in the Ten Commandments. The superego is a patriarchal legacy which, as such, is a conscious acquisition and an equally conscious possession. If it appears to be an almost unconscious factor in Freud's writings, this is due to his practical experience, which taught him that, in a surprising number of cases, the act of conscience takes place unconsciously, as in our example. Freud and his school rejected the hypothesis of inherited, instinctive modes of behaviour, termed by us archetypes, as mystical and unscientific, and accordingly explained unconscious acts of conscience as repressions caused by the superego.

831   The concept of the superego contains nothing that, in itself, would not be recognized as belonging to the common stock of thought. To that extent it is identical with what we call the "moral code." The only peculiar thing about it is that one or the other aspect of the moral tradition proves unconscious in the individual case. We should also mention that Freud admitted the existence of "archaic vestiges" in the superego – of acts of conscience, therefore, which are influenced by archaic motifs. But since Freud disputed the existence of archetypes, that is, of genuine archaic modes of behaviour, we can only assume that by "archaic vestiges" he meant certain conscious traditions which may be unconscious in certain individuals. In no circumstances can it be a question of inborn types, for otherwise they would be, on his own hypothesis, inherited ideas. But that is just what he does mean, though so far as I know there are no proofs of their existence. There are, however, proofs in abundance for the hypothesis of inherited, instinctive modes of behaviour, namely the archetypes. It is therefore probable that the "archaic vestiges" in the superego are a concession to the archetypes theory and imply a fundamental doubt as to the absolute dependence of unconscious contents on consciousness. There are indeed good grounds for doubting this dependence: first, the unconscious is, ontogenetically and phylogenetically, older than consciousness, and secondly, it is a well-known fact that it can hardly be influenced, if at all, by the conscious will. It can only be repressed or suppressed, and only temporarily at that. As a rule its account has to be settled sooner or later. Were that not so, psychotherapy would be no problem. If the unconscious were dependent on consciousness, we could, by insight and application of the will, finally get the better of the unconscious, and the psyche could be completely remodelled to suit our purpose. Only unworldly idealists, rationalists, and other fanatics can indulge in such dreams. The psyche is a phenomenon not subject to our will; it is nature, and though nature can, by skill, knowledge, and patience, be modified at

a few points, it cannot be changed into something artificial without profound injury to our humanity. Man can be transformed into a sick animal but not moulded into an intellectual ideal.

832   Although people still labour under the delusion that consciousness represents the whole of the psychic man, it is nevertheless only a part, of whose relation to the whole we know very little. Since the unconscious component really is unconscious, no boundaries can be assigned to it: we cannot say where the psyche begins or ends. We know that consciousness and its contents are the modifiable part of the psyche, but the more deeply we seek to penetrate, at least indirectly, into the realm of the unconscious, the more the impression forces itself on us that we are dealing with something autonomous. We must admit that our best results, whether in education or treatment, occur when the unconscious co-operates, that is to say when the goal we are aiming at coincides with the unconscious trend of development, and that, conversely, our best methods and intentions fail when nature does not come to our aid. Without at least some degree of autonomy the common experience of the complementary or compensatory function of the unconscious would not be possible. If the unconscious were really dependent on the conscious, it could not contain more than, and other things than, consciousness contains.

833   Our dream-example and many other cases of the kind suggest that, since the subliminal moral judgment accords with the moral code, the dream has behaved in the same way as a consciousness backed by traditional moral law, and that, consequently, ordinary morality is a basic law of the unconscious or at any rate influences it. This conclusion stands in flagrant contradiction to the common experience of the autonomy of the unconscious. Although morality as such is a universal attribute of the human psyche, the same cannot be maintained of a given moral code. It cannot, therefore, be an integral part of the psyche's structure. Nevertheless, the fact remains – as our example shows – that the act of conscience operates, in principle, in exactly the same way in the unconscious as in the conscious, follows the same moral precepts, and therefore evokes the impression that the moral code also controls the unconscious process.

834   This impression is deceptive, because in practice there are just as many, and perhaps even more, examples where the subliminal reaction does not conform at all to the moral code. Thus I was once consulted by a very distinguished lady – distinguished not only for her irreproachable conduct but also for her intensely "spiritual" attitude – on account of her "revolting" dreams. Her dreams did indeed deserve this epithet. She produced a whole series of extremely unsavoury dream-images all about drunken prostitutes, venereal diseases, and a lot more besides. She was horrified by these obscenities and could not understand why she, who had always striven for the highest, should be haunted by these apparitions from the abyss. She might just as well have asked why the saints are exposed to the vilest temptations. Here the moral code plays the contrary role – if

it plays any role at all. Far from uttering moral exhortions, the un-
concious delights in spawning every conceivable immorality, as though
it had what was morally repulsive exclusively in mind. Experiences of this
sort are so common and so regular that even St. Paul could confess: "For
the good that I would I do not, but the evil which I would not, that I do"
(Rom. 7 : 19).

835   In view of the fact that dreams lead astray as much as they exhort, it
seems doubtful whether what appears to be a judgement of conscience
should be evaluated as such – in other words, whether we should attribute
to the unconscious a function which appears moral to us. Obviously we
can understand dreams in a moral sense without at the same time assuming
that the unconscious, too, connects them with any moral tendency. It
seems, rather, that it pronounces moral judgements with the same objectivity with which it produces immoral fantasies. This paradox, or inner
contradictoriness of conscience, has long been know to investigators of
this question: besides the "right" kind of conscience there is a "wrong"
one, which exaggerates, perverts, and twists evil into good and good into
evil just as our own scruples do; and it does so with the same compulsive-
ness and with the same emotional consequences as the "right" kind of
conscience. Were it not for this paradox the question of conscience would
present no problem; we could then rely wholly on its decisions so far as
morality is concerned. But since there is great and justified uncertainty in
this regard, it needs unusual courage or – what amounts to the same
thing – unshakable faith for a person simply to follow the dictates of his
own conscience. As a rule one obeys only up to a certain point, which is
determined in advance by the moral code. This is where those dreaded
conflicts of duty begin. Generally they are answered according to the
precepts of the moral code, but only in a very few cases are they really
decided by an individual act of judgement. For as soon as the moral code
ceases to act as a support, conscience easily succumbs to a fit of weakness.

836   In practice it is indeed very difficult to distinguish conscience from the
traditional moral precepts. For this reason it is often thought that
conscience is nothing more than the suggestive effect of these precepts,
and that it would not exist if no moral laws had been invented. But the
phenomenon we call 'conscience" is found at every level of human
culture. Whether an Eskimo has a bad conscience about skinning an animal
with an iron knife instead of the traditional flint one, or about leaving a
friend in the lurch when he ought to help, in both cases he feels an inner
reproach, a "twinge of conscience," and in both cases the deviation from
an inveterate habit or generally accepted rule produces something like a
shock. For the primitive psyche anything unusual or not customary causes
an emotional reaction, and the more it runs counter to the "collective
representations" which almost invariably govern the prescribed mode of
behaviour, the more violent the reaction will be. It is a peculiarity of the
primitive mind to endow everything with mythical derivations that are

meant to explain it. Thus everything that we would call pure chance is understood to be intentional and is regarded as a magical influence. Such explanations are in no sense "inventions"; they are spontaneous fantasy-products which appear without premeditation in a natural and quite involuntary way; unconscious, archetypal reactions such as are peculiar to the human psyche. Nothing could be more mistaken than to assume that a myth is something "thought up." It comes into existence of its own accord, as can be observed in all authentic products of fantasy, and particularly in dreams. It is the hybris of consciousness to pretend that everything derives from *its* primacy, despite the fact that consciousness itself demonstrably comes from an older unconscious psyche. The unity and continuity of consciousness are such late acquisitions that there is still a fear that they might get lost again.

837   So, too, our moral reactions exemplify the original behaviour of the psyche, while moral laws are a late concomitant of moral behaviour, congealed into precepts. In consequence, they appear to be identical with the moral reaction, that is, with conscience. This delusion becomes obvious the moment a conflict of duty makes clear the difference between conscience and the moral code. It will then be decided which is the stronger: tradition and conventional morality, or conscience. Am I to tell the truth and thereby involve a fellow human being in catastrophe, or should I tell a lie in order to save a human life? In such dilemmas we are certainly not obeying our conscience if we stick obstinately and in all circumstances to the commandment: Thou shalt not lie. We have merely observed the moral code. But if we obey the judgment of conscience, we stand alone and have hearkened to a subjective voice, not knowing what the motives are on which it rests. No one can guarantee that he has only noble motives. We know – some of us – far too much about ourselves to pretend that we are one hundred per cent good and not egotists to the marrow. Always behind what we imagine are our best deeds stands the devil, patting us paternally on the shoulder and whispering, "Well done!"

838   Where does the true and authentic conscience, which rises above the moral code and refuses to submit to its dictates, get its justification from? What gives it the courage to assume that it is not a false conscience, a self-deception?

839   John says: "Try the spirits whether they are of God" (I John 4 : 1), an admonition we could profitably apply to ourselves. Since olden times conscience has been understood by many people less as a psychic function than as a divine intervention; indeed, its dictates were regarded as *vox Dei*, the voice of God. This view shows what value and significance were, and still are, attached to the phenomenon of conscience. The psychologist cannot disregard such an evaluation, for it too is a well-authenticated phenomenon that must be taken into account if we want to treat the idea of conscience psychologically. The question of "truth," which is usually raised here in a quite non-objective way, as to whether it has been proved

that God himself speaks to us with the voice of conscience, has nothing to do with the psychological problem. The *vox Dei* is an assertion and an opinion, like the assertion that there is such a thing as conscience at all. All psychological facts which cannot be verified with the help of scientific apparatus and exact methods of measurement are assertions and opinions, and, as such, are psychic realities. It is a *psychological truth* that the opinion exists that the voice of conscience is the voice of God.

840   Since, then, the phenomenon of conscience in itself does not coincide with the moral code, but is anterior to it, transcends its contents and, as already mentioned, can also be "false," the view of conscience as the voice of God becomes an extremely delicate problem. In practice it is very difficult to indicate the exact point at which the "right" conscience stops and the "false" one begins, and what the criterion is that divides one from the other. Presumably it is the moral code again, which makes it its business to know exactly what is good and what is evil. But if the voice of conscience is the voice of God, this voice must possess an incomparably higher authority than traditional morality. Anyone, therefore, who allows conscience this status should, for better or worse, put his trust in divine guidance and follow his conscience rather than give heed to conventional morality. If the believer had absolute confidence in his definition of God as the Summum Bonum, it would be easy for him to obey the inner voice, for he could be sure of never being led astray. But since, in the Lord's Prayer, we still beseech God not to lead us into temptation, this undermines the very trust the believer should have if, in the darkness of a conflict of duty, he is to obey the voice of conscience without regard to the "world" and, very possibly, act against the precepts of the moral code by "obeying God rather than men" (Acts 5 : 29).

841   Conscience – no matter on what it is based – commands the individual to obey his inner voice even at the risk of going astray. We can refuse to obey this command by an appeal to the moral code and the moral views on which it is founded, though with an uncomfortable feeling of having been disloyal. One may think what one likes about an ethos, yet an ethos is and remains an inner value, injury to which is no joke and can sometimes have very serious psychic consequences. These, admittedly, are known to relatively few people, for there are only a few who take objective account of psychic causality. The psyche is one of those things which people know least about, because no one likes to inquire into his own shadow. Even psychology is misused for the purpose of concealing the true causal connections from oneself. The more "scientific" it pretends to be, the more welcome is its so-called objectivity, because this is an excellent way of getting rid of the inconvenient emotional components of conscience, notwithstanding that these are the real dynamics of the moral reaction. Without its emotional dynamism the phenomenon of conscience loses all meaning – which is, of course the unconscious goal of the so-called "scientific" approach.

842 Conscience is, in itself, an autonomous psychic factor. All statements which do not directly deny it are agreed on this point. The clearest in this regard is the *vox Dei* concept. Here conscience is the voice of God, which often cuts sharply across our subjective intentions and may sometimes force an extremely disagreeable decision. If Freud himself attributed an almost daemonic power to the superego, although by definition it is not even a genuine conscience but merely human convention and tradition, this is in no sense an exaggeration: he was simply confirming the regular experience of the practising psychologist. Conscience is a demand that asserts itself in spite of the subject, or at any rate causes him considerable difficulties. This is not to deny that there are cases of lack of conscience. But the idea that conscience as such is only something learnt can be maintained only by those who imagine they were present on those prehistoric occasions when the first moral reactions came into existence. Conscience is far from being the only instance of an inner factor autonomously opposing the will of the subject. Every complex does that, and no one in his right senses would declare that it was "learnt" and that nobody would have a complex if it had not been hammered into him. Even domestic animals, to whom we erroneously deny a conscience, have complexes and moral reactions.

843 Primitive man regards the autonomy of the psyche as demonism and magic. This, we consider, is only what one would expect in primitive society. On closer inspection one finds, however, that the civilized man of antiquity, such as Socrates, still had his daemon and that there was a widespread and natural belief in superhuman beings who, we would suppose today, were personifications of projected unconscious contents. This belief has not, in principle, disappeared, but still persists in numerous variants. For instance, in the assumption that conscience is the voice of God, or that it is a very important psychic factor (and one which manifests itself according to temperament, seeing that it usually accompanies the most differentiated function, as in the case of a "thinking" or a "feeling" morality). Again, where conscience seems to play no role, it appears indirectly in the form of compulsions or obsessions. These manifestations all go to show that the moral reaction is the outcome of an autonomous dynamism, fittingly called man's daemon, genius, guardian angel, better self, heart, inner voice, the inner and higher man, and so forth. Close beside these, beside the positive, "right" conscience, there stands the negative, "false" conscience called the devil, seducer, tempter, evil spirit, etc. Everyone who examines his conscience is confronted with this fact, and he must admit that the good exceeds the bad only by a very little, if at all. It is therefore quite in order for St. Paul to admit to having his "messenger of Satan" (II Corinthians 12 : 7). We ought to avoid sin and occasionally we can; but, as experience shows, we fall into sin again at the very next step. Only unconscious and wholly uncritical people can imagine it possible to abide in a permanent state of moral goodness. But because most

people are devoid of self-criticism, permanent self-deception is the rule. A more developed consciousness brings the latent moral conflict to light, or else sharpens those opposites which are already conscious. Reason enough to eschew self-knowledge and psychology altogether and to treat the psyche with contempt!

844   There is scarcely any other psychic phenomenon that shows the polarity of the psyche in a clearer light than conscience. Its undoubted dynamism, in order to be understood at all, can only be explained in terms of energy, that is, as a potential based on opposites. Conscience brings these ever-present and necessary opposites to conscious perception. It would be a great mistake to suppose that one could ever get rid of this polarity, for it is an essential element in the psychic structure. Even if the moral reaction could be eliminated by training, the opposites would simply use a mode of expression other than the moral one. They would still continue to exist. But if the *vox Dei* conception of conscience is correct, we are faced logically with a metaphysical dilemma: either there is a dualism, and God's omnipotence is halved, or the opposites are contained in the monotheistic God-image, as for instance in the Old Testament image of Yahweh, which shows us morally contradictory opposites existing side by side. This figure corresponds to a unitary image of the psyche dynamically based on opposites, like Plato's charioteer driving the white and the black horses. Alternatively, we must admit with Faust: "Two souls, alas, are housed within my breast," which no human charioteer can master, as the fate of Faust clearly indicates.

845   The psychologist can criticize metaphysics as a human assertion, but he is not in a position to make such assertions himself. He can only establish that these assertions exist as a kind of exclamation, well knowing that neither one nor the other can be proved right and objectively valid, although he must acknowledge the legitimacy of subjective assertions as such. Assertions of this kind are manifestations of the psyche which belong to our human nature, and there is no psychic wholeness without them, even though one can grant them no more than subjective validity. Thus the *vox Dei* hypothesis is another subjective exclamation, whose purpose it is to underline the numinous character of the moral reaction. Conscience is a manifestation of *mana*, of the "extraordinarily powerful," a quality which is the especial peculiarity of archetypal ideas. For, in so far as the moral reaction is only apparently identical with the suggestive effect of the moral code, it falls within the sphere of the collective unconscious, exemplifying an archetypal pattern of behaviour reaching down into the animal psyche. Experience shows that the archetype, as a natural phenomenon, has a morally ambivalent character, or rather, it possesses no moral quality in itself but is amoral, like the Yahwistic God-image, and acquires moral qualities only through the act of cognition. Thus Yahweh is both just and unjust, kindly and cruel, truthful and deceitful. This is eminently true of the archetype as well. That is why the primitive form of conscience is

paradoxical: to burn a heretic is on the one hand a pious and meritorious act – as John Hus himself ironically recognized when, bound to the stake, he espied an old woman hobbling towards him with a bundle of faggots, and exclaimed, "*O sancta simplicitas!*" – and on the other hand a brutal manifestation of ruthless and savage lust for revenge.

846   Both forms of conscience, the right and the false, stem from the same source, and both therefore have approximately the same power of conviction. This is also apparent in the symbolic designation of Christ as Lucifer ("bringer of light"), lion, raven (or *nycticorax*: night-heron), serpent, son of God, etc., all of which he shares with Satan; in the idea that the good father-god of Christianity is so vindictive that it takes the cruel sacrifice of his son to reconcile him to humanity; in the belief that the Summum Bonum has a tendency to lead such an inferior and helpless creature as man into temptation, only to consign him to eternal damnation if he is not astute enough to spot the divine trap. Faced with these insufferable paradoxes, which are an affront to our religious feelings, I would suggest reducing the notion of the *vox Dei* to the hypothesis of the archetype, for this at least is understandable and accessible to investigation. The archetype is a pattern of behaviour that has always existed, that is morally indifferent as a biological phenomenon, but possesses a powerful dynamism by means of which it can profoundly influence human behaviour.

847   The concept of the archetype has been misunderstood so often that one can hardly mention it without having to explain it anew each time. It is derived from the repeated observation that, for instance, the myths and fairytales of world literature contain definite motifs which crop up everywhere. We meet these same motifs in the fantasies, dreams, deliriums, and delusions of individuals living today. These typical images and associations are what I call archetypal ideas. The more vivid they are, the more they will be coloured by particularly strong feeling-tones. This accentuation gives them a special dynamism in our psychic life. They impress, influence, and fascinate us. They have their origin in the archetype, which in itself is an irrepresentable, unconscious, pre-existent form that seems to be part of the inherited structure of the psyche and can therefore manifest itself spontaneously anywhere, at any time. Because of its instinctual nature, the archetype underlies the feeling-toned complexes and shares their autonomy. It is also the psychic precondition of religious assertions and is responsible for the anthropomorphism of all God-images. This fact, however, affords no ground for any metaphysical judgment, whether positive of negative.

848   With this view we remain within the framework of what can be experienced and known. The *vox Dei* hypothesis is then no more than an amplificatory tendency peculiar to the archetype – a mythological statement inseparably bound up with numinous experiences which expresses these occurrences and also seeks to explain them. By reducing them to

something empirically knowable, we do not in any way prejudice their transcendence. When, for example, someone was struck by lightning, the man of antiquity believed that Zeus had hurled a thunderbolt at him. Instead of this mythical dramatization we content ourselves with the more modest explanation that a sudden discharge of electrical tension happened to take place just at the spot where this unlucky man stood under a tree. The weak point in this argument, of course, is the so-called "accident," about which several things could be said. On the primitive level there are no accidents of this sort, but only intentional designs.

849   The reduction of the act of conscience to a collision with the archetype is, by and large, a tenable explanation. On the other hand we must admit that the *psychoid* archetype, that is, its irrepresentable and unconscious essence, is not just a postulate only, but possesses qualities of a parapsychological nature which I have grouped together under the term "synchronicity." I use this term to indicate the fact that, in cases of telepathy, precognition, and similar inexplicable phenomena, one can very frequently observe an archetypal situation. This may be connected with the collective nature of the archetype, for the collective unconscious, unlike the personal unconscious, is one and the same everywhere, in all individuals, just as all biological functions and all instincts are the same in members of the same species. Apart from the more subtle *synchronicity*, we can also observe in the instincts, for instance in the migratory instinct, a distinct *synchronism*. And since the parapsychological phenomena associated with the unconscious psyche show a peculiar tendency to relativize the categories of time and space, the collective unconscious must have a spaceless and timeless quality. Consequently, there is some probability that an archetypal situation will be accompanied by synchronistic phenomena, as in the case of death, in whose vicinity such phenomena are relatively frequent.

850   As with all archetypal phenomena, the synchronicity factor must be taken into account in considering conscience. For although the voice of genuine conscience (and not just the recollection of the moral code) may make itself heard in the context of an archetypal situation, it is by no means certain that the reason for this is always a subjective moral reaction. It sometimes happens that a person suffers from a decidedly bad conscience for no demonstrable reason. Naturally there are any number of cases where ignorance and self-deception offer a sufficient explanation. But this does not alter the fact that one can suddenly have a bad conscience when one is conversing with an unknown person who would have every reason to feel a bad conscience but is unconscious of it. The same is true of fear and other emotions arising from a collision with an archetype. When one is talking with somebody whose unconscious contents are "constellated," a parallel constellation arises in one's own unconscious. The same or similar archetype is activated, and since one is less unconscious than the other person and has no reason for repression, one becomes increasingly aware

of its feeling-tone in the form of a growing uneasiness of conscience. When this happens, we naturally tend to ascribe the moral reaction to ourselves, the more easily since no one, actually, has reason to enjoy a perfectly good conscience. But in the case we are discussing the self-criticism, laudable in itself, goes too far. We discover that, as soon as the conversation is ended, the bad conscience stops as suddenly as it began, and after a while it turns out that it is the other person who should take note of his bad conscience. By way of example, one thinks of cases like the one described by Heinrich Zschokke.[3] While in Brugg, he visited an inn, where he ate lunch. Opposite him sat a young man. Suddenly Zschokke saw in his mind's eye this young man standing at a desk, breaking it open, and pocketing the money he found. Zschokke even knew the exact amount and was so sure of it that he took the young man to task. The latter was so flabbergasted by Zschokke's knowledge that he made a confession on the spot.

851   This spontaneous reconstruction of an unknown fact can also be expressed in a dream, or give rise to a disagreeable feeling that cannot be put into words, or cause one to guess a situation without knowing to whom it refers. The psychoid archetype has a tendency to behave as though it were not localized in one person but were active in the whole environment. The fact or situation is transmitted in most cases through a subliminal perception of the affect it produces. Animals and primitives have a particularly fine nose for these things. This explanation, however, does not cover parapsychological events.

852   Experiences of this kind are the common lot of the psychotherapist, or of anybody who has frequent occasion to talk professionally, about their intimate affairs, with people with whom he has no personal relationship. One should not conclude from this that every subjective pang of conscience which seems unfounded is caused by the person one is conversing with. Such a conclusion is justified only when the ever-present guilt component in oneself proves, after mature reflection, to be an inadequate explanation of the reaction. The distinction is often a very delicate matter because, in therapy, ethical values must not be injured on either side if the treatment is to be successful. Yet what happens in the therapeutic process is only a special instance of human relationships in general. As soon as the dialogue between two people touches on something fundamental, essential, and numinous, and a certain rapport is felt, it gives rise to a phenomenon which Lévy-Bruhl fittingly called *participation mystique*. It is an unconscious identity in which two individual psychic spheres interpenetrate to such a degree that it is impossible to say what belongs to whom. If the problem is one of conscience, the guilt of one partner is the guilt of the other, and at first there is no possibility of breaking this emotional identity. For this a special act of reflection is required. I have dwelt at some length on this problem because I wanted to show that by the concept of the archetype nothing final is meant, and that it would be wrong

to suppose that the essence of conscience could be reduced to nothing but the archetype. The psychoid nature of the archetype contains very much more than can be included in a psychological explanation. It points to the sphere of the *unus mundus*, the unitary world, towards which the psychologist and the atomic physicist are converging along separate paths, producing independently of one another certain analogous auxiliary concepts. Although the first step in the cognitive process is to discriminate and divide, at the second step it will unite what has been divided, and an explanation will be satisfactory only when it achieves a synthesis.

853   For this reason I have not been able to confine myself exclusively to the psychological nature of conscience, but have had to consider its theological aspect. From this point of view it cannot be presupposed that the act of conscience is something that, of its own nature, can be treated exhaustively by means of a rational psychology. We have, rather, to give priority to the assertion which conscience itself makes – that it is a voice of God. This view is not a contrivance of the intellect, it is a primary assertion of the phenomenon itself: a numinous imperative which from ancient times has been accorded a far higher authority than the human intellect. The daemon of Socrates was not the empirical person of Socrates. Conscience as such, if regarded objectively, without rationalistic assumptions, behaves like a God so far as its demands and authority are concerned, and asserts that it is God's voice. This assertion cannot be overlooked by an objective psychology, which must also include the irrational. Nor can it be pinned down to the question of truth, for this is unanswerable anyway and for epistemological reasons has long since become obsolete. Human knowledge has to be content with constructing models which are "probable" – it would be thoughtless presumption to demand more. For just as knowledge is not faith, so faith is not knowledge. We are concerned here with things that can be disputed, that is, with knowledge, but not with indisputable faith, which precludes critical discussion at the outset. The oft-repeated paradox "knowledge through faith" seeks in vain to bridge the gulf that separates the two.

854   When, therefore, the psychologist explains genuine conscience as a collision of consciousness with a numinous archetype, he may be right. But he will have to add at once that the archetype *per se*, its psychoid essence, cannot be comprehended, that it possesses a transcendence which it shares with the unknown substance of the psyche in general. The mythical assertion of conscience that it is the voice of God is an inalienable part of its nature, the foundation of its numen. It is as much a phenomenon as conscience itself.

855   In conclusion I would like to say that conscience is a psychic reaction which one can call *moral* because it always appears when the conscious mind leaves the path of custom, of the *mores*, or suddenly recollects it. Hence in the great majority of cases conscience signifies primarily the reaction to a real or supposed deviation from the moral code, and is for

the most part identical with the primitive fear of anything unusual, not customary, and hence "immoral." As this behaviour is instinctive and, at best, only partly the result of reflection, it may be "moral" but can raise no claim to being *ethical*. It deserves this qualification only when it is reflective, when it is subjected to conscious scrutiny. And this happens only when a fundamental doubt arises as between two possible modes of moral behaviour, that is to say in a conflict of duty. A situation like this can be "solved" only by suppressing one moral reaction, upon which one has not reflected till now, in favour of another. In this case the moral code will be invoked in vain, and the judging intellect finds itself in the position of Buridan's ass between two bundles of hay. Only the creative power of the ethos that expresses the whole man can pronounce the final judgment. Like all the creative faculties in man, his ethos flows empirically from two sources: from rational consciousness and from the irrational unconscious. It is a special instance of what I have called the transcendent function, which is the discursive co-operation of conscious and unconscious factors or, in theological language, of reason and grace.

856   It is not the task of psychological understanding to broaden or narrow the concept of conscience. "Conscience," in ordinary usage, means the consciousness of a factor which in the case of a "good conscience" affirms that a decision or an act accords with morality and, if it does not, condemns it as "immoral." This view, deriving as it does from the *mores*, from what is customary, can properly be called "moral." Distinct from this is the ethical form of conscience, which appears when two decisions or ways of acting, both affirmed to be moral and therefore regarded as "duties," collide with one another. In these cases, not foreseen by the moral code because they are mostly very individual, a judgement is required which cannot properly be called "moral" or in accord with custom. Here the decision has no custom at its disposal on which it could rely. The deciding factor appears to be something else: it proceeds not from the traditional moral code but from the unconscious foundation of the personality. The decision is drawn from dark and deep waters. It is true that these conflicts of duty are solved very often and very conveniently by a decision in accordance with custom, that is, by suppressing one of the opposites. But this is not always so. If one is sufficiently conscientious the conflict is endured to the end, and a creative solution emerges which is produced by the constellated archetype and possesses that compelling authority not unjustly characterized as the voice of God. The nature of the solution is in accord with the deepest foundation of the personality as well as with its wholeness; it embraces conscious and unconscious and therefore transcends the ego.

857   The concept and phenomenon of conscience thus contains, when seen in a psychological light, two different factors: on the one hand a recollection of, and admonition by, the *mores*; on the other, a conflict of duty and its solution through the creation of a third standpoint. The first is the moral, and the second the ethical, aspect of conscience.

NOTES

1 [Originally published as "Das Gewissen in psychologischer Sicht," in *Universitas* (Stuttgart), June 1958; then in a symposium, *Das Gewissen* (Studien aus dem C. G. Jung-Institut, VII; Zurich, 1958). – EDITORS.]
2 [In the original, resp., *Gewissen, Wissen*, and *Bewusstsein*. Cf. L. *conscientia, scientia* (from *scire*, "to know"), *conscius* – EDITORS.]
3 *Eine Selbstschau* (1843).

10 Answer to Job

From: *CW* 11, paras 553–608, 628–42, 649–82, 688–717, 736–47

LECTORI BENEVOLO

> I am distressed for thee, my brother . . .
> II Samuel 1 : 26 (AV)

553 On account of its somewhat unusual content, my little book requires a short preface. I beg of you, dear reader, not to overlook it. For, in what follows, I shall speak of the venerable objects of religious belief. Whoever talks of such matters inevitably runs the risk of being torn to pieces by the two parties who are in mortal conflict about those very things. This conflict is due to the strange supposition that a thing is true only if it presents itself as a *physical* fact. Thus some people belief it to be physically true that Christ was born as the son of a virgin, while others deny this as a physical impossibility. Everyone can see that there is no logical solution to this conflict and that one would do better not to get involved in such sterile disputes. Both are right and both are wrong. Yet they could easily reach agreement if only they dropped the word "physical." "Physical" is not the only criterion of truth: there are also *psychic* truths which can neither be explained nor proved nor contested in any physical way. If, for instance, a general belief existed that the river Rhine had at one time flowed backwards from its mouth to its source, then this belief would in itself be a fact even though such an assertion, physically understood, would be deemed utterly incredible. Beliefs of this kind are psychic facts which cannot be contested and need no proof.

554 Religious statements are of this type. They refer without exception to things that cannot be established as physical facts. If they did not do this, they would inevitably fall into the category of the natural sciences. Taken as referring to anything physical, they make no sense whatever, and science would dismiss them as non-experienceable. They would be mere miracles, which are sufficiently exposed to doubt as it is, and yet they could not demonstrate the reality of the spirit of *meaning* that underlies them, because meaning is something that always demonstrates itself and is experienced on its own merits. The spirit and meaning of Christ are present and perceptible to us even without the aid of miracles. Miracles appeal

only to the understanding of those who cannot perceive the meaning. They are mere substitutes for the not understood reality of the spirit. This is not to say that the living presence of the spirit is not occasionally accompanied by marvellous physical happenings. I only wish to emphasize that these happenings can neither replace nor bring about an understanding of the spirit, which is the one essential thing.

555   The fact that religious statements frequently conflict with the observed physical phenomena proves that in contrast to physical perception the spirit is autonomous, and that psychic experience is to a certain extent independent of physical data. The psyche is an autonomous factor, and religious statements are psychic confessions which in the last resort are based on unconscious, i.e. on transcendental, processes. These processes are not accessible to physical perception but demonstrate their existence through the confessions of the psyche. The resultant statements are filtered through the medium of human consciousness: that is to say, they are given visible forms which in their turn are subject to manifold influences from within and without. That is why whenever we speak of religious contents we move in a world of images that point to something ineffable. We do not know how clear or unclear these images, metaphors, and concepts are in respect of their transcendental object. If, for instance, we say "God," we give expression to an image or verbal concept which has undergone many changes in the course of time. We are, however, unable to say with any degree of certainty – unless it be by faith – whether these changes affect only the images and concepts, or the Unspeakable itself. After all, we can imagine God as an eternally flowing current of vital energy that endlessly changes shape just as easily as we can imagine him as an eternally unmoved, unchangeable essence. Our reason is sure only of one thing: that it manipulates images and ideas which are dependent on human imagination and its temporal and local conditions, and which have therefore changed innumerable times in the course of their long history. There is no doubt that there is something behind these images that transcends consciousness and operates in such a way that the statements do not vary limitlessly and chaotically, but clearly all relate to a few basic principles or archetypes. These, like the psyche itself, or like matter, are unknowable as such. All we can do is to construct models of them which we know to be inadequate, a fact which is confirmed again and again by religious statements.

556   If, therefore, in what follows I concern myself with these "metaphysical" objects, I am quite conscious that I am moving in a world of images and that none of my reflections touches the essence of the Unknowable. I am also too well aware of how limited are our powers of conception – to say nothing of the feebleness and poverty of language – to imagine that my remarks mean anything more in principle than what a primitive man means when he conceives of his god as a hare or a snake. But, although our whole world of religious ideas consists of anthropomorphic images that could never stand up to rational criticism, we should

never forget that they are based on numinous archetypes, i.e. on an emotional foundation which is unassailable by reason. We are dealing with psychic facts which logic can overlook but not eliminate. In this connection Tertullian has already appealed, quite rightly, to the testimony of the soul. In his *De testimonio animae*, he says:

> These testimonies of the soul are as simple as they are true, as obvious as they are simple, as common as they are obvious, as natural as they are common, as divine as they are natural. I think that they cannot appear to any one to be trifling and ridiculous if he considers the majesty of Nature, whence the authority of the soul is derived. What you allow to the mistress you will assign to the disciple. Nature is the mistress, the soul is the disciple; what the one has taught, or the other has learned, has been delivered to them by God, who is, in truth, the Master even of the mistress herself. What notion the soul is able to conceive of her first teacher is in your power to judge, from that soul which is in you. Feel that which causes you to feel; think upon that which is in forebodings your prophet; in omens, your augur; in the events which befall you, your foreseer. Strange if, being given by God, she knows how to act the diviner for men! Equally strange if she knows Him by whom she has been given![1]

557   I would go a step further and say that the statements made in the Holy Scriptures are also utterances of the soul – even at the risk of being suspected of psychologism. The statements of the conscious mind may easily be snares and delusions, lies, or arbitrary opinions, but this is certainly not true of the statements of the soul: to begin with they always go over our heads because they point to realities that transcend consciousness. These *entia* are the archetypes of the collective unconscious, and they precipitate complexes of ideas in the form of mythological motifs. Ideas of this kind are never invented, but enter the field of inner perception as finished products, for instance in dreams. They are spontaneous phenomena which are not subject to our will, and we are therefore justified in ascribing to them a certain autonomy. They are to be regarded not only as objects but as subjects with laws of their own. From the point of view of consciousness, we can, of course, describe them as objects, and even explain them up to a point, in the same measure as we can describe and explain a living human being. But then we have to disregard their autonomy. If that is considered, we are compelled to treat them as subjects; in other words, we have to admit that they possess spontaneity and purposiveness, or a kind of consciousness and free will. We observe their behaviour and consider their statements. This dual standpoint, which we are forced to adopt towards every relatively independent organism, naturally has a dual result. On the one hand it tells me what I do to the object, and on the other hand what it does (possibly to me). It is obvious that this unavoidable dualism will create a certain amount of confusion in the minds of my readers, particularly as in what follows we shall have to do with the archetype of Deity.

558   Should any of my readers feel tempted to add an apologetic "only" to the God-images as we perceive them, he would immediately fall foul of experience, which demonstrates beyond any shadow of doubt the extraordinary numinosity of these images. The tremendous effectiveness (mana) of these images is such that they not only give one the feeling of pointing to the *Ens realissimum*, but make one convinced that they actually express it and establish it as a fact. This makes discussion uncommonly difficult, if not impossible. It is, in fact, impossible to demonstrate God's reality to oneself except by using images which have arisen spontaneously or are sanctified by tradition, and whose psychic nature and effects the naïve-minded person has never separated from their unknowable metaphysical background. He instantly equates the effective image with the transcendental x to which it points. The seeming justification for this procedure appears self-evident and is not considered a problem so long as the statements of religion are not seriously questioned. But if there is occasion for criticism, then it must be remembered that the image and the statement are psychic processes which are different from their transcendental object; they do not posit it, they merely point to it. In the realm of psychic processes criticism and discussion are not only permissible but are unavoidable.

559   In what follows I shall attempt just such a discussion, such a "coming to terms" with certain religious traditions and ideas. Since I shall be dealing with numinous factors, my feeling is challenged quite as much as my intellect. I cannot, therefore, write in a coolly objective manner, but must allow my emotional subjectivity to speak if I want to describe what I feel when I read certain books of the Bible, or when I remember the impressions I have received from the doctrines of our faith. I do not write as a biblical scholar (which I am not), but as a layman and physician who has been privileged to see deeply into the psychic life of many people. What I am expressing is first of all my own personal view, but I know that I also speak in the name of many who have had similar experiences.

ANSWER TO JOB

560   The Book of Job is a landmark in the long historical development of a divine drama. At the time the book was written, there were already many testimonies which had given a contradictory picture of Yahweh – the picture of a God who knew no moderation in his emotions and suffered precisely from this lack of moderation. He himself admitted that he was eaten up with rage and jealousy and that this knowledge was painful to him. Insight existed along with obtuseness, loving-kindness along with cruelty, creative power along with destructiveness. Everything was there, and none of these qualities was an obstacle to the other. Such a condition is only conceivable either when no reflecting consciousness is present at all, or when the capacity for reflection is very feeble and a more or less

adventitious phenomenon. A condition of this sort can only be described as *amoral*.

561   How the people of the Old Testament felt about their God we know from the testimony of the Bible. That is not what I am concerned with here, but rather with the way in which a modern man with a Christian education and background comes to terms with the divine darkness which is unveiled in the Book of Job, and what effect it has on him. I shall not give a cool and carefully considered exegesis that tries to be fair to every detail, but a purely subjective reaction. In this way I hope to act as a voice for many who feel the same way as I do, and to give expression to the shattering emotion which the unvarnished spectacle of divine savagery and ruthless-ness produces in us. Even if we know by hearsay about the suffering and discord in the Deity, they are so unconscious, and hence so ineffectual morally, that they arouse no human sympathy or understanding. Instead, they give rise to an equally ill-considered outburst of affect, and a smouldering resentment that may be compared to a slowly healing wound. And just as there is a secret tie between the wound and the weapon, so the affect corresponds to the violence of the deed that caused it.

562   The Book of Job serves as a paradigm for a certain experience of God which has a special significance for us today. These experiences come upon man from inside as well as from outside, and it is useless to interpret them rationalistically and thus weaken them by apotropaic means. It is far better to admit the affect and submit to its violence than to try to escape it by all sorts of intellectual tricks or by emotional value-judgments. Although, by giving way to the affect, one imitates all the bad qualities of the outrageous act that provoked it and thus makes oneself guilty of the same fault, that is precisely the point of the whole proceeding: the violence is meant to penetrate to a man's vitals, and he to succumb to its action. He must be affected by it, otherwise its full effect will not reach him. But he should know, or learn to know, what has affected him, for in this way he transforms the blindness of the violence on the one hand and of the affect on the other into knowledge.

563   For this reason I shall express my affect fearlessly and ruthlessly in what follows, and I shall answer injustice with injustice, that I may learn to know why and to what purpose Job was wounded, and what consequences have grown out of this for Yahweh as well as for man.

I

564   Job answers Yahweh thus:

> Behold, I am of small account; what shall I answer thee?
>   I lay my hand on my mouth.
> I have spoken once, and I will not answer;
>   twice, but I will proceed no further.[2]

565   And indeed, in the immediate presence of the infinite power of creation, this is the only possible answer for a witness who is still trembling in every limb with the terror of almost total annihilation. What else could a half-crushed human worm, grovelling in the dust, reasonably answer in the circumstances? In spite of his pitiable littleness and feebleness, this man knows that he is confronted with a superhuman being who is personally most easily provoked. He also knows that it is far better to withhold all moral reflections, to say nothing of certain moral requirements which might be expected to apply to a god.

566   Yahweh's "justice" is praised, so presumably Job could bring his complaint and the protestation of his innocence before him as the just judge. But he doubts this possibility. "How can a man be just before God?"[3] "If I summoned him and he answered me, I would not believe that he was listening to my voice."[4] "If it is a matter of justice, who can summon him?"[5] He "multiplies my wounds without cause."[6] "He destroys both the blameless and the wicked."[7] "If the scourge slay suddenly, he will laugh at the trial of the innocent."[8] "I know," Job says to Yahweh, "thou wilt not hold me innocent. I shall be condemned."[9] "If I wash myself . . . never so clean, yet shalt thou plunge me in the ditch."[10] "For he is not a man, as I am, that I should answer him, and we should come together in judgment."[11] Job wants to explain his point of view to Yahweh, to state his complaint, and tells him: "Thou knowest that I am not guilty, and there is none to deliver out of thy hand."[12] "I desire to argue my case with God."[13] "I will defend my ways to his face,"[14] "I know that I shall be vindicated."[15] Yahweh should summon him and render him an account or at least allow him to plead his cause. Properly estimating the disproportion between man and God, he asks: "Wilt thou break a leaf driven to and fro? and wilt thou pursue the dry stubble?"[16] God has put him in the wrong, but there is no justice.[17] He has "taken away my right."[18] "Till I die I will not put away my integrity from me. I hold fast to my righteousness, and will not let it go."[19] His friend Elihu the Buzite does not believe the injustice of Yahweh: "Of a truth, God will not do wickedly, and the Almighty will not pervert justice."[20] Illogically enough, he bases his opinion on God's *power*: "Is it fit to say to a king, Thou art wicked? and to princes, Ye are ungodly?"[21] One must "respect the persons of princes and esteem the high more than the low."[22] But Job is not shaken in his faith, and had already uttered an important truth when he said: "Behold, my witness is in heaven, and he that vouches for me is on high . . . my eye pours out tears to God, that he would maintain the right of a man with God, like that of a man with his neighbour."[23] And later: "For I know that my Vindicator lives, and at last he will stand upon the earth."[24]

567   These words clearly show that Job, in spite of his doubt as to whether man can be just before God, still finds it difficult to relinquish the idea of meeting God on the basis of justice and therefore of morality. Because, in

spite of everything, he cannot give up his faith in divine justice, it is not easy for him to accept the knowledge that divine arbitrariness breaks the law. On the other hand, he has to admit that no one except Yahweh himself is doing him injustice and violence. He cannot deny that he is up against a God who does not care a rap for any moral opinion and does not recognize any form of ethics as binding. This is perhaps the greatest thing about Job, that, faced with this difficulty, he does not doubt the unity of God. He clearly sees that God is at odds with himself – so totally at odds that he, Job, is quite certain of finding in God a helper and an "advocate" against God. As certain as he is of the evil in Yahweh, he is equally certain of the good. In a human being who renders us evil we cannot expect at the same time to find a helper. But Yahweh is not a human being: he is both a persecutor and a helper in one, and the one aspect is as real as the other. Yahweh is not split but is an *antinomy* – a totality of inner opposites – and this is the indispensable condition for his tremendous dynamism, his omniscience and omnipotence. Because of this knowledge Job holds on to his intention of "defending his ways to his face," i.e. of making his point of view clear to him, since notwithstanding his wrath, Yahweh is also man's advocate *against himself* when man puts forth his complaint.

568   One would be even more astonished at Job's knowledge of God if this were the first time one were hearing of Yahweh's amorality. His incalculable moods and devastating attacks of wrath had, however, been known from time immemorial. He had proved himself to be a jealous defender of morality and was specially sensitive in regard to justice. Hence he had always to be praised as "just," which, it seemed, was very important to him. Thanks to this circumstance or peculiarity of his, he had a *distinct personality*, which differed from that of a more or less archaic king only in scope. His jealous and irritable nature, prying mistrustfully into the faithless hearts of men and exploring their secret thoughts, compelled a personal relationship between himself and man, who could not help but feel personally called by him. That was the essential difference between Yahweh and the all-ruling Father Zeus, who in a benevolent and somewhat detached manner allowed the economy of the universe to roll along on its accustomed courses and punished only those who were disorderly. He did not moralize but ruled purely instinctively. He did not demand anything more *from* human beings than the sacrifices due to him; he did not want to do anything *with* human beings because he had no plans for them. Father Zeus is certainly a figure but not a personality. Yahweh, on the other hand, was interested in man. Human beings were a matter of first-rate importance to him. He needed them as they needed him, urgently and personally. Zeus too could throw thunderbolts about, but only at hopelessly disorderly individuals. Against mankind as a whole he had no objections – but then they did not interest him all that much. Yahweh, however, could get inordinately excited about man as a species and men as individuals if they did not behave as he desired or

expected, without ever considering that in his omnipotence he could easily have created something better than these "bad earthenware pots."

569   In view of this intense personal relatedness to his chosen people, it was only to be expected that a regular covenant would develop which also extended to certain individuals, for instance to David. As we learn from the Eighty-ninth Psalm, Yahweh told him:

> My steadfast love I will keep for him for ever,
>   and my covenant will stand firm for him.
>
> .   .   .   .
>
> I will not violate my covenant,
>   or alter the word that went forth from my lips.
> Once for all I have sworn by my holiness;
>   I will not lie to David.[25]

570   And yet it happened that he, who watched so jealously over the fulfilment of laws and contracts, broke his own oath. Modern man, with his sensitive conscience, would have felt the black abyss opening and the ground giving way under his feet, for the least he expects of his God is that he should be superior to mortal man in the sense of being better, higher, nobler – but not his superior in the kind of moral flexibility and unreliability that do not jib even at perjury.

571   Of course one must not tax an archaic god with the requirements of modern ethics. For the people of early antiquity things were rather different. In their gods there was absolutely everything: they teemed with virtues and vices. Hence they could be punished, put in chains, deceived, stirred up against one another without losing face, or at least not for long. The man of that epoch was so inured to divine inconsistencies that he was not unduly perturbed when they happened. With Yahweh the case was different because, from quite early on, the personal and moral tie began to play an important part in the religious relationship. In these circumstances a breach of contract was bound to have the effect not only of a personal but of a moral injury. One can see this from the way David answers Yahweh:

> How long, Lord? wilt thou hide thyself for ever?
>   shall thy wrath burn like fire?
> Remember how short my time is:
>   wherefore has thou made all men in vain?
>
> .   .   .   .
>
> Lord, where are thy former loving kindnesses,
>   which by thy faithfulness thou didst swear to David?[26]

572   Had this been addressed to a human being it would have run something like this: "For heaven's sake, man, pull yourself together and stop being such a senseless savage! It is really too grotesque to get into such a rage when it's partly your own fault that the plants won't flourish. You used to

be quite reasonable and took good care of the garden you planted, instead of trampling it to pieces."

573   Certainly our interlocutor would never dare to remonstrate with his almighty partner about this breach of contract. He knows only too well what a row he would get into if *he* were the wretched breaker of the law. Because anything else would put him in peril of his life, he must retire to the more exalted plane of reason. In this way, without knowing it or wanting it, he shows himself superior to his divine partner both intellectually and morally. Yahweh fails to notice that he is being humoured, just as little as he understands why he has continually to be praised as just. He makes pressing demands on his people to be praised[27] and propitiated in every possible way, for the obvious purpose of keeping him in a good temper at any price.

574   The character thus revealed fits a personality who can only convince himself that he exists through his relation to an object. Such dependence on the object is absolute when the subject is totally lacking in self-reflection and therefore has no insight into himself. It is as if he existed only by reason of the fact that he has an object which assures him that he is really there. If Yahweh, as we would expect of a sensible human being, were really conscious of himself, he would, in view of the true facts of the case, at least have put an end to the panegyrics on his justice. But he is too unconscious to be moral. Morality presupposes consciousness. By this I do not mean to say that Yahweh is imperfect or evil, like a gnostic demiurge. He is everything in its totality; therefore, among other things, he is total justice, and also its total opposite. At least this is the way he must be conceived if one is to form a unified picture of his character. We must only remember that what we have sketched is no more than an anthropomorphic picture which is not even particularly easy to visualize. From the way the divine nature expresses itself we can see that the individual qualities are not adequately related to one another, with the result that they fall apart into mutually contradictory acts. For instance, Yahweh regrets having created human beings, although in his omniscience he must have known all along what would happen to them.

II

575   Since the Omniscient looks into all hearts, and Yahweh's eyes "run to and fro through the whole earth,"[28] it were better for the interlocutor of the Eighty-ninth Psalm not to wax too conscious of his slight moral superiority over the more unconscious God. Better to keep it dark, for Yahweh is no friend of critical thoughts which in any way diminish the tribute of recognition he demands. Loudly as his power resounds through the universe, the basis of its existence is correspondingly slender, for it needs conscious reflection in order to exist in reality. Existence is only real when it is conscious to somebody. That is why the Creator needs

conscious man even though from sheer unconsciousness, he would like to prevent him from becoming conscious. And that is also why Yahweh needs the acclamation of a small group of people. One can imagine what would happen if this assembly suddenly decided to stop the applause: there would be a state of high excitation, with outbursts of blind destructive rage, then a withdrawal into hellish loneliness and the torture of non-existence, followed by a gradual reawakening of an unutterable longing for something which would make him conscious of himself. It is probably for this reason that all pristine things, even man before he becomes the canaille, have a touching, magical beauty, for in its nascent state "each thing after its kind" is the most precious, the most desirable, the tenderest thing in the world, being a reflection of the infinite love and goodness of the Creator.

576   In view of the undoubted frightfulness of divine wrath, and in an age when men still knew what they were talking about when they said "Fear God," it was only to be expected that man's slight superiority should have remained unconscious. The powerful personality of Yahweh, who, in addition to everything else, lacked all biographical antecedents (his original relationship to the Elohim had long since been sunk in oblivion), had raised him above all the numina of the Gentiles and had immunized him against the influence that for several centuries had been undermining the authority of the pagan gods. It was precisely the details of their mythological biography that had become their nemesis, for with his growing capacity for judgment man had found these stories more and more incomprehensible and indecent. Yahweh, however, had no origin and no past, except his creation of the world, with which all history began, and his relation to that part of mankind whose forefather Adam he had fashioned in his own image as the Anthropos, the original man, by what appears to have been a special act of creation. One can only suppose that the other human beings who must also have existed at that time had been formed previously on the divine potter's wheel along with the various kinds of beasts and cattle – those human beings, namely, from whom Cain and Seth chose their wives. If one does not approve of this conjecture, then the only other possibility that remains is the far more scandalous one that they incestuously married their sisters (for whom there is no evidence in the text), as was still surmised by the philosopher Karl Lamprecht at the end of the nineteenth century.

577   The special providence which singled out the Jews from among the divinely stamped portion of humanity and made them the "chosen people" had burdened them from the start with a heavy obligation. As usually happens with such mortgages, they quite understandably tried to circumvent it as much as possible. Since the chosen people used every opportunity to break away from him, and Yahweh felt it of vital importance to tie this indispensable object (which he had made "godlike" for this very purpose) definitely to himself, he proposed to the patriarch Noah a

contract between himself on the one hand, and Noah, his children, and all their animals, both tame and wild, on the other – a contract that promised advantages to both parties. In order to strengthen this contract and keep it fresh in the memory, he instituted the rainbow as a token of the covenant. If, in future, he summoned the thunder-clouds which hide within them floods of water and lightning, then the rainbow would appear, reminding him and his people of the contract. The temptation to use such an accumulation of clouds for an experimental deluge was no small one, and it was therefore a good idea to associate it with a sign that would give timely warning of possible catastrophe.

578   In spite of these precautions the contract had gone to pieces with David, an event which left behind it a literary deposit in the Scriptures and which grieved some few of the devout, who upon reading it became reflective. As the Psalms were zealously read, it was inevitable that certain thoughtful people were unable to stomach the Eighty-ninth Psalm. However that may be, the fatal impression made by the breach of contract survived.[29] It is historically possible that these considerations influenced the author of the Book of Job.

579   The Book of Job places this pious and faithful man, so heavily afflicted by the Lord, on a brightly lit stage where he presents his case to the eyes and ears of the world. It is amazing to see how easily Yahweh, quite without reason, had let himself be influenced by one of his sons, by a *doubting thought*,[30] and made unsure of Job's faithfulness. With his touchiness and suspiciousness the mere possibility of doubt was enough to infuriate him and induce that peculiar double-faced behaviour of which he had already given proof in the Garden of Eden, when he pointed out the tree to the First Parents and at the same time forbade them to eat of it. In this way he precipitated the Fall, which he apparently never intended. Similarly, his faithful servant Job is now to be exposed to a rigorous moral test, quite gratuitously and to no purpose, although Yahweh is convinced of Job's faithfulness and constancy, and could moreover have assured himself beyond all doubt on this point had he taken counsel with his own omniscience. Why, then, is the experiment made at all, and a bet with the unscrupulous slanderer settled, without a stake, on the back of a powerless creature? It is indeed no edifying spectacle to see how quickly Yahweh abandons his faithful servant to the evil spirit and lets him fall without compunction or pity into the abyss of physical and moral suffering. From the human point of view Yahweh's behaviour is so revolting that one has to ask oneself whether there is not a deeper motive hidden behind it. Has Yahweh some secret resistance against Job? That would explain his yielding to Satan. But what does man possess that God does not have? Because of his littleness, puniness, and defencelessness against the Almighty, he possesses, as we have already suggested, a somewhat keener consciousness based on self-reflection: he must, in order to survive, always be mindful of his impotence. God has no need of this circumspection, for

nowhere does he come up against an insuperable obstacle that would force him to hesitate and hence make him reflect on himself. Could a suspicion have grown up in God that man possesses an infinitely small yet more concentrated light than he, Yahweh, possesses? A jealousy of that kind might perhaps explain his behaviour. It would be quite explicable if some such dim, barely understood deviation from the definition of a mere "creature" had aroused his divine suspicions. Too often already these human beings had not behaved in the prescribed manner. Even his trusty servant Job might have something up his sleeve. . . . Hence Yahweh's surprising readiness to listen to Satan's insinuations against his better judgment.

580   Without further ado Job is robbed of his herds, his servants are slaughtered, his sons and daughters are killed by a whirlwind, and he himself is smitten with sickness and brought to the brink of the grave. To rob him of peace altogether, his wife and his old friends are let loose against him, all of whom say the wrong things. His justified complaint finds no hearing with the judge who is so much praised for his justice. Job's right is refused in order that Satan be not disturbed in his play.

581   One must bear in mind here the dark deeds that follow one another in quick succession: robbery, murder, bodily injury with premeditation, and denial of a fair trial. This is further exacerbated by the fact that Yahweh displays no compunction, remorse, or compassion, but only ruthlessness and brutality. The plea of unconsciousness is invalid, seeing that he flagrantly violates at least three of the commandments he himself gave out on Mount Sinai.

582   Job's friends do everything in their power to contribute to his moral torments, and instead of giving him, whom God has perfidiously abandoned, their warm-hearted support, they moralize in an all too human manner, that is, in the stupidest fashion imaginable, and "fill him with wrinkles." They thus deny him even the last comfort of sympathetic participation and human understanding, so that one cannot altogether suppress the suspicion of connivance in high places.

583   Why Job's torments and the divine wager should suddenly come to an end is not quite clear. So long as Job does not actually die, the pointless suffering could be continued indefinitely. We must, however, keep an eye on the background of all these events: it is just possible that something in this background will gradually begin to take shape as a compensation for Job's undeserved suffering – something to which Yahweh, even if he had only a faint inkling of it, could hardly remain indifferent. Without Yahweh's knowledge and contrary to his intentions, the tormented though guiltless Job had secretly been lifted up to a superior knowledge of God which God himself did not possess. Had Yahweh consulted his omniscience, Job would not have had the advantage of him. But then, so many other things would not have happened either.

584   Job realizes God's inner antinomy, and in the light of his realization his

knowledge attains a divine numinosity. The possibility of this development lies, one must suppose, in man's "godlikeness," which one should
certainly not look for in human morphology. Yahweh himself had guarded
against this error by expressly forbidding the making of images. Job, by
his insistence on bringing his case before God, even without hope of a
hearing, had stood his ground and thus created the very obstacle that forced
God to reveal his true nature. With this dramatic climax Yahweh abruptly
breaks off his cruel game of cat and mouse. But if anyone should expect
that his wrath will now be turned against the slanderer, he will be severely
disappointed. Yahweh does not think of bringing this mischief-making son
of his to account, nor does it ever occur to him to give Job at least the
moral satisfaction of explaining his behaviour. Instead, he comes riding
along on the tempest of his almightiness and thunders reproaches at the
half-crushed human worm:

> Who is this that darkens counsel
>   by words without insight?[31]

585   In view of the subsequent words of Yahweh, one must really ask oneself:
Who is darkening *what* counsel? The only dark thing here is how Yahweh
ever came to make a bet with Satan. It is certainly not Job who has
darkened anything and least of all a counsel, for there was never any talk
of this nor will there be in what follows. The bet does not contain any
"counsel" so far as one can see – unless, of course, it was Yahweh himself
who egged Satan on for the ultimate purpose of exalting Job. Naturally
this development was foreseen in omniscience, and it may be that the word
"counsel" refers to this eternal and absolute knowledge. If so, Yahweh's
attitude seems the more illogical and incomprehensible, as he could then
have enlightened Job on this point – which, in view of the wrong done to
him, would have been only fair and equitable. I must therefore regard this
possibility as improbable.

586   *Whose* words are without insight? Presumably Yahweh is not referring
to the words of Job's friends, but is rebuking Job. But what is Job's guilt?
The only thing he can be blamed for is his incurable optimism in believing
that he can appeal to divine justice. In this he is mistaken, as Yahweh's
subsequent words prove. God does not want to be just; he merely flaunts
might over right. Job could not get that into his head, because he looked
upon God as a moral being. He had never doubted God's might, but had
hoped for right as well. He had, however, already taken back this error
when he recognized God's contradictory nature, and by so doing he
assigned a place to God's justice and goodness. So one can hardly speak
of lack of insight.

587   The answer to Yahweh's conundrum is therefore: it is Yahweh himself
who darkens his own counsel and who has no insight. He turns the tables
on Job and blames him for what he himself does: man is not permitted to
have an opinion about him, and, in particular, is to have no insight which

he himself does not possess. For seventy-one verses he proclaims his world-creating power to his miserable victim, who sits in ashes and scratches his sores with potsherds, and who by now has had more than enough of superhuman violence. Job has absolutely no need of being impressed by further exhibitions of this power. Yahweh, in his omniscience, could have known just how incongruous his attempts at intimidation were in such a situation. He could easily have seen that Job believes in his omnipotence as much as ever and has never doubted it or wavered in his loyalty. Altogether, he pays so little attention to Job's real situation that one suspects him of having an ulterior motive which is more important to him: Job is no more than the outward occasion for an inward process of dialectic in God. His thunderings at Job so completely miss the point that one cannot help but see how much he is occupied with himself. The tremendous emphasis he lays on his omnipotence and greatness makes no sense in relation to Job, who certainly needs no more convincing, but only becomes intelligible when aimed at a listener *who doubts it*. This "doubting thought" is Satan, who after completing his evil handiwork has returned to the paternal bosom in order to continue his subversive activity there. Yahweh must have seen that Job's loyalty was unshakable and that Satan had lost his bet. He must also have realized that, in accepting this bet, he had done everything possible to drive his faithful servant to disloyalty, even to the extent of perpetrating a whole series of crimes. Yet it is not remorse and certainly not moral horror that rises to his consciousness, but an obscure intimation of something that questions his omnipotence. He is particularly sensitive on this point, because "might" is the great argument. But omniscience knows that might excuses nothing. The said intimation refers, of course, to the extremely uncomfortable fact that Yahweh had let himself be bamboozled by Satan. This weakness of his does not reach full consciousness, since Satan is treated with remarkable tolerance and consideration. Evidently Satan's intrigue is deliberately overlooked at Job's expense.

588   Luckily enough, Job had noticed during this harangue that everything else had been mentioned except his right. He has understood that it is at present impossible to argue the question of right, as it is only too obvious that Yahweh has no interest whatever in Job's cause but is far more preoccupied with his own affairs. Satan, that is to say, has somehow to disappear, and this can best be done by casting suspicion on Job as a man of subversive opinions. The problem is thus switched on to another track, and the episode with Satan remains unmentioned and unconscious. To the spectator it is not quite clear why Job is treated to this almighty exhibition of thunder and lightning, but the performance as such is sufficiently magnificent and impressive to convince not only a larger audience but above all Yahweh himself of his unassailable power. Whether Job realizes what violence Yahweh is doing to his own omniscience by behaving like this we do not know, but his silence and submission leave a number of

possibilities open. Job has no alternative but formally to revoke his demand for justice, and he therefore answers in the words quoted at the beginning: "I lay my hand on my mouth."

589   He betrays not the slightest trace of mental reservation – in fact, his answer leaves us in no doubt that he has succumbed completely and without question to the tremendous force of the divine demonstration. The most exacting tyrant should have been satisfied with this, and could be quite sure that his servant – from terror alone, to say nothing of his undoubted loyalty – would not dare to nourish a single improper thought for a very long time to come.

590   Strangely enough, Yahweh does not notice anything of the kind. He does not see Job and his situation at all. It is rather as if he had another powerful opponent in the place of Job, one who was better worth challenging. This is clear from his twice-repeated taunt:

> Gird up your loins like a man;
>   I will question you, and you shall declare to me.[32]

591   One would have to choose positively grotesque examples to illustrate the disproportion between the two antagonists. Yahweh sees something in Job which we would not ascribe to him but to God, that is, an equal power which causes him to bring out his whole power apparatus and parade it before his opponent. Yahweh projects on to Job a sceptic's face which is hateful to him because it is his own, and which gazes at him with an uncanny and critical eye. He is afraid of it, for only in face of something frightening does one let off a cannonade of references to one's power, cleverness, courage, invincibility, etc. What has all that to do with Job? Is it worth the lion's while to terrify a mouse?

592   Yahweh cannot rest satisfied with the first victorious round. Job has long since been knocked out, but the great antagonist whose phantom is projected on to the pitiable sufferer still stands menacingly upright. Therefore Yahweh raises his arm again:

> Will you even put me in the wrong?
>   Will you condemn me that you may be justified?
> Have you an arm like God,
>   and can you thunder with a voice like his?[33]

593   Man, abandoned without protection and stripped of his rights, and whose nothingness is thrown in his face at every opportunity, evidently appears to be so dangerous to Yahweh that he must be battered down with the heaviest artillery. What irritates Yahweh can be seen from his challenge to the ostensible Job:

> Look on every one that is proud, and bring him low;
>   and tread down the wicked where they stand.
> Hide them in the dust together;

> bind their faces in the hidden place.
>   Then will I also acknowledge to you
>   that your own right hand can give you victory.[34]

594   Job is challenged as though he himself were a god. But in the contemporary metaphysics there was no *deuteros theos*, no other god except Satan, who owns Yahweh's ear and is able to influence him. He is the only one who can pull the wool over his eyes, beguile him, and put him up to a massive violation of his own penal code. A formidable opponent indeed, and, because of his close kinship, so compromising that he must be concealed with the utmost discretion – even to the point of God's hiding him from his own consciousness in his own bosom! In his stead God must set up his miserable servant as the bugbear whom he has to fight, in the hope that by banishing the dreaded countenance to "the hidden place" he will be able to maintain himself in a state of unconsciousness.

595   The stage-managing of this imaginary duel, the speechifying, and the impressive performance given by the prehistoric menagerie would not be sufficiently explained if we tried to reduce them to the purely negative factor of Yahweh's fear of becoming conscious and of the relativization which this entails. The conflict becomes acute for Yahweh as a result of a new factor, which is, however, not hidden from omniscience – though in this case the existing knowledge is not accompanied by any conclusion. The new factor is something that has never occurred before in the history of the world, the unheard-of fact that, without knowing it or wanting it, a mortal man is raised by his moral behaviour above the stars in heaven, from which position of advantage he can behold the back of Yahweh, the abysmal world of "shards."[35]

596   Does Job know what he has seen? If he does, he is astute or canny enough not to betray it. But his words speak volumes:

> I know that thou canst do all things,
>   and that no purpose of thine can be thwarted.[36]

597   Truly, Yahweh can do all things and permits himself all things without batting an eyelid. With brazen countenance he can project his shadow side and remain unconscious at man's expense. He can boast of his superior power and enact laws which mean less than air to him. Murder and manslaughter are mere bagatelles, and if the mood takes him he can play the feudal grand seigneur and generously recompense his bondslave for the havoc wrought in his wheat-fields. "So you have lost your sons and daughters? No harm done, I will give you new and better ones."

598   Job continues (no doubt with downcast eyes and in a low voice):

> "Who is this that hides counsel without insight?"
> Therefore I have uttered what I did not understand,
>   things too wonderful for me, which I did not know.

> "Hear, and I will speak;
>   I will question you, and you declare to me."
> I had heard of thee by the hearing of the ear,
>   but now my eye sees thee;
> therefore I abhor myself,
>   and repent in dust and ashes.[37]

599   Shrewdly, Job takes up Yahweh's aggressive words and prostrates himself at his feet as if he were indeed the defeated antagonist. Guileless as Job's speech sounds, it could just as well be equivocal. He has learnt his lesson well and experienced "wonderful things" which are none too easily grasped. Before, he had known Yahweh "by the hearing of the ear," but now he has got a taste of his reality, more so even than David – an incisive lesson that had better not be forgotten. Formerly he was naïve, dreaming perhaps of a "good" God, or of a benevolent ruler and just judge. He had imagined that a "covenant" was a legal matter and that anyone who was party to a contract could insist on his rights as agreed; that God would be faithful and true or at least just, and, as one could assume from the Ten Commandments, would have some recognition of ethical values or at least feel committed to his own legal standpoint. But, to his horror, he has discovered that Yahweh is not human but, in certain respects, less than human, that he is just what Yahweh himself says of Leviathan (the crocodile):

> He beholds everything that is high:
> He is king over all proud beasts.[38]

600   Unconsciousness has an animal nature. Like all old gods Yahweh has his animal symbolism with its unmistakable borrowings from the much older theriomorphic gods of Egypt, especially Horus and his four sons. Of the four animals of Yahweh only one has a human face. That is probably Satan, the god-father of man as a spiritual being. Ezekiel's vision attributes three-fourths animal nature and only one-fourth human nature to the animal deity, while the upper deity, the one above the "sapphire throne," merely had the "likeness" of a man.[39] This symbolism explains Yahweh's behaviour, which, from the human point of view, is so intolerable: it is the behaviour of an unconscious being who cannot be judged morally. Yahweh is a *phenomenon* and, as Job says, "not a man."[40]

601   One could, without too much difficulty, impute such a meaning to Job's speech. Be that as it may, Yahweh calmed down at last. The therapeutic measure of unresisting acceptance had proved its value yet again. Nevertheless, Yahweh is still somewhat nervous of Job's friends – they "have not spoken of me what is right."[41] The projection of his doubt-complex extends – comically enough, one must say – to these respectable and slightly pedantic old gentlemen, as though God-knows-what depended on what they thought. But the fact that men should think at all, and especially

about him, is maddeningly disquieting and ought somehow to be stopped. It is far too much like the sort of thing his vagrant son is always springing on him, thus hitting him in his weakest spot. How often already has he bitterly regretted his unconsidered outbursts!

602   One can hardly avoid the impression that Omniscience is gradually drawing near to a realization, and is threatened with an insight that seems to be hedged about with fears of self-destruction. Fortunately, Job's final declaration is so formulated that one can assume with some certainty that, for the protagonists, the incident is closed for good and all.

603   We, the commenting chorus on this great tragedy, which has never at any time lost its vitality, do not feel quite like that. For our modern sensibilities it is by no means apparent that with Job's profound obeisance to the majesty of the divine presence, and his prudent silence, a real answer has been given to the question raised by the Satanic prank of a wager with God. Job has not so much answered as reacted in an adjusted way. In so doing he displayed remarkable self-discipline, but an unequivocal answer has still to be given.

604   To take the most obvious thing, what about the moral wrong Job has suffered? Is man so worthless in God's eyes that not even a *tort moral* can be inflicted on him? That contradicts the fact that man is desired by Yahweh and that it obviously matters to him whether men speak "right" of him or not. He needs Job's loyalty, and it means so much to him that he shrinks at nothing in carrying out his test. This attitude attaches an almost divine importance to man, for what else is there in the whole wide world that could mean anything to one who has everything? Yahweh's divided attitude, which on the one hand tramples on human life and happiness without regard, and on the other hand must have man for a partner, puts the latter in an impossible position. At one moment Yahweh behaves as irrationally as a cataclysm; the next moment he wants to be loved, honoured, worshipped, and praised as just. He reacts irritably to every word that has the faintest suggestion of criticism, while he himself does not care a straw for his own moral code if his actions happen to run counter to its statutes.

605   One can submit to such a God only with fear and trembling, and can try indirectly to propitiate the despot with unctuous praises and ostentatious obedience. But a relationship of trust seems completely out of the question to our modern way of thinking. Nor can moral satisfaction be expected from an unconscious nature god of this kind. Nevertheless, Job got his satisfaction, without Yahweh's intending it and possibly without himself knowing it, as the poet would have it appear. Yahweh's allocutions have the unthinking yet none the less transparent purpose of showing Job the brutal power of the demiurge: "This is I, the creator of all the un-governable, ruthless forces of Nature, which are not subject to any ethical laws. I, too, am an amoral force of Nature, a purely phenomenal person-ality that cannot see its own back."

606   This is, or at any rate could be, a moral satisfaction of the first order for Job, because through this declaration man, in spite of his impotence, is set up as a judge over God himself. We do not know whether Job realizes this, but we do know from the numerous commentaries on Job that all succeeding ages have overlooked the fact that a kind of Moira or Dike rules over Yahweh, causing him to give himself away so blatantly. Anyone can see how he unwittingly raises Job by humiliating him in the dust. By so doing he pronounces judgment on himself and gives man the moral satisfaction whose absence we found so painful in the Book of Job.

607   The poet of this drama showed a masterly discretion in ringing down the curtain at the very moment when his hero gave unqualified recognition to the ἀπόφασις μεγάλη of the Demiurge by prostrating himself at the feet of His Divine Majesty. No other impression was permitted to remain. An unusual scandal was blowing up in the realm of metaphysics, with supposedly devastating consequences, and nobody was ready with a saving formula which would rescue the monotheistic conception of God from disaster. Even in those days the critical intellect of a Greek could easily have seized on this new addition to Yahweh's biography and used it in his disfavour (as indeed happened, though very much later)[42] so as to mete out to him the fate that had already overtaken the Greek gods. But a relativization of God was utterly unthinkable at that time, and remained so for the next two thousand years.

608   The unconscious mind of man sees correctly even when conscious reason is blind and impotent. The drama has been consummated for all eternity: Yahweh's dual nature has been revealed, and somebody or something has seen and registered this fact. Such a revelation, whether it reached man's consciousness or not, could not fail to have far-reaching consequences.

V

628   The older son of the first parents was corrupted by Satan and not much of a success. He was an eidolon of Satan, and only the younger son, Abel, was pleasing to God. In Cain the God-image was distorted, but in Abel it was considerably less dimmed. If Adam is thought of as a copy of God, then God's successful son, who served as a model for Abel (and about whom, as we have seen, there are no available documents), is the prefiguration of the God-man. Of the latter we know positively that, as the Logos, he is preexistent and coeternal with God, indeed of the same substance (ὁμοούσιος) as he. One can therefore regard Abel as the imperfect prototype of God's son who is about to be begotten in Mary. Just as Yahweh originally undertook to create a chthonic equivalent of himself in the first man, Adam, so now he intends something similar, but much better. The extraordinary precautionary measures above-mentioned are designed to serve this purpose. The new son, Christ, shall on the one

hand be a chthonic man like Adam, mortal and capable of suffering, but on the other hand he shall not be, like Adam, a mere copy, but God himself, begotten by himself as the Father, and rejuvenating the Father as the Son. As God he has always been God, and as the son of Mary, who is plainly a copy of Sophia, he is the Logos (synonymous with Nous), who, like Sophia, is a master workman, as stated by the Gospel according to St. John.[43] This identity of mother and son is borne out over and over again in the myths.

629   Although the birth of Christ is an event that occurred but once in history, it has always existed in eternity. For the layman in these matters, the identity of a nontemporal, eternal event with a unique historical occurrence is something that is extremely difficult to conceive. He must, however, accustom himself to the idea that "time" is a relative concept and needs to be complemented by that of the "simultaneous" existence, in the Bardo or pleroma, of all historical processes. What exists in the pleroma as an eternal process appears in time as an aperiodic sequence, that is to say, it is repeated many times in an irregular pattern. To take but one example: Yahweh had one good son and one who was a failure. Cain and Abel, Jacob and Esau, correspond to this prototype, and so, in all ages and in all parts of the world, does the motif of the hostile brothers, which in innumerable modern variants still causes dissension in families and keeps the psychotherapists busy. Just as many examples, no less instructive, could be found for the two women prefigured in eternity. When these things occur as modern variants, therefore, they should not be regarded merely as personal episodes, moods, or chance idiosyncrasies in people, but as fragments of the pleromatic process itself, which, broken up into individual events occurring in time, is an essential component or aspect of the divine drama.

630   When Yahweh created the world from his *prima materia*, the "Void," he could not help breathing his own mystery into the Creation which is himself in every part, as every reasonable theology has long been convinced. From this comes the belief that it is possible to know God from his Creation. When I say that he could not help doing this, I do not imply any limitation of his omnipotence; on the contrary, it is an acknowledgment that all possibilities are contained in him, and that there are in consequence no other possibilities than those which express him.

631   All the world is God's, and God is in all the world from the very beginning. Why, then, the *tour de force* of the Incarnation? one asks oneself, astonished. God is in everything already, and yet there must be something missing if a sort of second entrance into Creation has now to be staged with so much care and circumspection. Since Creation is universal, reaching to the remotest stellar galaxies, and since it has also made organic life infinitely variable and capable of endless differentiation, we can hardly see where the defect lies. The fact that Satan has everywhere intruded his corrupting influence is no doubt regrettable for many reasons, but it makes no difference in principle. It is not easy to give an answer to

this question. One would like to say that Christ had to appear in order to deliver mankind from evil. But when one considers that evil was originally slipped into the scheme of things by Satan, and still is, then it would seem much simpler if Yahweh would, for once, call this "practical joker" severely to account, get rid of his pernicious influence, and thus eliminate the root of all evil. He would then not need the elaborate arrangement of a special Incarnation with all the unforeseeable consequences which this entails. One should make clear to oneself what it means when God becomes man. It means nothing less than a world-shaking transformation of God. It means more or less what Creation meant in the beginning, namely an objectivation of God. At the time of the Creation he revealed himself in Nature; now he wants to be more specific and become man. It must be admitted, however, that there was a tendency in this direction right from the start. For, when those other human beings, who had evidently been created before Adam, appeared on the scene along with the higher mammals, Yahweh created on the following day, by a special act of creation, a man who was the image of God. This was the first prefiguration of his becoming man. He took Adam's descendants, especially the people of Israel, into his personal possession, and from time to time he filled this people's prophets with his spirit. All these things were preparatory events and symptoms of a tendency within God to become man. But in omniscience there had existed from all eternity a knowledge of the human nature of God or of the divine nature of man. That is why, long before Genesis was written, we find corresponding testimonies in the ancient Egyptian records. These intimations and prefigurations of the Incarnation must strike one as either completely incomprehensible or superfluous, since all creation *ex nihilo* is God's and consists of nothing but God, with the result that man, like the rest of creation, is simply God become concrete. Prefigurations, however, are not in themselves creative events, but are only stages in the process of becoming conscious. It was only quite late that we realized (or rather, are beginning to realize) that God is Reality itself and therefore – last but not least – man. This realization is a millennial process.

VI

632   In view of the immense problem which we are about to discuss, this excursus on pleromatic events is not out of place as an introduction.

633   What, then, is the real reason for the Incarnation as an historical event?

634   In order to answer this question we have to go rather far back. As we have seen, Yahweh evidently has a disinclination to take his absolute knowledge into account as a counterbalance to the dynamism of omnipotence. The most instructive example of this is his relation to Satan: it always looks as if Yahweh were completely uninformed about his son's intentions. That is because he never consults his omniscience. We can only

explain this on the assumption that Yahweh was so fascinated by his successive acts of creation, so taken up with them, that he forgot about his omniscience altogether. It is quite understandable that the magical bodying forth of the most diverse objects, which had never before existed in such pristine splendour, should have caused God infinite delight. Sophia's memory is not at fault when she says:

> when he marked out the foundations of the earth,
>> then I was by him, like a master workman,
> and I was daily his delight.[44]

635   The Book of Job still rings with the proud joy of creating when Yahweh points to the huge animals he has successfully turned out:

> Behold, Behemoth,
>> which I made as I made you.
> . . . .
>
> He is the first of the works of God,
>> made to be lord over his companions.[45]

636   So even in Job's day Yahweh is still intoxicated with the tremendous power and grandeur of his creation. Compared with this, what are Satan's pinpricks and the lamentations of human beings who were created with the behemoth, even if they do bear God's image? Yahweh seems to have forgotten this fact entirely, otherwise he would never have ridden so roughshod over Job's human dignity.

637   It is only the careful and farsighted preparations for Christ's birth which show us that omniscience has begun to have a noticeable effect on Yahweh's actions. A certain philanthropic and universalistic tendency makes itself felt. The "children of Israel" take something of a second place in comparison with the "children of men." After Job, we hear nothing further about new covenants. Proverbs and gnomic utterances seem to be the order of the day, and a real *novum* now appears on the scene, namely apocalyptic communications. This points to metaphysical acts of cognition, that is, to "constellated" unconscious contents which are ready to irrupt into consciousness. In all this, as we have said, we discern the helpful hand of Sophia.

638   If we consider Yahweh's behaviour, up to the appearance of Sophia, as a whole, one indubitable fact strikes us – the fact that his actions are accompanied by an inferior consciousness. Time and again we miss reflection and regard for absolute knowledge. His consciousness seems to be not much more than a primitive "awareness" which knows no reflection and no morality. One merely perceives and acts blindly, without conscious inclusion of the subject, whose individual existence raises no problems. Today we would call such a state psychologically "un-conscious," and in the eyes of the law it would be described as *non compos mentis*. The fact that consciousness does not perform acts of thinking does

not, however, prove that they do not exist. They merely occur unconsciously and make themselves felt indirectly in dreams, visions, revelations, and "instinctive" changes of consciousness, whose very nature tells us that they derive from an "unconscious" knowledge and are the result of unconscious acts of judgment or unconscious conclusions.

639   Some such process can be observed in the curious change which comes over Yahweh's behaviour after the Job episode. There can be no doubt that he did not immediately become conscious of the moral defeat he had suffered at Job's hands. In his omniscience, of course, this fact had been known from all eternity, and it is not unthinkable that the knowledge of it unconsciously brought him into the position of dealing so harshly with Job in order that he himself should become conscious of something through this conflict, and thus gain new insight. Satan who, with good reason, later on received the name of "Lucifer," knew how to make more frequent and better use of omniscience than did his father.[46] It seems he was the only one among the sons of God who developed that much initiative. At all events, it was he who placed those unforeseen incidents in Yahweh's way, which omniscience knew to be necessary and indeed indispensable for the unfolding and completion of the divine drama. Among these the case of Job was decisive, and it could only have happened thanks to Satan's initiative.

640   The victory of the vanquished and oppressed is obvious: Job stands morally higher than Yahweh. In this respect the creature has surpassed the creator. As always when an external event touches on some unconscious knowledge, this knowledge can reach consciousness. The event is recognized as a *déjà vu*, and one remembers a pre-existent knowledge about it. Something of the kind must have happened to Yahweh. Job's superiority cannot be shrugged off. Hence a situation arises in which real reflection is needed. That is why Sophia steps in. She reinforces the much needed self-reflection and thus makes possible Yahweh's decision to become man. It is a decision fraught with consequences: he raises himself above his earlier primitive level of consciousness by indirectly acknowledging that the man Job is morally superior to him and that therefore he has to catch up and become human himself. Had he not taken this decision he would have found himself in flagrant opposition to his omniscience. Yahweh must become man precisely because he has done man a wrong. He, the guardian of justice, knows that every wrong must be expiated, and Wisdom knows that moral law is above even him. Because his creature has surpassed him he must regenerate himself.

641   As nothing can happen without a pre-existing pattern, not even creation *ex nihilo*, which must always resort to the treasurehouse of eternal images in the fabulous mind of the "master workman," the choice of a model for the son who is now about to be begotten lies between Adam (to a limited extent) and Abel (to a much greater extent). Adam's limitation lies in the fact that, even if he is the Anthropos, he is chiefly a creature and a father.

Abel's advantage is that he is the son well pleasing to God, begotten and not directly created. One disadvantage has to be accepted: he met with an early death by violence, too early to leave behind him a widow and children, which ought really to be part of human fate if lived to the full. Abel is not the authentic archetype of the son well pleasing to God; he is a copy, but the first of the kind to be met with in the Scriptures. The young dying god is also well known in the contemporary pagan religions, and so is the fratricide motif. We shall hardly be wrong in assuming that Abel's fate refers back to a metaphysical event which was played out between Satan and another son of God with a "light" nature and more devotion to his father. Egyptian tradition can give us information on this point (Horus and Set). As we have said, the disadvantage prefigured in the Abel type can hardly be avoided, because it is an integral part of the mythical-son drama, as the numerous pagan variants of this motif show. The short, dramatic course of Abel's fate serves as an excellent paradigm for the life and death of a God become man.

642   To sum up: the immediate cause of the Incarnation lies in Job's elevation, and its purpose is the differentiation of Yahweh's consciousness. For this a situation of extreme gravity was needed, a *peripeteia* charged with affect, without which no higher level of consciousness can be reached.

VIII

649   When one remembers the earlier acts of creation, one wonders what has happened to Satan and his subversive activities. Everywhere he sows his tares among the wheat. One suspects he had a hand in Herod's massacre of the innocents. What is certain is his attempt to lure Christ into the role of a worldly ruler. Equally obvious is the fact, as is evidenced by the remarks of the man possessed of devils, that he is very well informed about Christ's nature. He also seems to have inspired Judas, without, however, being able to influence or prevent the sacrificial death.

650   His comparative ineffectiveness can be explained on the one hand by the careful preparations for the divine birth, and on the other hand by a curious metaphysical phenomenon which Christ witnessed: he saw Satan fall like lightning from heaven.[47] In this vision a metaphysical event has become temporal; it indicates the historic and – so far as we know – final separation of Yahweh from his dark son. Satan is banished from heaven and no longer has any opportunity to inveigle his father into dubious undertakings. This event may well explain why he plays such an inferior role wherever he appears in the history of the Incarnation. His role here is in no way comparable to his former confidential relationship to Yahweh. He has obviously forfeited the paternal affection and been exiled. The punishment which we missed in the story of Job has at last caught up with him, though in a strangely limited form. Although he is banished from the heavenly court he has kept his dominion over the sublunary world. He is

not cast directly into hell, but upon earth. Only at the end of time shall he be locked up and made permanently ineffective. Christ's death cannot be laid at his door, because, through its prefiguration in Abel and in the young dying gods, the sacrificial death was a fate chosen by Yahweh as a reparation for the wrong done to Job on the one hand, and on the other hand as a fillip to the spiritual and moral development of man. There can be no doubt that man's importance is enormously enhanced if God himself deigns to become one.

651 As a result of the partial neutralization of Satan, Yahweh identifies with his light aspect and becomes the good God and loving father. He has not lost his wrath and can still mete out punishment, but he does it with justice. Cases like the Job tragedy are apparently no longer to be expected. He proves himself benevolent and gracious. He shows mercy to the sinful children of men and is defined as Love itself. But although Christ has complete confidence in his father and even feels at one with him, he cannot help inserting the cautious petition – and warning – into the Lord's Prayer: "Lead us not into temptation, but deliver us from evil." God is asked not to entice us outright into doing evil, but rather to deliver us from it. The possibility that Yahweh, in spite of all the precautionary measures and in spite of his express intention to become the Summum Bonum, might yet revert to his former ways is not so remote that one need not keep one eye open for it. At any rate, Christ considers it appropriate to remind his father of his destructive inclinations towards mankind and to beg him to desist from them. Judged by any human standards it is after all unfair, indeed extremely immoral, to entice little children into doing things that might be dangerous for them, simply in order to test their moral stamina! Especially as the difference between a child and a grown-up is immeasurably smaller than that between God and his creatures, whose moral weakness is particularly well known to him. The incongruity of it is so colossal that if this petition were not in the Lord's Prayer one would have to call it sheer blasphemy, because it really will not do to ascribe such contradictory behaviour to the God of Love and Summum Bonum.

652 The sixth petition indeed allows a deep insight, for in face of this fact Christ's immense certainty with regard to his father's character becomes somewhat questionable. It is, unfortunately, a common experience that particularly positive and categorical assertions are met with wherever there is a slight doubt in the background that has to be stifled. One must admit that it would be contrary to all reasonable expectations to suppose that a God who, for all his lavish generosity, had been subject to intermittent but devastating fits of rage ever since time began could suddenly become the epitome of everything good. Christ's unadmitted but none the less evident doubt in this respect is confirmed in the New Testament, and particularly in the Apocalypse. There Yahweh again delivers himself up to an unheard-of fury of destruction against the human race, of whom a mere hundred and forty-four thousand specimens appear to survive.[48]

653   One is indeed at a loss to bring such reaction into line with the behaviour of a loving father, whom we would expect to glorify his creation with patience and love. It looks as if the attempt to secure an absolute and final victory for good is bound to lead to a dangerous accumulation of evil and hence to catastrophe. Compared with the end of the world, the destruction of Sodom and Gomorrah and even the Deluge are mere child's play; for this time the whole of creation goes to pieces. As Satan was locked up for a time, then conquered and cast into a lake of fire,[49] the destruction of the world can hardly be the work of the devil, but must be an "act of God" not influenced by Satan.

654   The end of the world is, however, preceded by the circumstance that even Christ's victory over his brother Satan – Abel's counterstroke against Cain – is not really and truly won, because, before this can come to pass, a final and mighty manifestation of Satan is to be expected. One can hardly suppose that God's incarnation in his son Christ would be calmly accepted by Satan. It must certainly have stirred up his jealousy to the highest pitch and evoked in him a desire to imitate Christ (a role for which he is particularly well suited as the πνεῦμα ἀντίμιμον), and to become incarnate in his turn as the *dark* God. (As we know, numerous legends were later woven round this theme.) This plan will be put into operation by the figure of the Antichrist after the preordained thousand years are over, the term allotted by astrology to the reign of Christ. This expectation, which is already to be found in the New Testament, reveals a doubt as to the immediate finality or universal effectiveness of the work of salvation. Unfortunately it must be said that these expectations gave rise to thought-less revelations which were never even discussed with other aspects of the doctrine of salvation, let alone brought into harmony with them.

IX

655   I mention these future apocalyptic events only to illustrate the doubt which is indirectly expressed in the sixth petition of the Lord's Prayer, and not in order to give a general interpretation of the Apocalypse. I shall come back to this theme later on. But, before doing so, we must turn to the question of how matters stood with the Incarnation after the death of Christ. We have always been taught that the Incarnation was a unique historical event. No repetition of it was to be expected, any more than one could expect a further revelation of the Logos, for this too was included in the uniqueness of God's appearance on earth, in human form, nearly two thousand years ago. The sole source of revelation, and hence the final authority, is the Bible. God is an authority only in so far as he authorized the writings in the New Testament, and with the conclusion of the New Testament the authentic communications of God cease. Thus far the Protestant standpoint. The Catholic Church, the direct heir and continuator of historical Christianity, proves to be somewhat more cautious in this

regard, believing that with the assistance of the Holy Ghost the dogma can progressively develop and unfold. This view is in entire agreement with Christ's own teachings about the Holy Ghost and hence with the further continuance of the Incarnation. Christ is of the opinion that whoever believes in him – believes, that is to say, that he is the son of God – can "do the works that I do, and greater works than these."[50] He reminds his disciples that he had told them they were gods.[51] The believers or chosen ones are children of God and "fellow heirs with Christ."[52] When Christ leaves the earthly stage, he will ask his father to send his flock a Counsellor (the "Paraclete"), who will abide with them and in them for ever.[53] The Counsellor is the Holy Ghost, who will be sent from the father. This "Spirit of truth" will teach the believers "all things" and guide them "into all truth."[54] According to this, Christ envisages a continuing realization of God in his children, and consequently in his (Christ's) brothers and sisters in the spirit, so that his own works need not necessarily be considered the greatest ones.

656   Since the Holy Ghost is the Third Person of the Trinity and God is present entire in each of the three Persons at any time, the indwelling of the Holy Ghost means nothing less than an approximation of the believer to the status of God's son. One can therefore understand what is meant by the remark "you are gods." The deifying effect of the Holy Ghost is naturally assisted by the *imago Dei* stamped on the elect. God, in the shape of the Holy Ghost, puts up his tent in man, for he is obviously minded to realize himself continually not only in Adam's descendants, but in an indefinitely large number of believers, and possibly in mankind as a whole. Symptomatic of this is the significant fact that Barnabas and Paul were identified in Lystra with Zeus and Hermes: "The gods have come down to us in the likeness of men."[55] This was certainly only the more naïve, pagan view of the Christian transmutation, but precisely for that reason it convinces. Tertullian must have had something of the sort in mind when he described the "sublimiorem Deum" as a sort of lender of divinity "who has made gods of men."[56]

657   God's Incarnation in Christ requires continuation and completion because Christ, owing to his virgin birth and his sinlessness, was not an empirical human being at all. As stated in the first chapter of St. John, he represented a light which, though it shone in the darkness, was not comprehended by the darkness. He remained outside and above mankind. Job, on the other hand, was an ordinary human being, and therefore the wrong done to him, and through him to mankind, can, according to divine justice, only be repaired by an incarnation of God in an empirical human being. This act of expiation is performed by the Paraclete; for, just as man must suffer from God, so God must suffer from man. Otherwise there can be no reconciliation between the two.

658   The continuing, direct operation of the Holy Ghost on those who are called to be God's children implies, in fact, a broadening process of

incarnation. Christ, the son begotten by God, is the first-born who is succeeded by an ever-increasing number of younger brother and sisters. These are, however, neither begotten by the Holy Ghost nor born of a virgin. This may be prejudicial to their metaphysical status, but their merely human birth will in no sense endanger their prospects of a future position of honour at the heavenly court, nor will it diminish their capacity to perform miracles. Their lowly origin (possibly from the mammals) does not prevent them from entering into a close kinship with God as their father and Christ as their brother. In a metaphorical sense, indeed, it is actually a "kinship by blood," since they have received their share of the blood and flesh of Christ, which means more than mere adoption. These profound changes in man's status are the direct result of Christ's work of redemption. Redemption or deliverance has several different aspects, the most important of which is the expiation wrought by Christ's sacrificial death for the misdemeanours of mankind. His blood cleanses us from the evil consequences of sin. He reconciles God with man and delivers him from the divine wrath, which hangs over him like doom, and from eternal damnation. It is obvious that such ideas still picture God the father as the dangerous Yahweh who has to be propitiated. The agonizing death of his son is supposed to give him satisfaction for an affront he has suffered, and for this "moral injury" he would be inclined to take a terrible vengeance. Once more we are appalled by the incongruous attitude of the world creator towards his creatures, who to his chagrin never behave according to his expectations. It is as if someone started a bacterial culture which turned out to be a failure. He might curse his luck, but he would never seek the reason for the failure in the bacilii and want to punish them morally for it. Rather, he would select a more suitable culture medium. Yahweh's behaviour towards his creatures contradicts all the requirements of so-called "divine" reason whose possession is supposed to distinguish men from animals. Moreover, a bacteriologist might make a mistake in his choice of a culture medium, for he is only human. But God in his omniscience would never make mistakes if only he consulted with it. He has equipped his human creatures with a modicum of consciousness and a corresponding degree of free will, but he must also know that by so doing he leads them into the temptation of falling into a dangerous independence. That would not be too great a risk if man had to do with a creator who was only kind and good. But Yahweh is forgetting his son Satan, to whose wiles even he occasionally succumbs. How then could he expect man with his limited consciousness and imperfect knowledge to do any better? He also overlooks the fact that the more consciousness a man possesses the more he is separated from his instincts (which at least give him an inkling of the hidden wisdom of God) and the more prone he is to error. He is certainly not up to Satan's wiles if even his creator is unable, or unwilling, to restrain this powerful spirit.

XI

662   To believe that God is the Summum Bonum is impossible for a reflecting consciousness. Such a consciousness does not feel in any way delivered from the fear of God, and therefore asks itself, quite rightly, what Christ means to it. That, indeed, is the great question: can Christ still be interpreted in our day and age, or must one be satisfied with the historical interpretation?

663   One thing, anyway, cannot be doubted: Christ is a highly numinous figure. The interpretation of him as God and the son of God is in full accord with this. The old view, which is based on Christ's own view of the matter, asserts that he came into the world, suffered, and died in order to save mankind from the wrath to come. Furthermore he believed that his own bodily resurrection would assure all God's children of the same future.

664   We have already pointed out at some length how curiously God's salvationist project works out in practice. All he does is, in the shape of his own son, to rescue mankind from himself. This thought is as scurrilous as the old rabbinical view of Yahweh hiding the righteous from his wrath under his throne, where of course he cannot see them. It is exactly as if God the father were a different God from the son, which is not the meaning at all. Nor is there any psychological need for such an assumption, since the undoubted lack of reflection in God's consciousness is sufficient to explain his peculiar behaviour. It is quite right, therefore, that fear of God should be considered the beginning of all wisdom. On the other hand, the much-vaunted goodness, love, and justice of God should not be regarded as mere propitiation, but should be recognized as a genuine experience, for God is a *coincidentia oppositorum*. Both are justified, the fear of God as well as the love of God.

665   A more differentiated consciousness must, sooner or later, find it difficult to love, as a kind father, a God whom on account of his unpredictable fits of wrath, his unreliability, injustice, and cruelty, it has every reason to fear. The decay of the gods of antiquity has proved to our satisfaction that man does not relish any all-too-human inconsistencies and weaknesses in his gods. Likewise, it is probable that Yahweh's moral defeat in his dealings with Job had its hidden effects: man's unintended elevation on the one hand, and on the other hand a disturbance of the unconscious. For a while the first-mentioned effect remains a mere fact, not consciously realized though registered by the unconscious. This contributes to the disturbance in the unconscious, which thereby acquires a higher potential than exists in consciousness. Man then counts for more in the unconscious than he does consciously. In these circumstances the potential starts flowing from the unconscious towards consciousness, and the unconscious breaks through in the form of dreams, visions and revelations. Unfortunately the Book of Job cannot be dated with any certainty. As mentioned above, it was written somewhere between 600 and

300 B.C. During the first half of the sixth century, Ezekiel,[57] the prophet with the so-called "pathological" features, appears on the scene. Although laymen are inclined to apply this epithet to his visions, I must, as a psychiatrist, emphatically state that visions and their accompanying phenomena cannot be uncritically evaluated as morbid. Visions, like dreams, are unusual but quite natural occurrences which can be designated as "pathological" only when their morbid nature has been proved. From a strictly clinical standpoint Ezekiel's visions are of an archetypal nature and are not morbidly distorted in any way. There is no reason to regard them as pathological.[58] They are a symptom of the split which already existed at that time between conscious and unconscious. The first great vision is made up of two well-ordered compound quaternities, that is, conceptions of totality, such as we frequently observe today as spontaneous phenomena. Their *quinta essentia* is represented by a figure which has "the likeness of a human form."[59] Here Ezekiel has seen the essential content of the unconscious, namely *the idea of the higher man* by whom Yahweh was morally defeated and who he was later to become.

666   In India, a more or less simultaneous symptom of the same tendency was Gautama the Buddha (b. 562 B.C.), who gave the maximum differentiation of consciousness supremacy even over the highest Brahman gods. This development was a logical consequence of the *purusha-atman* doctrine and derived from the inner experience of yoga practice.

667   Ezekiel grasped, in a symbol, the fact that Yahweh was drawing closer to man. This is something which came to Job as an experience but probably did not reach his consciousness. That is to say, he did not realize that his consciousness was higher than Yahweh's, and that consequently God wants to become man. What is more, in Ezekiel we meet for the first time the title "Son of Man," which Yahweh significantly uses in addressing the prophet, presumably to indicate that he is a son of the "Man" on the throne, and hence a prefiguration of the much later revelation in Christ. It is with the greatest right, therefore, that the four seraphim on God's throne became the emblems of the evangelists, for they form the quaternity which expresses Christ's totality, just as the four gospels represent the four pillars of his throne.

668   The disturbance of the unconscious continued for several centuries. Around 165 B.C., Daniel had a vision of four beasts and the "Ancient of Days," to whom "with the clouds of heaven there came one like a son of man."[60] Here the "son of man" is no longer the prophet but a son of the "Ancient of Days" in his own right, and a son whose task it is to rejuvenate the father.

669   The Book of Enoch, written around 100 B.C., goes into considerably more detail. It gives a revealing account of the advance of the sons of God into the world of men, another prefiguration which has been described as the "fall of the angels." Whereas, according to Genesis,[61] Yahweh resolved that his spirit should not "abide in man for ever," and that men

should not live to be hundreds of years old as they had before, the sons of God, by way of compensation, fell in love with the beautiful daughters of men. This happened at the time of the giants. Enoch relates that after conspiring with one another, two hundred angels under the leadership of Samiazaz descended to earth, took the daughters of men to wife, and begat with them giants three thousand ells long.[62] The angels, among whom Azazel particularly excelled, taught mankind the arts and sciences. They proved to be extraordinarily progressive elements who broadened and developed man's consciousness, just as the wicked Cain had stood for progress as contrasted with the stay-at-home Abel. In this way they enlarged the significance of man to "gigantic" proportions, which points to an inflation of the cultural consciousness at that period. An inflation, however, is always threatened with a counterstroke from the unconscious, and this actually did happen in the form of the Deluge. So corrupt was the earth before the Deluge that the giants "consumed all the acquisitions of men" and then began to devour each other, while men in their turn devoured the beasts, so that "the earth laid accusation against the lawless ones."[63]

670   The invasion of the human world by the sons of God therefore had serious consequences, which make Yahweh's precautions prior to his appearance on the earthly scene the more understandable. Man was completely helpless in face of his superior divine force. Hence it is of the greatest interest to see how Yahweh behaves in this matter. As the later Draconian punishment proves, it was a not unimportant event in the heavenly economy when no less than two hundred of the sons of God departed from the paternal household to carry out experiments on their own in the human world. One would have expected that information concerning this mass exodus would have trickled through to the court (quite apart from the fact of divine omniscience). But nothing of the sort happened. Only after the giants had long been begotten and had already started to slaughter and devour mankind did four archangels, apparently by accident, hear the weeping and wailing of men and discover what was going on on earth. One really does not know which is the more astonishing, the bad organization of the angelic hosts or the faulty communications in heaven. Be that as it may, this time the archangels felt impelled to appear before God with the following peroration:

> All things are naked and open in Thy sight, and Thou seest all things, and nothing can hide itself from Thee. Thou seest what Azazel hath done, who taught all unrighteousness on earth and revealed the eternal secrets which were preserved in heaven. . . . [And enchantments hath Samiazaz taught], to whom Thou has given authority to bear rule over his associates. . . . And Thou knowest all things before they come to pass, and Thou seest these things and Thou dost suffer them, and Thou dost not say to us what we are to do to them in regard to these.[64]

671   Either all that the archangels say is a lie, or Yahweh, for some incomprehensible reason, has drawn no conclusions from his omniscience, or – what is more likely – the archangels must remind him that once again he has preferred to know nothing of his omniscience. At any rate it is only on their intervention that retaliatory action is released on a global scale, but it is not really a just punishment, seeing that Yahweh promptly drowns all living creatures with the exception of Noah and his relatives. This intermezzo proves that the sons of God are somehow more vigilant, more progressive, and more conscious than their father. Yahweh's subsequent transformation is therefore to be rated all the higher. The preparations for his Incarnation give one the impression that he has really learnt something from experience and is setting about things more consciously than before. Undoubtedly the recollection of Sophia has contributed to this increase of consciousness. Parallel with this, the revelation of the metaphysical structure becomes more explicit. Whereas in Ezekiel and Daniel we find only vague hints about the quaternity and the Son of Man, Enoch gives us clear and detailed information on these points. The underworld, a sort of Hades, is divided into four hollow places which serve as abodes for the spirits of the dead until the Last Judgment. Three of these hollow places are dark, but one is bright and contains a "fountain of water."[65] This is the abode of the righteous.

672   With statements of this type we enter into a definitely psychological realm, namely that of mandala symbolism, to which also belongs the ratios 1 : 3 and 3 : 4. The quadripartite Hades of Enoch corresponds to a chthonic quaternity, which presumably stands in everlasting contrast to a pneumatic or heavenly one. The former corresponds in alchemy to the *quaternio* of the elements, the latter to a fourfold, or total, aspect of the deity, as for instance Barbelo, Kolorbas, *Mercurius quadratus*, and the four-faced gods all indicate.

673   In fact, Enoch in his vision sees the four faces of God. Three of them are engaged in praising, praying, and supplicating, but the fourth in "fending off the Satans and forbidding them to come before the Lord of Spirits to accuse them who dwell on earth."[66]

674   The vision shows us an essential differentiation of the God-image: God now has four faces, or rather, four angels of his face, who are four hypostases or emanations, of which one is exclusively occupied in keeping his elder son Satan, now changed into many, away from him, and preventing further experiments after the style of the Job episode.[67] The Satans still dwell in the heavenly regions, since the fall of Satan has not yet occurred. The above-mentioned proportions are also suggested here by the fact that three of the angels perform holy or beneficial functions, while the fourth is a militant figure who has to keep Satan at bay.

675   This quaternity has a distinctly pneumatic nature and is therefore expressed by angels, who are generally pictured with wings, i.e. as aerial

beings. This is the more likely as they are presumably the descendants of Ezekiel's four seraphim.[68] The doubling and separation of the quaternity into an upper and a lower one, like the exclusion of the Satans from the heavenly court, points to a metaphysical split that had already taken place. But the pleromatic split is in its turn a symptom of a much deeper split in the divine will: the father wants to become the son, God wants to become man, the amoral wants to become exclusively good, the unconscious wants to become consciously responsible. So far everything exists only *in statu nascendi*.

676   Enoch's unconscious is vastly excited by all this and its contents burst out in a spate of apocalyptic visions. It also causes him to undertake the *peregrinatio*, the journey to the four quarters of heaven and to the centre of the earth, so that he draws a mandala with his own movements, in accordance with the "journeys" of the alchemistic philosophers and the corresponding fantasies of our modern unconscious.

677   When Yahweh addressed Ezekiel as "Son of Man," this was no more at first than a dark and enigmatic hint. But now it becomes clear: the man Enoch is not only the recipient of divine revelation but is at the same time a participant in the divine drama, as though he were at least one of the sons of God himself. This can only be taken as meaning that in the same measure as God sets out to become man, man is immersed in the pleromatic process. He becomes, as it were, baptized in it and is made to participate in the divine quaternity (i.e. is crucified with Christ). That is why even today, in the rite of the *benedictio fontis*, the water is divided into a cross by the hand of the priest and then sprinkled to the four quarters.

678   Enoch is so much under the influence of the divine drama, so gripped by it, that one could almost suppose he had a quite special understanding of the coming Incarnation. The "Son of Man" who is with the "Head [or Ancient] of Days" looks like an angel (i.e. like one of the sons of God). He "hath righteousness"; "with him dwelleth righteousness"; the Lord of Spirits has "chosen him"; "his lot hath the preeminence before the Lord of Spirits in uprightness."[69] It is probably no accident that so much stress is laid on righteousness, for it is the one quality that Yahweh lacks, a fact that could hardly have remained hidden from such a man as the author of the Book of Enoch. Under the reign of the Son of Man ". . . the prayer of the righteous has been heard, and the blood of the righteous . . . [avenged] before the Lord of Spirits."[70] Enoch sees a "fountain of righteousness which was inexhaustible."[71] The Son of Man

> . . . shall be a staff to the righteous. . . .
>
> For this reason hath he been chosen and hidden before
>   him,
> Before the creation of the world and for evermore.
> And the wisdom of the Lord of Spirits hath revealed
>   him . . . ,
> For he hath preserved the lot of the righteous.[72]

> For wisdom is poured out like water. . . .
> He is mighty in all the secrets of righteousness,
> And unrighteousness shall disappear as a shadow. . . .
> In him dwells the spirit of wisdom,
> And the spirit which gives insight,
> And the spirit of understanding and of might.[73]

679   Under the reign of the Son of Man

> . . . shall the earth also give back that which has been
>   entrusted to it,
> And Sheol also shall give back that which it has received,
> And hell[74] shall give back that which it owes. . . .

> The Elect One shall in those days sit on My Throne,
> And his mouth shall pour forth all the secrets of
>   wisdom and counsel.[75]

680   "All shall become angels in heaven." Azazel and his hosts shall be cast into the burning fiery furnace for "becoming subject to Satan and leading astray those who dwell on the earth."[76]

681   At the end of the world the Son of Man shall sit in judgment over all creatures. "The darkness shall be destroyed, and the light established for ever."[77] Even Yahweh's two big exhibits, Leviathan and Behemoth, are forced to succumb: they are carved up and eaten. In this passage[78] Enoch is addressed by the revealing angel with the title "Son of Man," a further indication that he, like Ezekiel, has been assimilated by the divine mystery, is included in it, as is already suggested by the bare fact that he witnesses it. Enoch is wafted away and takes his seat in heaven. In the "heaven of heavens" he beholds the house of God built of crystal, with streams of living fire about it, and guarded by winged beings that never sleep.[79] The "Head of Days" comes forth with the angelic quaternity (Michael, Gabriel, Raphael, Phanuel) and speaks to him, saying: "This is the Son of Man who is born unto righteousness, and righteousness abides over him, and the righteousness of the Head of Days forsakes him not."[80]

682   It is remarkable that the Son of Man and what he means should be associated again and again with righteousness. It seems to be his leitmotif, his chief concern. Only where injustice threatens or has already occurred does such an emphasis on righteousness make any sense. No one, only God, can dispense justice to any noticeable degree, and precisely with regard to him there exists the justifiable fear that he may forget his justice. In this case his righteous son would intercede with him on man's behalf. Thus "the righteous shall have peace."[81] The justice that shall prevail under the son is stressed to such an extent that one has the impression that formerly, under the reign of the father, injustice was paramount, and that only with the son is the era of law and order inaugurated. It looks as though, with this, Enoch had unconsciously given an answer to Job.

XII

688   Jesus first appears as a Jewish reformer and prophet of an exclusively good God. In so doing he saves the threatened religious continuity, and in this respect he does in fact prove himself a σωτήρ, a saviour. He preserves mankind from loss of communion with God and from getting lost in mere consciousness and rationality. That would have brought something like a dissociation between consciousness and the unconscious, an unnatural and even pathological condition, a "loss of soul" such as has threatened man from the beginning of time. Again and again and in increasing measure he gets into danger of overlooking the necessary irrationalities of his psyche, and of imagining that he can control everything by will and reason alone, and thus paddle his own canoe. This can be seen most clearly in the great socio-political movements, such as Socialism and Communism: under the former the state suffers, and under the latter, man.

689   Jesus, it is plain, translated the existing tradition into his own personal reality, announcing the glad tidings: "God has good pleasure in mankind. He is a loving father and loves you as I love you, and has sent me as his son to ransom you from the old debt." He offers himself as an expiatory sacrifice that shall effect the reconciliation with God. The more desirable a real relationship of trust between man and God, the more astonishing becomes Yahweh's vindictiveness and irreconcilability towards his creatures. From a God who is a loving father, who is actually Love itself, one would expect understanding and forgiveness. So it comes as a nasty shock when this supremely good God only allows the purchase of such an act of grace through a human sacrifice, and, what is worse, through the killing of his own son. Christ apparently overlooked this anticlimax; at any rate all succeeding centuries have accepted it without opposition. One should keep before one's eyes the strange fact that the God of goodness is so unforgiving that he can only be appeased by a human sacrifice! This is an insufferable incongruity which modern man can no longer swallow, for he must be blind if he does not see the glaring light it throws on the divine character, giving the lie to all talk about love and the Summum Bonum.

690   Christ proves to be a mediator in two ways: he helps men against God and assuages the fear which man feels towards this being. He holds an important position midway between the two extremes, man and God, which are so difficult to unite. Clearly the focus of the divine drama shifts to the mediating God-man. He is lacking neither in humanity nor in divinity, and for this reason he was long ago characterized by totality symbols, because he was understood to be all-embracing and to unite all opposites. The quaternity of the Son of Man, indicating a more differentiated consciousness, was also ascribed to him (*vide* Cross and tetramorph). This corresponds by and large to the pattern in Enoch, but with one important deviation: Ezekiel and Enoch, the two bearers of the title "Son of Man," were ordinary human beings, whereas Christ by his

descent,[82] conception, and birth is a hero and half-god in the classical sense. He is virginally begotten by the Holy Ghost and, as he is not a creaturely human being, has no inclination to sin. The infection of evil was in his case precluded by the preparations for the Incarnation. Christ therefore stands more on the divine than on the human level. He incarnates God's good will to the exclusion of all else and therefore does not stand exactly in the middle, because the essential thing about the creaturely human being, sin, does not touch him. Sin originally came from the heavenly court and entered into creation with the help of Satan, which enraged Yahweh to such an extent that in the end his own son had to be sacrificed in order to placate him. Strangely enough, he took no steps to remove Satan from his entourage. In Enoch a special archangel, Phanuel, was charged with the task of defending Yahweh from Satan's insinuations, and only at the end of the world shall Satan, in the shape of a star,[83] be bound hand and foot, cast into the abyss, and destroyed. (This is not the case in the Book of Revelation, where he remains eternally alive in his natural element.)

691   Although it is generally assumed that Christ's unique sacrifice broke the curse of original sin and finally placated God, Christ nevertheless seems to have had certain misgivings in this respect. What will happen to man, and especially to his own followers, when the sheep have lost their shepherd, and when they miss the one who interceded for them with the father? He assures his disciples that he will always be with them, nay more, that he himself abides within them. Nevertheless this does not seem to satisfy him completely, for in addition he promises to send them from the father another παράκλητος (advocate, "Counsellor"), in his stead, who will assist them by word and deed and remain with them forever.[84] One might conjecture from this that the "legal position" has still not been cleared up beyond a doubt, or that there still exists a factor of uncertainty.

692   The sending of the Paraclete has still another aspect. This Spirit of Truth and Wisdom is the Holy Ghost by whom Christ was begotten. He is the spirit of physical and spiritual procreation who from now on shall make his abode in creaturely man. Since he is the Third Person of the Deity, this is as much as to say that *God will be begotten in creaturely man*. This implies a tremendous change in man's status, for he is now raised to sonship and almost to the position of a man-god. With this the pre-figuration in Ezekiel and Enoch, where, as we saw, the title "Son of Man" was already conferred on the creaturely man, is fulfilled. But that puts man, despite his continuing sinfulness, in the position of the mediator, the unifier of God and creature. Christ probably had this incalculable pos-sibility in mind when he said: ". . . he who believes in me, will also do the works that I do; and greater works than these will he do,"[85] and, referring to the sixth verse of the Eighty-second Psalm, "I say, 'You are gods, sons of the Most High, all of you,'" he added, "and scripture cannot be broken."[86]

693   The future indwelling of the Holy Ghost in man amounts to a continuing incarnation of God. Christ, as the begotten son of God and pre-existing mediator, is a first-born and a divine paradigm which will be followed by further incarnations of the Holy Ghost in the empirical man. But man participates in the darkness of the world, and therefore, with Christ's death, a critical situation arises which might well be a cause for anxiety. When God became man all darkness and evil were carefully kept outside. Enoch's transformation into the Son of Man took place entirely in the realm of light, and to an even greater extent this is true of the incarnation in Christ. It is highly unlikely that the bond between God and man was broken with the death of Christ; on the contrary, the continuity of this bond is stressed again and again and is further confirmed by the sending of the Paraclete. But the closer this bond becomes, the closer becomes the danger of a collision with evil. On the basis of a belief that had existed quite early, the expectation grew up that the light manifestation would be followed by an equally dark one, and Christ by an Antichrist. Such an opinion is the last thing one would expect from the metaphysical situation, for the power of evil is supposedly overcome, and one can hardly believe that a loving father, after the whole complicated arrangement of salvation in Christ, the atonement and declaration of love for mankind, would again let loose his evil watch-dog on his children in complete disregard of all that had gone before. Why this wearisome forbearance towards Satan? Why this stubborn projection of evil on man, whom he has made so weak, so faltering, and so stupid that we are quite incapable of resisting his wicked sons? Why not pull up evil by the roots?

694   God, with his good intentions, begot a good and helpful son and thus created an image of himself as the good father – unfortunately, we must admit, again without considering that there existed in him a knowledge that spoke a very different truth. Had he only given an account of his action to himself, he would have seen what a fearful dissociation he had got into through his incarnation. Where, for instance, did his darkness go – that darkness by means of which Satan always manages to escape his well-earned punishment? Does he think he is completely changed and that his amorality has fallen from him? Even his "light" son, Christ, did not quite trust him in this respect. So now he sends to men the "spirit of truth," with whose help they will discover soon enough what happens when God incarnates only in his light aspect and believes he is goodness itself, or at least wants to be regarded as such. An enantiodromia in the grand style is to be expected. This may well be the meaning of the belief in the coming of the Antichrist, which we owe more than anything else to the activity of the "spirit of truth."

695   Although the Paraclete is of the greatest significance metaphysically, it was, from the point of view of the organization of the Church, most undesirable, because, as is authoritatively stated in scripture, the Holy Ghost is not subject to any control. In the interests of continuity and the

Church the uniqueness of the incarnation and of Christ's work of redemption has to be strongly emphasized, and for the same reason the continuing indwelling of the Holy Ghost is discouraged and ignored as much as possible. No further individualistic digressions can be tolerated. Anyone who is inclined by the Holy Ghost towards dissident opinions necessarily becomes a heretic, whose persecution and elimination take a turn very much to Satan's liking. On the other hand one must realize that if everybody had tried to thrust the intuitions of his own private Holy Ghost upon others for the improvement of the universal doctrine, Christianity would rapidly have perished in a Babylonian confusion of tongues – a fate that lay threateningly close for many centuries.

696   It is the task of the Paraclete, the "spirit of truth," to dwell and work in individual human beings, so as to remind them of Christ's teachings and lead them into the light. A good example of this activity is Paul, who knew not the Lord and received his gospel not from the apostles but through revelation. He is one of those people whose unconscious was disturbed and produced revelatory ecstasies. The life of the Holy Ghost reveals itself through its own activity, and through effects which not only confirm the things we all know, but go beyond them. In Christ's sayings there are already indications of ideas which go beyond the traditionally "Christian" morality – for instance the parable of the unjust steward, the moral of which agrees with the Logion of the Codex Bezae,[87] and betrays an ethical standard very different from what is expected. Here the moral criterion is *consciousness*, and not law or convention. One might also mention the strange fact that it is precisely Peter, who lacks self-control and is fickle in character, whom Christ wishes to make the rock and foundation of his Church. These seem to me to be ideas which point to the inclusion of evil in what I would call a *differential moral valuation*. For instance, it is good if evil is sensibly covered up, but to act unconsciously is evil. One might almost suppose that such views were intended for a time when consideration is given to evil as well as to good, or rather, when it is not suppressed below the threshold on the dubious assumption that we always know exactly what evil is.

697   Again, the expectation of the Antichrist is a far-reaching revelation or discovery, like the remarkable statement that despite his fall and exile the devil is still "prince of this world" and has his habitation in the all-surrounding air. In spite of his misdeeds and in spite of God's work of redemption for mankind, the devil still maintains a position of considerable power and holds all sublunary creatures under his sway. This situation can only be described as critical; at any rate it does not correspond to what could reasonably have been expected from the "glad tidings." Evil is by no means fettered, even though its days are numbered. God still hesitates to use force against Satan. Presumably he still does not know how much his own dark side favours the evil angel. Naturally this situation could not remain indefinitely hidden from the "spirit of truth"

who has taken up his abode in man. He therefore created a disturbance in man's unconscious and produced, at the beginning of the Christian era, another great revelation which, because of its obscurity, gave rise to numerous interpretations and misinterpretations in the centuries that followed. This is the Revelation of St. John.

XIII

698   One could hardly imagine a more suitable personality for the John of the Apocalypse than the author of the Epistles of John. It was he who declared that God is light and that "in him is no darkness at all."[88] (Who said there was any darkness in God?) Nevertheless, he knows that when we sin we need an "advocate with the Father," and this is Christ, "the expiation for our sins,"[89] even though for his sake our sins are already forgiven. (Why then do we need an advocate?) The Father has bestowed his great love upon us (though it had to be bought at the cost of a human sacrifice!), and we are the children of God. He who is begotten by God commits no sin[90] (Who commits *no* sin?) John then preaches the message of love. God himself is love; perfect love casteth out fear. But he must warn against false prophets and teachers of false doctrines, and it is he who announces the coming of the Antichrist.[91] His conscious attitude is orthodox, but he has evil forebodings. He might easily have dreams that are not listed on his conscious programme. He talks as if he knew not only a sinless state but also a perfect love, unlike Paul, who was not lacking in the necessary self-reflection. John is a bit too sure, and therefore he runs the risk of a dissociation. Under these circumstances a counterposition is bound to grow up in the unconscious, which can then irrupt into consciousness in the form of a revelation. If this happens, the revelation will take the form of a more or less subjective myth, because, among other things, it compensates the one-sidedness of an individual consciousness. This contrasts with the visions of Ezekiel or Enoch, whose conscious situation was mainly characterized by an ignorance (for which they were not to blame) and was therefore compensated by a more or less objective and universally valid configuration of archetypal material.

699   So far as we can see, the Apocalypse conforms to these conditions. Even in the initial vision a fear-inspiring figure appears: Christ blended with the Ancient of Days, having the likeness of a man and the Son of Man. Out of his mouth goes a "sharp two-edged sword," which would seem more suitable for fighting and the shedding of blood than for demonstrating brotherly love. Since this Christ says to him, "Fear not," we must assume that John was not overcome by love when he fell "as though dead,"[92] but rather by fear. (What price now the perfect love which casts out fear?)

700   Christ commands him to write seven epistles to the churches in the province of Asia. The church in Ephesus is admonished to repent; otherwise it is threatened with deprivation of the light ("I will come . . . and

remove your candlestick from its place").[93] We also learn from this letter that Christ "hates" the Nicolaitans. (How does this square with love of your neighbour?)

701   The church in Smyrna does not come off so badly. Its enemies supposedly are Jews, but they are "a synagogue of Satan," which does not sound too friendly.

702   Pergamum is censured because a teacher of false doctrines is making himself conspicuous there, and the place swarms with Nicolaitans. Therefore it must repent – if not, I will come to you soon." This can only be interpreted as a threat.

703   Thyatira tolerates the preaching of "that woman Jezebel, who calls herself a prophetess." He will "throw her on a sickbed" and "strike her children dead." But "he who . . . keeps my works until the end, I will give him power over the nations, and he shall rule them with a rod of iron, as when earthen pots are broken in pieces, even as I myself have received power from my Father; and I will give him the morning star."[94] Christ, as we know, teaches "Love your enemies," but here he threatens a massacre of children all too reminiscent of Bethlehem!

704   The works of the church in Sardis are not perfect before God. Therefore, "repent." Otherwise he will come like a thief, "and you will not know at what hour I will come upon you"[95] – a none too friendly warning.

705   In regard to Philadelphia, there is nothing to be censured. But Laodicea he will spew out of his mouth, because they are lukewarm. They too must repent. His explanation is characteristic: "Those whom I love, I reprove and chasten."[96] It would be quite understandable if the Laodiceans did not want too much of this "love."

706   Five of the seven churches get bad reports. This apocalyptic "Christ" behaves rather like a bad-tempered, power-conscious "boss" who very much resembles the "shadow" of a love-preaching bishop.

707   As if in confirmation of what I have said, there now follows a vision in the style of Ezekiel. But he who sat upon the throne did not look like a man, but was to look upon "like jasper and carnelian."[97] Before him was "a sea of glass, like crystal"; around the throne, four "living creatures" (ζῷα), which were "full of eyes in front and behind . . . all round and within."[98] The symbol of Ezekiel appears here strangely modified: stone, glass, crystal – dead and rigid things deriving from the inorganic realm – characterize the Deity. One is inevitably reminded of the preoccupation of the alchemists during the following centuries, when the mysterious "Man," the *homo altus*, was named λίθος οὐ λίθος, "the stone that is no stone," and multiple eyes gleamed in the ocean of the unconscious.[99] At any rate, something of John's psychology comes in here, which has caught a glimpse of things beyond the Christian cosmos.

708   Hereupon follows the opening of the Book with Seven Seals by the "Lamb." The latter has put off the human features of the "Ancient of Days" and now appears in purely theriomorphic but monstrous form, like

one of the many other horned animals in the Book of Revelation. It has seven eyes and seven horns, and is therefore more like a ram than a lamb. Altogether it must have looked pretty awful. Although it is described as "standing, as though it had been slain,"[100] it does not behave at all like an innocent victim, but in a very lively manner indeed. From the first four seals it lets loose the four sinister apocalyptic horsemen. With the opening of the fifth seal, we hear the martyrs crying for vengeance ("O sovereign Lord, holy and true, how long before thou wilt judge and avenge our blood on those who dwell upon the earth?").[101] The sixth seal brings a cosmic catastrophe, and everything hides from the "wrath of the Lamb," "for the great day of his wrath is come."[102] We no longer recognize the meek Lamb who lets himself be led unresistingly to the slaughter; there is only the aggressive and irascible ram whose rage can at last be vented. In all this I see less a metaphysical mystery than the outburst of long pent-up negative feelings such as can frequently be observed in people who strive for perfection. We can take it as certain that the author of the Epistles of John made every effort to practise what he preached to his fellow Christians. For this purpose he had to shut out all negative feelings, and, thanks to a helpful lack of self-reflection, he was able to forget them. But though they disappeared from the conscious level they continued to rankle beneath the surface, and in the course of time spun an elaborate web of resentments and vengeful thoughts which then burst upon consciousness in the form of a revelation. From this there grew up a terrifying picture that blatantly contradicts all ideas of Christian humility, tolerance, love of your neighbour and your enemies, and makes nonsense of a loving father in heaven and rescuer of mankind. A veritable orgy of hatred, wrath, vindictiveness, and blind destructive fury that revels in fantastic images of terror breaks out and with blood and fire overwhelms a world which Christ had just endeavoured to restore to the original state of innocence and loving communion with God.

709   The opening of the seventh seal naturally brings a new flood of miseries which threaten to exhaust even St. John's unholy imagination. As if to fortify himself, he must now eat a "little scroll" in order to go on with his "prophesying."

710   When the seventh angel had finally ceased blowing his trumpet, there appeared in heaven, after the destruction of Jerusalem, a vision of the *sun-woman*, "with the moon under her feet, and on her head a crown of twelve stars."[103] She was in the pangs of birth, and before her stood a great red dragon that wanted to devour her child.

711   This vision is altogether out of context. Whereas with the previous visions one has the impression that they were afterwards revised, re-arranged, and embellished, one feels that this image is original and not intended for any educational purpose. The vision is introduced by the opening of the temple in heaven and the sight of the Ark of the Covenant.[104] This is probably a prelude to the descent of the heavenly

bride, Jerusalem, an equivalent of Sophia, for it is all part of the heavenly *hieros gamos*, whose fruit is a divine man-child. He is threatened with the fate of Apollo, the son of Leto, who was likewise pursued by a dragon. But here we must dwell for a moment on the figure of the mother. She is "a woman clothed with the sun." Note the simple statement "a woman" – an ordinary woman, not a goddess and not an eternal virgin immaculately conceived. No special precautions exempting her from complete woman-hood are noticeable, except the cosmic and naturalistic attributes which mark her as an *anima mundi* and peer of the primordial cosmic man, or Anthropos. She is the feminine Anthropos, the counterpart of the masculine principle. The pagan Leto motif is eminently suited to illustrate this, for in Greek mythology matriarchal and patriarchal elements are about equally mixed. The stars above, the moon below, in the middle the sun, the rising Horus and the setting Osiris, and the maternal night all round, οὐρνὸς ἄνω, οὐρανος κάτω[105] – this symbolism reveals the whole mystery of the "woman": she contains in her darkness the sun of "masculine" consciousness, which rises as a child out of the nocturnal sea of the unconscious, and as an old man sinks into it again. She adds the dark to the light, symbolizes the hierogamy of opposites, and reconciles nature with spirit.

712   The son who is born of these heavenly nuptials is perforce a *complexio oppositorum*, a uniting symbol, a totality of life. John's unconscious, certainly not without reason, borrowed from Greek mythology in order to describe this strange eschatological experience, for it was not on any account to be confused with the birth of the Christ-child which had occurred long before under quite different circumstances. Though obviously the allusion is to the "wrathful Lamb," i.e. the apocalyptic Christ, the new-born man-child is represented as his duplicate, as one who will "rule the nations with a rod of iron."[106] He is thus assimilated to the predominant feelings of hatred and vengeance, so that it looks as if he will needlessly continue to wreak his judgment even in the distant future. This interpretation does not seem consistent, because the Lamb is already charged with this task and, in the course of the revelation, carries it to an end without the newborn man-child ever having an opportunity to act on his own. He never reappears afterwards. I am therefore inclined to believe that the depiction of him as a son of vengeance, if it is not an interpretative interpolation, must have been a familiar phrase to John and that it slipped out as the obvious interpretation. This is the more probable in that the intermezzo could not at the time have been understood in any other way, even though this interpretation is quite meaningless. As I have already pointed out, the sun-woman episode is a foreign body in the flow of the visions. Therefore, I believe, it is not too far-fetched to conjecture that the author of the Apocalypse, or perhaps a perplexed transcriber, felt the need to interpret this obvious parallel with Christ and somehow bring it into line with the text as a whole. This could easily be done by using the

familiar image of the shepherd with the iron crook. I cannot see any other reason for this association.

713   The man-child is "caught up" to God, who is manifestly his father, and the mother is hidden in the wilderness. This would seem to indicate that the child-figure will remain latent for an indefinite time and that its activity is reserved for the future. The story of Hagar may be a prefiguration of this. The similarity between this story and the birth of Christ obviously means no more than that the birth of the man-child is an analogous event, like the previously mentioned enthronement of the Lamb in all his metaphysical glory, which must have taken place long before at the time of the ascension. In the same way the dragon, i.e. the devil, is described as being thrown down to earth,[107] although Christ had already observed the fall of Satan very much earlier. This strange repetition or duplication of the characteristic events in Christ's life gave rise to the conjecture that a second Messiah is to be expected at the end of the world. What is meant here cannot be the return of Christ himself, for we are told that he would come "in the clouds of heaven," but not be *born* a second time, and certainly not from a sun-moon conjunction. The epiphany at the end of the world corresponds more to the content of Revelation I and 19 : 11ff. The fact that John uses the myth of Leto and Apollo in describing the birth may be an indication that the vision, in contrast to the Christian tradition, is a product of the unconscious.[108] But in the unconscious is everything that has been rejected by consciousness, and the more Christian one's consciousness is, the more heathenishly does the unconscious behave, if in the rejected heathenism there are values which are important for life – if, that is to say, the baby has been thrown out with the bath water, as so often happens. The unconscious does not isolate or differentiate its objects as consciousness does. It does not think abstractly or apart from the subject: the person of the ecstatic or visionary is always drawn into the process and included in it. In this case it is John himself whose unconscious personality is more or less identified with Christ; that is to say, he is born like Christ, and born to a like destiny. John is so completely captivated by the archetype of the divine son that he sees its activity in the unconscious; in other words, he sees how God is born again in the (partly pagan) unconscious, indistinguishable from the self of John, since the "divine child" is a symbol of the one as much as the other, just as Christ is. Consciously, of course, John was very far from thinking of Christ as a symbol. For the believing Christian, Christ is everything, but certainly not a symbol, which is an expression for something unknown or not yet knowable. And yet he is a symbol by his very nature. Christ would never have made the impression he did on his followers if he had not expressed something that was alive and at work in their unconscious. Christianity itself would never have spread through the pagan world with such astonishing rapidity had its ideas not found an analogous psychic readiness to receive them. It is this fact which also makes it possible to say that

whoever believes in Christ is not only contained in him, but that Christ then dwells in the believer as the perfect man formed in the image of God, the second Adam. Psychologically, it is the same relationship as that in Indian philosophy between man's ego-consciousness and *purusha*, or *atman*. It is the ascendency of the "complete" – τέλειος – or total human being, consisting of the totality of the psyche, of conscious and un-conscious, over the ego, which represents only consciousness and its contents and knows nothing of the unconscious, although in many respects it is dependent on the unconscious and is often decisively influenced by it. This relationship of the self to the ego is reflected in the relationship of Christ to man. Hence the unmistakable analogies between certain Indian and Christian ideas, which have given rise to conjectures of Indian influence on Christianity.

714   This parallelism, which has so far remained latent in John, now bursts into consciousness in the form of a vision. That this invasion is authentic can be seen from the use of pagan mythological material, a most improb-able procedure for a Christian of that time, especially as it contains traces of astrological influence. That may explain the thoroughly pagan remark, "And the earth helped the woman."[109] Even though the consciousness of that age was exclusively filled with Christian ideas, earlier or contempor-aneous pagan contents lay just below the surface, as for example in the case of St. Perpetua.[110] With a Judaeo-Christian – and the author of the Apocalypse was probably such – another possible model to be considered is the cosmic Sophia, to whom John refers on more than one occasion. She could easily be taken as the mother of the divine child,[111] since she is obviously a woman in heaven, i.e. a goddess or consort of a god. Sophia comes up to this definition, and so does the transfigured Mary. If the vision were a modern dream one would not hesitate to interpret the birth of the divine child as the coming to consciousness of the self. In John's case the conscious attitude of faith made it possible for the Christ-image to be received into the material of the unconscious; it activated the archetype of the divine virgin mother and of the birth of her son-lover, and brought it face to face with his Christian consciousness. As a result, John became personally involved in the divine drama.

715   His Christ-image, clouded by negative feelings, has turned into a savage avenger who no longer bears any real resemblance to a saviour. One is not at all sure whether this Christ-figure may not in the end have more of the human John in it, with his compensating shadow, than of the divine saviour who, as the *lumen de lunine*, contains "no darkness." The grotesque paradox of the "wrathful Lamb" should have been enough to arouse our suspicions in this respect. We can turn and twist it as we like, but, seen in the light of the gospel of love, the avenger and judge remains a most sinister figure. This, one suspects, may have been the reason which moved John to assimilate the newborn man-child to the figure of the avenger, thereby blurring his mythological character as the lovely and lovable

divine youth whom we know so well in the figures of Tammuz, Adonis, and Balder. The enchanting springlike beauty of this divine youth is one of those pagan values which we miss so sorely in Christianity, and particularly in the sombre world of the Apocalypse – the indescribable morning glory of a day in spring, which after the deathly stillness of winter causes the earth to put forth and blossom, gladdens the heart of man and makes him believe in a kind and loving God.

716   As a totality, the self is by definition always a *complexio oppositorum*, and the more consciousness insists on its own luminous nature and lays claim to moral authority, the more the self will appear as something dark and menacing. We may assume such a condition in John, since he was a shepherd of his flock and also a fallible human being. Had the Apocalypse been a more or less personal affair of John's, and hence nothing but an outburst of personal resentment, the figure of the wrathful Lamb would have satisfied this need completely. Under those conditions the new-born man-child would have been bound to have a noticeably positive aspect, because, in accordance with his symbolic nature, he would have compensated the intolerable devastation wrought by the outburst of long pent-up passions, being the child of the conjunction of opposites, of the sunfilled day world and the moonlit night world. He would have acted as a mediator between the loving and the vengeful sides of John's nature, and would thus have become a beneficent saviour who restored the balance. This positive aspect, however, must have escaped John's notice, otherwise he could never have conceived of the child as standing on the same level as the avenging Christ.

717   But John's problem was not a personal one. It was not a question of his personal unconscious or of an outburst of ill humour, but of visions which came up from a far greater and more comprehensive depth, namely from the collective unconscious. His problem expresses itself far too much in collective and archetypal forms for us to reduce it to a merely personal situation. To do so would be altogether too easy as well as being wrong in theory and practice. As a Christian, John was seized by a collective, archetypal process, and he must therefore be explained first and foremost in that light. He certainly also had his personal psychology, into which we, if we may regard the author of the Epistles and the apocalyptist as one and the same person, have some insight. That the imitation of Christ creates a corresponding shadow in the unconscious hardly needs demonstrating. The fact that John had visions at all is evidence of an unusual tension between conscious and unconscious. If he is identical with the author of the Epistles, he must have been quite old when he wrote the Book of Revelation. *In confinio mortis* and in the evening of a long and eventful life a man will often see immense vistas of time stretching out before him. Such a man no longer lives in the everyday world and in the vicissitudes of personal relationships, but in the sight of many aeons and in the movement of ideas as they pass from century to century. The eye of John

penetrates into the distant future of the Christian aeon and into the dark abyss of those forces which his Christianity kept in equilibrium. What burst upon him is the storm of the times, the premonition of a tremendous enantiodromia which he could only understand as the final annihilation of the darkness which had not comprehended the light that appeared in Christ. He failed to see that the power of destruction and vengeance is that very darkness from which God had split himself off when he became man. Therefore he could not understand, either, what that sun-moon-child meant, and he could only interpret it as another figure of vengeance. The passion that breaks through in his revelation bears no trace of the feebleness or serenity of old age, because it is infinitely more than personal resentment: it is the spirit of God itself, which blows through the weak mortal frame and again demands man's *fear* of the unfathomable Godhead.

XVII

736   Let us turn back to the question of coming to terms with the paradoxical idea of God which the Apocalypse reveals to us. Evangelical Christianity, in the strict sense, has no need to bother with it, because it has as an essential doctrine an idea of God that, unlike Yahweh, coincides with the epitome of good. It would have been very different if the John of the Epistles had been obliged to discuss these matters with the John of Revelation. Later generations could afford to ignore the dark side of the Apocalypse, because the specifically Christian achievement was something that was not to be frivolously endangered. But for modern man the case is quite otherwise. We have experienced things so unheard of and so staggering that the question of whether such things are in any way reconcilable with the idea of a good God has become burningly topical. It is no longer a problem for experts in theological seminaries, but a universal religious nightmare, to the solution of which even a layman in theology like myself can, or perhaps must, make a contribution.

737   I have tried to set forth above the inescapable conclusions which must, I believe, be reached if one looks at tradition with critical common sense. If, in this wise, one is confronted with a paradoxical idea of God, and if, as a religious person, one considers at the same time the full extent of the problem, one finds oneself in the situation of the author of Revelation, who we may suppose was a convinced Christian. His possible identity with the writer of the letters brings out the acuteness of the contradiction: What is the relationship of this man to God? How does he endure the intolerable contradiction in the nature of Deity? Although we know nothing of his conscious decision, we believe we may find some clue in the vision of the sun-woman in travail.

738   The paradoxical nature of God has a like effect on man: it tears him asunder into opposites and delivers him over to a seemingly insoluble conflict. What happens in such a condition? Here we must let psychology

speak, for psychology represents the sum of all the observations and insights it has gained from the empirical study of severe states of conflict. There are, for example, conflicts of duty no one knows how to solve. Consciousness only knows: *tertium non datur*! The doctor therefore advises his patient to wait and see whether the unconscious will not produce a dream which proposes an irrational and therefore unexpected third thing as a solution. As experience shows, symbols of a reconciling and unitive nature do in fact turn up in dreams, the most frequent being the motif of the child-hero and the squaring of the circle, signifying the union of opposites. Those who have no access to these specifically medical experiences can derive practical instruction from fairy tales, and part-icularly from alchemy. The real subject of Hermetic philosophy is the *coniunctio oppositorum*. Alchemy characterizes its "child" on the one hand as the stone (e.g. the carbuncle), and on the other hand as the homunculus, or the *filius sapientiae* or even the *homo altus*. This is precisely the figure we meet in the Apocalypse as the son of the sun-woman, whose birth story seems like a paraphrase of the birth of Christ – a paraphrase which was repeated in various forms by the alchemists. In fact, they posit their stone as a parallel to Christ (this, with one exception, without reference to the Book of Revelation). This motif appears again in corresponding form and in corresponding situations in the dreams of modern man, with no connection with alchemy, and always it has to do with the bringing together of the light and the dark, as though modern man, like the alchemists, had divined what the problem was that the Apocalypse set the future. It was this problem on which the alchemists laboured for nearly seventeen centuries, and it is the same problem that distresses modern man. Though in one respect he knows more, in another respect he knows less than the alchemists. The problem for him is no longer projected upon matter, as it was for them; but on the other hand it has become psychologically acute, so that the psychotherapist has more to say on these matters than the theologian, who has remained caught in his archaic figures of speech. The doctor, often very much against his will, is forced by the problems of psychoneurosis to look more closely at the religious problem. It is not without good reason that I myself have reached the age of seventy-six before venturing to catechize myself as to the nature of those "ruling ideas" which decide our ethical behaviour and have such an important influence on our practical life. They are in the last resort the principles which, spoken or unspoken, determine the moral decisions upon which our existence depends, for weal or woe. All these dominants culminate in the positive or negative concept of God.[112]

739   Ever since John the apocalyptist experienced for the first time (perhaps unconsciously) the conflict into which Christianity inevitably leads, mankind has groaned under this burden: *God wanted to become man, and still wants to*. That is probably why John experienced in his vision a second birth of a son from the mother Sophia, a divine birth which was

characterized by a *coniunctio oppositorum* and which anticipated the *filius sapientiae*, the essence of the individuation process. This was the effect of Christianity on a Christian of early times, who had lived long and resolutely enough to be able to cast a glance into the distant future. The mediation between the opposites was already indicated in the symbolism of Christ's fate, in the crucifixion scene where the mediator hangs between two thieves, one of whom goes to paradise, the other down to hell. Inevitably, in the Christian view, the opposition had to lie between God and man, and man was always in danger of being identified with the dark side. This, and the predestinarian hints dropped by our Lord, influenced John strongly: only the few preordained from eternity shall be saved, while the great mass of mankind shall perish in the final catastrophe. The opposition between God and man in the Christian view may well be a Yahwistic legacy from olden times, when the metaphysical problem consisted solely in Yahweh's relations with his people. The fear of Yahweh was still too great for anybody to dare – despite Job's gnosis – to lodge the antinomy in Deity itself. But if you keep the opposition between God and man, then you finally arrive, whether you like it or not, at the Christian conclusion "omne bonum a Deo, omne malum ab homine," with the absurd result that the creature is placed in opposition to its creator and a positively cosmic or daemonic grandeur in evil is imputed to man. The terrible destructive will that breaks out in John's ecstasies gives some idea of what it means when man is placed in opposition to the God of goodness: it burdens him with the dark side of God, which in Job is still in its right place. But either way man is identified with evil, with the result that he sets his face against goodness or else tries to be as perfect as his father in heaven.

740   Yahweh's decision to become man is a symbol of the development that had to supervene when man becomes conscious of the sort of God-image he is confronted with.[113] God acts out of the unconscious of man and forces him to harmonize and unite the opposing influences to which his mind is exposed from the unconscious. The unconscious wants both: to divide and to unite. In his striving for unity, therefore, man may always count on the help of a metaphysical advocate, as Job clearly recognized. The unconscious wants to flow into consciousness in order to reach the light, but at the same time it continually thwarts itself, because it would rather remain unconscious. That is to say, God wants to become man, but not quite. The conflict in his nature is so great that the incarnation can only be bought by an expiatory self-sacrifice offered up to the wrath of God's dark side.

741   At first, God incarnated his good side in order, as we may suppose, to create the most durable basis for a later assimilation of the other side. From the promise of the Paraclete we may conclude that God wants to become *wholly* man; in other words, to reproduce himself in his own dark creature (man not redeemed from original sin). The author of Revelation has left

us a testimony to the continued operation of the Holy Ghost in the sense of a continuing incarnation. He was a creaturely man who was invaded by the dark God of wrath and vengeance – a *ventus urens*, a "burning wind." (This John was possibly the favourite disciple, who in old age was vouchsafed a premonition of future developments.) This disturbing invasion engendered in him the image of the divine child, of a future saviour, born of the divine consort whose reflection (the anima) lives in every man – that child whom Meister Eckhart also saw in a vision. It was he who knew that God alone in his Godhead is not in a state of bliss, but must be born in the human soul ("Gott ist selig in der Seele"). The incarnation in Christ is the prototype which is continually being transferred to the creature by the Holy Ghost.

742   Since our moral conduct can hardly be compared with that of an early Christian like John, all manner of good as well as evil can still break through in us, particularly in regard to love. A sheer will for destruction, such as was evident in John, is not to be expected in our case. In all my experience I have never observed anything like it, except in cases of severe psychoses and criminal insanity. As a result of the spiritual differentiation fostered by the Reformation, and by the growth of the sciences in particular (which were originally taught by the fallen angels), there is already a considerable admixture of darkness in us, so that, compared with the purity of the early Christian saints (and some of the later ones too), we do not show up in a very favourable light. Our comparative blackness naturally does not help us a bit. Though it mitigates the impact of evil forces, it makes us more vulnerable and less capable of resisting them. We therefore need more light, more goodness and moral strength, and must wash off as much of the obnoxious blackness as possible, otherwise we shall not be able to assimilate the dark God who also wants to become man, and at the same time endure him without perishing. For this all the Christian virtues are needed and something else besides, for the problem is not only moral: we also need the Wisdom that Job was seeking. But at that time she was still hidden in Yahweh, or rather, she was not yet remembered by him. That higher and "complete" (τέλειος) man is begotten by the "unknown" father and born from Wisdom, and it is he who, in the figure of the *puer aeternus* – "vultu mutabilis albus et ater"[114] – represents our totality, which transcends consciousness. It was this boy into whom Faust had to change, abandoning his inflated onesidedness which saw the devil only outside. Christ's "Except ye become as little children" prefigures this change, for in them the opposites lie close together; but what is meant is the boy who is born from the maturity of the adult man, and not the unconscious child we would like to remain. Looking ahead, Christ also hinted, as I mentioned before, at a morality of evil.

743   Strangely, suddenly, as if it did not belong there, the sun-woman with her child appears in the stream of apocalyptic visions. He belongs to another, future world. Hence, like the Jewish Messiah, the child is "caught

up" to God, and his mother must stay for a long time hidden in the wilderness, where she is nourished by God. For the immediate and urgent problem in those days was not the union of opposites, which lay in the future, but the incarnation of the light and the good, the subjugation of *concupiscentia*, the lust of this world, and the consolidation of the *civitas Dei* against the advent of the Antichrist, who would come after a thousand years to announce the horrors of the last days, the epiphany of the wrathful and avenging God. The Lamb, transformed into a demonic ram, reveals a new gospel, the *Evangelium Aerternum*, which, going right beyond the love of God, has the fear of God as its main ingredient. Therefore the Apocalypse closes, like the classical individuation process, with the symbol of the *hieros gamos*, the marriage of the son with the mother-bride. But the marriage takes place in heaven, where "nothing unclean" enters, high above the devastated world. Light consorts with light. That is the programme for the Christian aeon which must be fulfilled before God can incarnate in the creaturely man. Only in the last days will the vision of the sun-woman be fulfilled. In recognition of this truth, and evidently inspired by the workings of the Holy Ghost, the Pope has recently announced the dogma of the *Assumptio Mariae*, very much to the astonishment of all rationalists. Mary as the bride is united with the son in the heavenly bridal-chamber, and, as Sophia, with the Godhead.[115]

744   This dogma is in every respect timely. In the first place it is a symbolical fulfilment of John's vision.[116] Secondly, it contains an allusion to the marriage of the Lamb at the end of time, and, thirdly, it repeats the Old Testament anamnesis of Sophia. These three references foretell the Incarnation in Christ,[117] but the first foretells the Incarnation in creaturely man.

XVIII

745   Everything now depends on man: immense power of destruction is given into his hand, and the question is whether he can resist the will to use it, and can temper his will with the spirit of love and wisdom. He will hardly be capable of doing so on his own unaided resources. He needs the help of an "advocate" in heaven, that is, of the child who was caught up to God and who brings the "healing" and making whole of the hitherto fragmentary man. Whatever man's wholeness, or the self, may mean *per se*, empirically it is an image of the goal of life spontaneously produced by the unconscious, irrespective of the wishes and fears of the conscious mind. It stands for the goal of the total man, for the realization of his wholeness and individuality with or without the consent of his will. The dynamic of this process is instinct, which ensures that everything which belongs to an individual's life shall enter into it, whether he consents or not, or is conscious of what is happening to him or not. Obviously, it makes a great deal of difference subjectively whether he knows what he is living out, whether he understands what he is doing, and whether he accepts

responsibility for what he proposes to do or has done. The difference between conscious realization and the lack of it has been roundly formulated in the saying of Christ already quoted: "Man, if indeed thou knowest what thou doest, thou art blessed: but if thou knowest not, thou art cursed, and a transgressor of the law."[118] Before the bar of nature and fate, unconsciousness is never accepted as an excuse; on the contrary there are very severe penalties for it. Hence all unconscious nature longs for the light of consciousness while frantically struggling against it at the same time.

746   The conscious realization of what is hidden and kept secret certainly confronts us with an insoluble conflict; at least this is how it appears to the conscious mind. But the symbols that rise up out of the unconscious in dreams show it rather as a confrontation of opposites, and the images of the goal represent their successful reconciliation. Something empirically demonstrable comes to our aid from the depths of our unconscious nature. It is the task of the conscious mind to understand these hints. If this does not happen, the process of individuation will nevertheless continue. The only difference is that we become its victims and are dragged along by fate towards that inescapable goal which we might have reached walking upright, if only we had taken the trouble and been patient enough to understand in time the meaning of the numina that cross our path. The only thing that really matters now is whether man can climb up to a higher moral level, to a higher plane of consciousness, in order to be equal to the superhuman powers which the fallen angels have played into his hands. But he can make no progress with himself unless he becomes very much better acquainted with his own nature. Unfortunately, a terrifying ignorance prevails in this respect, and an equally great aversion to increasing the knowledge of his intrinsic character. However, in the most unexpected quarters nowadays we find people who can no longer blink the fact that something *ought* to be done with man in regard to his psychology. Unfortunately, the little word "ought" tells us that they do not know what to do, and do not know the way that leads to the goal. We can, of course, hope for the undeserved grace of God, who hears our prayers. But God, who also does *not* hear our prayers, wants to become man, and for that purpose he has chosen, through the Holy Ghost, the creaturely man filled with darkness – the natural man who is tainted with original sin and who learnt the divine arts and sciences from the fallen angels. The guilty man is eminently suitable and is therefore chosen to become the vessel for the continuing incarnation, not the guiltless one who holds aloof from the world and refuses to pay his tribute to life, for in him the dark God would find no room.

747   Since the Apocalypse we now know again that God is not only to be loved, but also to be feared. He fills us with evil as well as with good, otherwise he would not need to be feared; and because he wants to become man, the uniting of his antinomy must take place in man. This involves man in a new responsibility. He can no longer wriggle out of it on the plea

of his littleness and nothingness, for the dark God has slipped the atom bomb and chemical weapons into his hands and given him the power to empty out the apocalyptic vials of wrath on his fellow creatures. Since he has been granted an almost godlike power, he can no longer remain blind and unconscious. He must know something of God's nature and of metaphysical processes if he is to understand himself and thereby achieve gnosis of the Divine.

NOTES

1 Cap. V, in Migne, *P.L.*, vol. 1, cols. 615f. (trans. by C. Dodgson, I, pp. 138f., slightly modified.

2 Job 40 : 4–5. [Quotations throughout are from the Revised Standard Version (RSV), except where the Authorized Version (AV) is closer to the text of the Zürcher Bibel (ZB) used by the author in conjunction with the original Hebrew and Greek sources. Where neither RSV nor AV fits, I have translated direct from ZB. The poetic line-arrangement of RSV is followed in so far as possible. – TRANS.]

3 Job 9 : 2.
4 9 : 16.
5 9 : 19.
6 9 : 17.
7 9 : 22.
8 9 : 23 (AV).
9 9 : 28, 29.
10 9 : 30–1 (AV).
11 9 : 32 (AV).
12 10 : 7.
13 13 : 3.
14 13 : 15.
15 13 : 18.
16 13 : 25 (AV).
17 19 : 6–7.
18 27 : 2.
19 27 : 5–6.
20 34 : 12.
21 34 : 18.
22 34 : 19 (ZB).
23 16 : 19–21.
24 19 : 25. ["Vindicator" is RSV alternative reading for "Redeemer," and comes very close to the ZB *Anwalt*, "advocate." – TRANS.]
25 Verses 28, 34, 35.
26 Psalm 89 : 46, 47, 49 (AV; last line from RSV).
27 Or to be "blessed," which is even more captious of him.
28 Zechariah 4 : 10 (AV). Cf. also the Wisdom of Solomon 1 : 10 (AV): "For the ear of jealousy heareth all things: and the noise of murmurings is not hid."
29 The 89th Psalm is attributed to David and is supposed to have been a community song written in exile.
30 Satan is presumably one of God's eyes which "go to and fro in the earth and walk up and down in it" (Job 1 : 7). In Persian tradition, Ahriman proceeded from one of Ormuzd's doubting thoughts.

31 Job 38 : 2 (ZB).

32 Job 38 : 3 and 40 : 7.

33 40 : 8–9.

34 40 : 12–14 ("in the hidden place" is RSV alternative reading for "in the world below").

35 This is an allusion to an idea found in the later cabalistic philosophy. [These "shards," also called "shells" (Heb. *kelipot*), form ten counterpoles to the ten *sefiroth*, which are the ten stages in the revelation of God's creative power. The shards, representing the forces of evil and darkness, were originally mixed with the light of the *sefiroth*. The *Zohar* describes evil as the by-product of the life process of the *sefiroth*. Therefore the *sefiroth* had to be cleansed of the evil admixture of the shards. This elimination of the shards took place in what is described in the cabalistic writings – particularly of Luria and his school – as the "breaking of the vessels." Through this the powers of evil assumed a separate and real existence. Cf. Scholem, *Major Trends in Jewish Mysticism*, p. 267 – EDITORS.]

36 42 : 2.

37 42 : 3–6 (modified).

38 Job 41 : 25 (ZB); cf. 41 : 34 (AV and RSV).

39 Ezekiel 1 : 26.

40 The naïve assumption that the creator of the world is a conscious being must be regarded as a disastrous prejudice which later gave rise to the most incredible dislocations of logic. For example, the nonsensical doctrine of the *privatio boni* would never have been necessary had one not had to assume in advance that it is impossible for the consciousness of a good God to produce evil deeds. Divine unconsciousness and lack of reflection, on the other hand, enable us to form a conception of God which puts his actions beyond moral judgment and allows no conflict to arise between goodness and beastliness.

41 Job 42 : 7.

42 [Cf. Gnostic interpretation of Yahweh as Saturn-Ialdabaoth in "Transformation Symbolism in the Mass," par. 350, above; *Aion*, par. 128 – EDITORS.]

43 John 1 : 3: "All things were made through him, and without him was not anything made that was made."

44 Proverbs 8 : 29–30.

45 Job 40 : 15, 19 (last line, ZB).

46 In Christian tradition, too, there is a belief that God's intention to become man was known to the Devil many centuries before, and that this was why he instilled the Dionysus myth into the Greeks, so that they could say, when the joyful tidings reached them in reality: "So what? We knew all that long ago." When the conquistadores later discovered the crosses of the Mayas in Yucatán, the Spanish bishops used the same argument.

47 Luke 10 : 18.

48 Revelation 7 : 4.

49 Revelation 19 : 20.

50 John 14 : 12.

51 10 : 34.

52 Romans 8 : 17.

53 John 14 : 16f.

54 14 : 26 and 16 : 13.

55 Acts 14 : 11.

56 "Mancipem quendam divinitatis qui ex hominibus deos fecerit." *Apologeticus*, XI, in Migne, *P.L.*, vol. 1, col. 386.

57 The vision in which he received his call occurred in 592 B.C.

58 It is altogether wrong to assume that visions as such are pathological. They occur

with normal people also – not very frequently, it is true, but they are by no means rare.

59 Ezekiel 1 : 26.
60 Daniel 7 : 13.
61 Genesis 6 : 3f.
62 Enoch 7 : 2.
63 Enoch 7 : 3–6. [The translations of the Book of Enoch are from Charles, ed., *The Apocrypha and Pseudepigrapha of the Old Testament in English*, II, sometimes slightly modified. – TRANS.]
64 Enoch 9 : 5–11.
65 22 : 2.
66 Enoch 40 : 7.
67 Cf. also ch. 87f. Of the four "beings who were like white men," three take Enoch by the hand, while the other seizes a star and hurls it into the abyss.
68 Three had animal faces, one a human face.
69 Enoch 46 : 1–3.
70 47 : 4.
71 48 : 1.
72 48 : 4, 6–7.
73 Enoch 49 : 1–3.
74 Synonym for Sheol.
75 51 : 1, 3.
76 54 : 6. Here at last we hear that the exodus of the two hundred angels was a prank of Satan's.
77 58 : 6 (mod.).
78 60 : 10.
79 71 : 5–6.
80 71 : 14.
81 71 : 17.
82 As a consequence of her immaculate conception Mary is already different from other mortals, and this fact is confirmed by her assumption.
83 Presumably the "morning star" (cf. Revelation 2 : 28 and 22 : 16). This is the planet Venus in her psychological implications and not, as one might think, either of the two *malefici*, Saturn and Mars.
84 John 14 : 16.
85 John 14 : 12.
86 10 : 35.
87 An apocryphal insertion at Luke 6 : 4. ["Man, if indeed thou knowest what thou doest, thou art blessed; but if thou knowest not, thou art cursed, and a transgressor of the law" (trans. in James, *The Apocryphal New Testament*, p. 33). – TRANS.]
88 John 1 : 5.
89 2 : 1–2.
90 3 : 9.
91 18f., 4 : 3.
92 Cf. Rev. 1 : 16–17.
93 Rev. 2 : 5.
94 2 : 20f.
95 3 : 3.
96 3 : 19.
97 4 : 3.
98 4 : 6f.
99 This refers to the "luminosity" of the archetypes. [Cf. Jung, "On the Nature of the Psyche," pp. 190ff. – EDITORS.]
100 Rev. 5 : 6.

101 6 : 10.

102 6 : 17 (AV).

103 Rev. 12 : 1.

104 Rev. 11 : 19. The *arca foederis* is an *allegoria Mariae*.

105 "Heaven above, heaven below."

106 Rev. 12 : 5; cf. 2 : 27.

107 Rev. 12 : 9.

108 It is very probable that John knew the Leto myth and used it consciously. What was unconscious and most unexpected, however, was the fact that his unconscious used this pagan myth to describe the birth of the second Messiah.

109 Rev. 12 : 16 (AV).

110 [Cf. Marie-Louise von Franz, "Die Passio Perpetuae." – EDITORS.]

111 The son would then correspond to the *filius sapientiae* of medieval alchemy.

112 Psychologically the God-concept includes every idea of the ultimate, of the first or last, of the highest or lowest. The name makes no difference.

113 The God-concept, as the idea of an all-embracing totality, also includes the unconscious, and hence, in contrast to consciousness, it includes the objective psyche, which so often frustrates the will and intentions of the conscious mind. Prayer, for instance, reinforces the potential of the unconscious, thus accounting for the sometimes unexpected effects of prayer.

114 "Of changeful countenance, both white and black." Horace, *Epistulae*, II, 2.

115 *Apostolic Constitution ("Munificentissimus Deus") of . . . Pius XII*, §22: "Oportebat sponsam, quam Pater desponsaverat, in thalamis caelestibus habitare" (The place of the bride whom the Father had espoused was in the heavenly courts). – St. John Damascene, *Encomium in Dormitionem, etc.*, Homily II, 14 (cf. Migne, *P.G.*, vol. 96, col. 742). §30: Comparison with the Bride in the Song of Solomon. §33: ". . . ita pariter surrexit et Arca sanctificationis suae, cum in hac die Virgo Mater ad aethereum thalamum est assumpta" (. . . so in like manner arose the Ark which he had sanctified, when on this day the Virgin Mother was taken up to her heavenly bridal-chamber). – St. Anthony of Padua, *Sermones Dominicales, etc.*, (ed. Locatelli, III, p. 730).

116 *Apostolic Constitution*, §31: "Ac praeterea scholastici doctores non modo in variis Veteris Testamenti figuris, sed in illa etiam Muliere amicta sole, quam Joannes Apostolus in insula Patmo [Rev. 12 : 1ff.] contemplatus est, Assumptionem Deiparae Virginis significatam viderunt" (Moreover, the Scholastic doctors saw the Assumption of the Virgin Mother of God signified not only in the various figures of the Old Testament, but also in the Woman clothed with the sun, whom the Apostle John contemplated on the island of Patmos).

117 The marriage of the Lamb repeats the Annunciation and the Overshadowing of Mary.

118 Codex Bezae, apocryphal insertion at Luke 6 : 4. [Trans. by James; see above, par. 696. n. 6. – TRANS.]

11 The fight with the shadow[1]

From: *CW* 10, paras 444–57

444   The indescribable events of the last decade lead one to suspect that a peculiar psychological disturbance was a possible cause. If you ask a psychiatrist what he thinks about these things, you must naturally expect to get an answer from his particular point of view. Even so, as a scientist, the psychiatrist makes no claim to omniscience, for he regards his opinion merely as one contribution to the enormously complicated task of finding a comprehensive solution.

445   When one adopts the standpoint of psychopathology, it is not easy to address an audience which may include people who know nothing of this specialized and difficult field. But there is one simple rule that you should bear in mind: the psychopathology of the masses is rooted in the psychology of the individual. Psychic phenomena of this class can be investigated in the individual. Only if one succeeds in establishing that certain phenomena or symptoms are common to a number of different individuals can one begin to examine the analogous mass phenomena.

446   As you perhaps already know, I take account of the psychology both of the conscious and of the unconscious, and this includes the investigation of dreams. Dreams are the natural products of unconscious psychic activity. We have known for a long time that there is a biological relationship between the unconscious processes and the activity of the conscious mind. This relationship can best be described as a compensation, which means that any deficiency in consciousness – such as exaggeration, one-sidedness, or lack of a function – is suitably supplemented by an unconscious process.

447   As early as 1918, I noticed peculiar disturbances in the unconscious of my German patients which could not be ascribed to their personal psychology. Such non-personal phenomena always manifest themselves in dreams as mythological motifs that are also to be found in legends and fairytales throughout the world. I have called these mythological motifs *archetypes*: that is, typical modes or forms in which these collective phenomena are experienced. There was a disturbance of the collective unconscious in every single one of my German patients. One can explain these disorders causally, but such an explanation is apt to be

unsatisfactory, as it is easier to understand archetypes by their aim rather than by their causality. The archetypes I had observed expressed primitivity, violence, and cruelty. When I had seen enough of such cases, I turned my attention to the peculiar state of mind then prevailing in Germany. I could only see signs of depression and a great restlessness, but this did not allay my suspicions. In a paper which I published at that time, I suggested that the "blond beast" was stirring in an uneasy slumber and that an outburst was not impossible.[2]

448   This condition was not by any means a purely Teutonic phenomenon, as became evident in the following years. The onslaught of primitive forces was more or less universal. The only difference lay in the German mentality itself, which proved to be more susceptible because of the marked proneness of the Germans to mass psychology. Moreover, defeat and social disaster had increased the herd instinct in Germany, so that it became more and more probable that Germany would be the first victim among the Western nations – victim of a mass movement brought about by an upheaval of forces lying dormant in the unconscious, ready to break through all moral barriers. These forces, in accordance with the rule I have mentioned, were meant to be a compensation. If such a compensatory move of the unconscious is not integrated into consciousness in an individual, it leads to a neurosis or even to a psychosis, and the same would apply to a collectivity. Clearly there must be something wrong with the conscious attitude for a compensatory move of this kind to be possible; something must be amiss or exaggerated, because only a faulty consciousness can call forth a countermove on the part of the unconscious. Well, innumerable things were wrong, as you know, and opinions are thoroughly divided about them. Which is the correct opinion will be learned only *ex effectu*; that is, we can only discover what the defects in the consciousness of our epoch are by observing the kind of reaction they call forth from the unconscious.

449   As I have already told you, the tide that rose in the unconscious after the First World War was reflected in individual dreams, in the form of collective, mythological symbols which expressed primitivity, violence, cruelty: in short, all the powers of darkness. When such symbols occur in a large number of individuals and are not understood, they begin to draw these individuals together as if by magnetic force, and thus a mob is formed. Its leader will soon be found in the individual who has the least resistance, the least sense of responsibility and, because of his inferiority, the greatest will to power. He will let loose everything that is ready to burst forth, and the mob will follow with the irresistible force of an avalanche.

450   I had observed the German revolution in the test-tube of the individual, so to speak, and I was fully aware of the immense dangers involved when such people crowd together. But I did not know at the time whether there were enough of them in Germany to make a general explosion inevitable.

However, I was able to follow up quite a number of cases and to observe how the uprush of the dark forces deployed itself in the individual test-tube. I could watch these forces as they broke through the individual's moral and intellectual self-control, and as they flooded his conscious world. There was often terrific suffering and destruction; but when the individual was able to cling to a shred of reason, or to preserve the bonds of a human relationship, a new compensation was brought about in the unconscious by the very chaos of the conscious mind, and this compensation could be integrated into consciousness. New symbols then appeared, of a collective nature, but this time reflecting the forces of *order*. There was measure, proportion, and symmetrical arrangement in these symbols, expressed in their peculiar mathematical and geometrical structure. They represent a kind of axial system and are known as *mandalas*. I am afraid I cannot go into an explanation of these highly technical matters here, but, however incomprehensible they may sound, I must mention them in passing because they represent a gleam of hope, and we need hope very badly in this time of dissolution and chaotic disorder.

451   The world-wide confusion and disorder reflect a similar condition in the mind of the individual, but this lack of orientation is compensated in the unconscious by the archetypes of order. Here again I must point out that if these symbols of order are not integrated into consciousness, the forces they express will accumulate to a dangerous degree, just as the forces of destruction and disorder did twenty-five years ago. The integration of unconscious contents is an individual act of realization, of understanding, and moral evaluation. It is a most difficult task, demanding a high degree of ethical responsibility. Only relatively few individuals can be expected to be capable of such an achievement, and they are not the political but the moral leaders of mankind. The maintenance and further development of civilization depend on such individuals, for it is obvious enough that the consciousness of the masses has not advanced since the First World War. Only certain reflective minds have been enriched, and their moral and intellectual horizon has been considerably enlarged by the realization of the immense and overwhelming power of evil, and of the fact that mankind is capable of becoming merely its instrument. But the average man is still where he was at the end of the First World War. Therefore it is only too obvious that the vast majority are incapable of integrating the forces of order. On the contrary, it is even probable that these forces will encroach upon consciousness and take it by surprise and violence, against our will. We see the first symptoms everywhere: totalitarianism and State slavery. The value and importance of the individual are rapidly decreasing and the chances of his being heard will vanish more and more.

452   This process of deterioration will be long and painful, but I fear it is inevitable. Yet in the long run it will prove to be the only way by which man's lamentable unconsciousness, his childishness and individual weakness, can be replaced by a future man, who knows that he himself is the

maker of his fate and that the State is his servant and not his master. But man will reach this level only when he realizes that, through his unconsciousness, he has gambled away the fundamental *droits de l'homme*. Germany has given us a most instructive example of the psychological development in question. There the First World War released the hidden power of evil, just as the war itself was released by the accumulation of unconscious masses and their blind desires. The so-called "Friedenskaiser" was one of the first victims and, not unlike Hitler, he voiced these lawless, chaotic desires and was thus led into war, and into the inevitable catastrophe. The Second World War was a repetition of the same psychic process but on an infinitely greater scale.

453   As I have said, the uprush of mass instincts was symptomatic of a compensatory move of the unconscious. Such a move was possible because the conscious state of the people had become estranged from the natural laws of human existence. Thanks to industrialization, large portions of the population were uprooted and were herded together in large centres. This new form of existence – with its mass psychology and social dependence on the fluctuation of markets and wages – produced an individual who was unstable, insecure, and suggestible. He was aware that his life depended on boards of directors and captains of industry, and he supposed, rightly or wrongly, that they were chiefly motivated by financial interests. He knew that, no matter how conscientiously he worked, he could still fall a victim at any moment to economic changes which were utterly beyond his control. And there was nothing else for him to rely on. Moreover, the system of moral and political education prevailing in Germany had already done its utmost to permeate everybody with a spirit of dull obedience, with the belief that every desirable thing must come from above, from those who by divine decree sat on top of the law-abiding citizen, whose feelings of personal responsibility were overruled by a rigid sense of duty. No wonder, therefore, that it was precisely Germany that fell a prey to mass psychology, though she is by no means the only nation threatened by this dangerous germ. The influence of mass psychology has spread far and wide.

454   The individual's feeling of weakness, indeed of non-existence, was thus compensated by the eruption of hitherto unknown desires for power. It was the revolt of the powerless, the insatiable greed of the "have-nots." By such devious means the unconscious compels man to become conscious of himself. Unfortunately, there were no values in the conscious mind of the individual which would have enabled him to understand and integrate the reaction when it reached consciousness. Nothing but materialism was preached by the highest intellectual authorities. The Churches were evidently unable to cope with this new situation; they could do nothing but protest and that did not help very much. Thus the avalanche rolled on in Germany and produced its leader, who was elected as a tool to complete the ruin of the nation. But what was his original intention? He dreamed of

a "new order." We should be badly mistaken if we assumed that he did not really intend to create an international order of some kind. On the contrary, deep down in his being he was motivated by the forces of order, which became operative in him the moment desirousness and greed had taken complete possession of his conscious mind. Hitler was the exponent of a "new order," and that is the real reason why practically every German fell for him. The Germans wanted order, but they made the fatal mistake of choosing the principal victim of disorder and unchecked greed for their leader. Their individual attitude remained unchanged: just as they were greedy for power, so they were greedy for order. Like the rest of the world, they did not understand wherein Hitler's significance lay, that he symbolized something in every individual. He was the most prodigious personification of all human inferiorities. He was an utterly incapable, unadapted, irresponsible, psychopathic personality, full of empty, infantile fantasies, but cursed with the keen intuition of a rat or a guttersnipe. He represented the shadow, the inferior part of everybody's personality, in an overwhelming degree, and this was another reason why they fell for him.

455   But what could they have done? In Hitler, every German should have seen his own shadow, his own worst danger. It is everybody's allotted fate to become conscious of and learn to deal with this shadow. But how could the Germans be expected to understand this, when nobody in the world can understand such a simple truth? The world will never reach a state of order until this truth is generally recognized. In the meantime, we amuse ourselves by advancing all sorts of external and secondary reasons why it cannot be reached, though we know well enough that conditions depend very largely on the way we take them. If, for instance, the French Swiss should assume that the German Swiss were all devils, we in Switzerland could have the grandest civil war in no time, and we could also discover the most convincing economic reasons why such a war was inevitable. Well – we just don't, for we learned our lesson more than four hundred years ago. We came to the conclusion that it is better to avoid external wars, so we went home and took the strife with us. In Switzerland we have built up the "perfect democracy," where our warlike instincts expend themselves in the form of domestic quarrels called "political life." We fight each other within the limits of the law and the constitution, and we are inclined to think of democracy as a chronic state of mitigated civil war. We are far from being at peace with ourselves: on the contrary, we hate and fight each other because we have succeeded in introverting war. Our peaceful outward demeanour merely serves to safeguard our domestic quarrels from foreign intruders who might disturb us. Thus far we have succeeded, but we are still a long way from the ultimate goal. We still have enemies in the flesh, and we have not yet managed to introvert our political disharmonies. We still labour under the unwholesome delusion that we should be at peace within ourselves. Yet even our national, mitigated state of war would soon come to and end if everybody could see his own shadow

and begin the only struggle that is really worth while: the fight against the overwhelming power-drive of the shadow. We have a tolerable social order in Switzerland because we fight among ourselves. Our order would be perfect if only everybody could direct his aggressiveness inwards, into his own psyche. Unfortunately, our religious education prevents us from doing this, with its false promises of an immediate peace within. Peace may come in the end, but only when victory and defeat have lost their meaning. What did our Lord mean when he said: "I came not to send peace, but a sword"?

456   To the extent that we are able to found a true democracy – a conditional fight among ourselves, either collective or individual – we realize, we make real, the factors of order, because then it becomes absolutely necessary to live in orderly circumstances. In a democracy you simply cannot afford the disturbing complications of outside interference. How can you run a civil war properly when you are attacked from without? When, on the other hand, you are seriously at variance with yourself, you welcome your fellow human beings as possible sympathizers with your cause, and on this account you are disposed to be friendly and hospitable. But you politely avoid people who want to be helpful and relieve you of your troubles. We psychologists have learned, through long and painful experience, that you deprive a man of his best resource when you help him to get rid of his complexes. You can only help him to become sufficiently aware of them and to start a conscious conflict within himself. In this way the complex becomes a focus of life. Anything that disappears from your psychological inventory is apt to turn up in the guise of a hostile neighbour, who will inevitably arouse your anger and make you aggressive. It is surely better to know that your worst enemy is right there in your own heart. Man's warlike instincts are ineradicable – therefore a state of perfect peace is unthinkable. Moreover, peace is uncanny because it breeds war. True democracy is a highly psychological institution which takes account of human nature as it is and makes allowances for the necessity of conflict within its own national boundaries.

457   If you now compare the present state of mind of the Germans with my argument you will appreciate the enormous task with which the world is confronted. We can hardly expect the demoralized German masses to realize the import of such psychological truths, no matter how simple. But the great Western democracies have a better chance, so long as they can keep out of those wars that always tempt them to believe in external enemies and in the desirability of internal peace. The marked tendency of the Western democracies to internal dissension is the very thing that could lead them into a more hopeful path. But I am afraid that this hope will be deferred by powers which still believe in the contrary process, in the destruction of the individual and the increase of the fiction we call the State. The psychologist believes firmly in the individual as the sole carrier of mind and life. Society and the State derive their quality from the individual's mental condition, for they are made up of individuals and the

way they are organized. Obvious as this fact is, it has still not permeated collective opinion sufficiently for people to refrain from using the word "State" as if it referred to a sort of super-individual endowed with inexhaustible power and resourcefulness. The State is expected nowadays to accomplish what nobody would expect from an individual. The dangerous slope leading down to mass psychology begins with this plausible thinking in large numbers, in terms of powerful organizations where the individual dwindles to a mere cipher. Everything that exceeds a certain human size evokes equally inhuman powers in man's unconscious. Totalitarian demons are called forth, instead of the realization that all that can really be accomplished is an infinitesimal step forward in the moral nature of the individual. The destructive power of our weapons has increased beyond all measure, and this forces a psychological question on mankind: Is the mental and moral condition of the men who decide on the use of these weapons equal to the enormity of the possible consequences?

NOTES

1 [A broadcast talk in the Third Programme of the British Broadcasting Corporation, on November 3, 1946. First published in *The Listener* (London), XXXVI (1946), no. 930, 615–16; reprinted as an introduction to *Essays on Contemporary Events* (1947); also published, under the title "Individual and Mass Psychology," in *Chimera* (New York and Princeton, N.J.), V (1947):3, 3–11. Here slightly revised. – EDITORS.]
2 Cf. "The Role of the Unconscious," par. 17.

12   After the catastrophe[1]

From: *CW* 10, paras 400–43

400   This is the first time since 1936 that the fate of Germany again drives me to take up my pen. The quotation from the *Voluspo* with which I ended the article[2] I wrote at that time, about Wotan "murmuring with Mimir's head," pointed prophetically to the nature of the coming apocalyptic events. The myth has been fulfilled, and the greater part of Europe lies in ruins.

401   Before the work of reconstruction can begin, there is a good deal of clearing up to be done, and this calls above all for *reflection*. Questions are being asked on all sides about the meaning of the whole tragedy. People have even turned to me for an explanation, and I have had to answer them there and then to the best of my ability. But as the spoken word very quickly gives rise to legends, I have decided – not without considerable hesitations and misgivings – to set down my views once again in the form of an article. I am only too well aware that "Germany" presents an immense problem, and that the subjective views of a medical psychologist can touch on only a few aspects of this gigantic tangle of questions. I must be content with a modest contribution to the work of clearing up, without even attempting to look as far ahead as reconstruction.

402   While I was working on this article I noticed how churned up one still is in one's own psyche, and how difficult it is to reach anything approaching a moderate and relatively calm point of view in the midst of one's emotions. No doubt we should be cold-blooded and superior; but we are, on the whole, much more deeply involved in the recent events in Germany than we like to admit. Nor can we feel compassion, for the heart harbours feelings of a very different nature, and these would like to have the first say. Neither the doctor nor the psychologist can afford to be *only* cold-blooded – quite apart from the fact that they would find it impossible. Their relationship to the world involves them and all their affects, otherwise their relationship would be incomplete. That being so, I found myself faced with the task of steering my ship between Scylla and Charybdis, and – as is usual on such a voyage – stopping my ears to one side of my being and lashing the other to the mast. I must confess that no article has ever given me so much trouble, from a moral as well as a human point of view. I had

not realized how much I myself was affected. There are others, I am sure, who will share this feeling with me. This inner identity or *participation mystique* with events in Germany has caused me to experience afresh how painfully wide is the scope of the psychological concept of *collective guilt*. So when I approach this problem it is certainly not with any feelings of cold-blooded superiority, but rather with an avowed sense of inferiority.

403   The psychological use of the word "guilt" should not be confused with guilt in the legal or moral sense. Psychologically, it connotes the irrational presence of a subjective feeling (or conviction) of guilt, or an objective imputation of, or imputed share in, guilt. As an example of the latter, suppose a man belongs to a family which has the misfortune to be disgraced because one of its members has committed a crime. It is clear that he cannot be held responsible, either legally or morally. Yet the atmosphere of guilt makes itself felt in many ways. His family name appears to have been sullied, and it gives him a painful shock to hear it bandied about in the mouths of strangers. Guilt can be restricted to the lawbreaker only from the legal, moral, and intellectual point of view, but as a psychic phenomenon it spreads itself over the whole neighbourhood. A house, a family, even a village where a murder has been committed feels the psychological guilt and is made to feel it by the outside world. Would one take a room where one knows a man was murdered a few days before? Is it particularly pleasant to marry the sister or daughter of a criminal? What father is not deeply wounded if his son is sent to prison, and does he not feel injured in his family pride if a cousin of the same name brings dishonour on his house? Would not every decent Swiss feel ashamed – to put it mildly – if our Government had erected a human slaughterhouse like Maidenek in our country? Would we then be surprised if, travelling abroad with our Swiss passports, we heard such remarks at the frontier as "Ces cochons de Suisses!"? Indeed, are we not all a little ashamed – precisely because we are patriots – that Switzerland should have bred so many traitors?

404   Living as we do in the middle of Europe, we Swiss feel comfortably far removed from the foul vapours that arise from the morass of German guilt. But all this changes the moment we set foot, as Europeans, on another continent or come into contact with an Oriental people. What are we to say to an Indian who asks us: "You are anxious to bring us your Christian culture, are you not? May I ask if Auschwitz and Buchenwald are examples of European civilization?" Would it help matters if we hastened to assure him that these things did not take place where we live, but several hundred miles further east – not in our country at all but in a neighbouring one? How would we react if an Indian pointed out indignantly that India's black spot lay not in Travancore but in Hyderabad? Undoubtedly we'd say, "Oh well, India is India!" Similarly, the view all over the East is "Oh well, Europe is Europe!" The moment we so-called innocent Europeans cross the frontiers of our own continent we are made to feel something of the

collective guilt that weighs upon it, despite our good conscience. (One might also ask: Is Russia so primitive that she can still feel our "guilt-by-contagion" – as collective guilt might also be called – and for that reason accuses us of Fascism?) The world sees Europe as the continent on whose soil the shameful concentration camps grew, just as Europe singles out Germany as the land and the people that are enveloped in a cloud of guilt; for the horror happened in Germany and its perpetrators were Germans. No German can deny this, any more than a European or a Christian can deny that the most monstrous crime of all ages was committed in his house. The Christian Church should put ashes on her head and rend her garments on account of the guilt of her children. The shadow of their guilt has fallen on her as much as upon Europe, the mother of monsters. Europe must account for herself before the world, just as Germany must before Europe. The European can no more convince the Indian that Germany is no concern of his, or that he knows nothing at all about that country, than the German can rid himself of his collective guilt by protesting that he did not know. In that way he merely compounds his collective guilt by the sin of unconsciousness.

405   Psychological collective guilt is a *tragic fate*. It hits everybody, just and unjust alike, everybody who was anywhere near the place where the terrible thing happened. Naturally no reasonable and conscientious person will lightly turn collective into individual guilt by holding the individual responsible without giving him a hearing. He will know enough to distinguish between the individually guilty and the merely collectively guilty. But how many people are either reasonable or conscientious, and how many take the trouble to become so? I am not very optimistic in this respect. Therefore, although collective guilt, viewed on the archaic and primitive level, is a state of *magical uncleanness*, yet precisely because of the general unreasonableness it is a very real fact, which no European outside Europe and no German outside Germany can leave out of account. If the German intends to live on good terms with Europe, he must be conscious that in the eyes of Europeans he is a guilty man. As a German, he has betrayed European civilization and all its values; he has brought shame and disgrace on his European family, so that one must blush to hear oneself called a European; he has fallen on his European brethren like a beast of prey, and tortured and murdered them. The German can hardly expect other Europeans to resort to such niceties as to inquire at every step whether the criminal's name was Müller or Meier. Neither will he be deemed worthy of being treated as a gentleman until the contrary has been proved. Unfortunately, for twelve long years it has been demonstrated with the utmost clarity that the official German was no gentleman.

406   If a German is prepared to acknowledge his moral inferiority as collective guilt before the whole world, without attempting to minimize it or explain it away with flimsy arguments, then he will stand a reasonable chance, after a time, of being taken for a more or less decent man, and will

thus be absolved of his collective guilt at any rate in the eyes of individuals.

407   It may be objected that the whole concept of psychological collective guilt is a prejudice and a sweepingly unfair condemnation. Of course it is, but that is precisely what constitutes the irrational nature of collective guilt: it cares nothing for the just and the unjust, it is the dark cloud that rises up from the scene of an unexpiated crime. It is a psychic phenomenon, and it is therefore no condemnation of the German people to say that they are collectively guilty, but simply a statement of fact. Yet if we penetrate more deeply into the psychology of this phenomenon, we shall soon discover that the problem of collective guilt has another and more questionable aspect than that merely of a collective judgment.

408   Since no man lives within his own psychic sphere like a snail in its shell, separated from everybody else, but is connected with his fellow-men by his unconscious humanity, no crime can ever be what it appears to our consciousness to be: an isolated psychic happening. In reality, it always happens over a wide radius. The sensation aroused by a crime, the passionate interest in tracking down the criminal, the eagerness with which the court proceedings are followed, and so on, all go to prove the exciting effect which the crime has on everybody who is not abnormally dull or apathetic. Everybody joins in, feels the crime in his own being, tried to understand and explain it. Something is set aflame by that great fire of evil that flared up in the crime. Was not Plato aware that the sight of ugliness produces something ugly in the soul? Indignation leaps up, angry cries of "Justice!" pursue the murderer, and they are louder, more impassioned, and more charged with hate the more fiercely burns the fire of evil that has been lit in our souls. It is a fact that cannot be denied: the wickedness of others becomes our own wickedness because it kindles something evil in our own hearts. The murder has been suffered by everyone, and everyone has committed it; lured by the irresistible fascination of evil, we have all made this collective psychic murder possible; and the closer we were to it and the better we could see, the greater our guilt. In this way we are unavoidably drawn into the uncleanness of evil, no matter what our conscious attitude may be. No one can escape this, for we are all so much a part of the human community that every crime calls forth a secret satisfaction in some corner of the fickle human heart. It is true that, in persons with a strong moral disposition, this reaction may arouse contrary feelings in a neighbouring compartment of the mind. But a strong moral disposition is a comparative rarity, so that when the crimes mount up, indignation may easily get pitched too high, and evil then becomes the order of the day. Everyone harbours his "statistical criminal" in himself, just as he has his own private madman or saint. Owing to this basic peculiarity in our human make-up, a corresponding suggestibility, or susceptibility to infection, exists everywhere. It is our age in particular – the last half century – that has prepared the way for crime. Has it never

occurred to anybody, for instance, that the vogue for the thriller has a rather questionable side?

409   Long before 1933 there was a smell of burning in the air, and people were passionately interested in discovering the locus of the fire and in tracking down the incendiary. And when denser clouds of smoke were seen to gather over Germany, and the burning of the Reichstag gave the signal, then at last there was no mistake where the incendiary, evil in person, dwelt. Terrifying as this discovery was, in time it brought a sense of relief: now we knew for certain where all unrighteousness was to be found, whereas we ourselves were securely entrenched in the opposite camp, among respectable people whose moral indignation could be trusted to rise higher and higher with every fresh sign of guilt on the other side. Even the call for mass executions no longer offended the ears of the righteous, and the saturation bombing of German cities was looked upon as the judgment of God. Hate had found respectable motives and had ceased to be a personal idiosyncracy, indulged in secret. And all the time the esteemed public had not the faintest idea how closely they themselves were living to evil.

410   One should not imagine for a moment that anybody could escape this play of opposites. Even a saint would have to pray unceasingly for the souls of Hitler and Himmler, the Gestapo and the S.S., in order to repair without delay the damage done to his own soul. The sight of evil kindles evil in the soul – there is no getting away from this fact. The victim is not the only sufferer; everybody in the vicinity of the crime, including the murderer, suffers with him. Something of the abysmal darkness of the world has broken in on us, poisoning the very air we breathe and befouling the pure water with the stale, nauseating taste of blood. True, we are innocent, we are the victims, robbed, betrayed, outraged; and yet for all that, or precisely because of it, the flame of evil glowers in our moral indignation. It must be so, for it is necessary that someone should feel indignant, that someone should let himself be the sword of judgment wielded by fate. Evil calls for expiation, otherwise the wicked will destroy the world utterly, or the good suffocate in their rage which they cannot vent, and in either case no good will come of it.

411   When evil breaks at any point into the order of things, our whole circle of psychic protection is disrupted. Action inevitably calls up reaction, and, in the matter of destructiveness, this turns out to be just as bad as the crime, and possibly even worse, because the evil must be exterminated root and branch. In order to escape the contaminating touch of evil we need a proper *rite de sortie*, a solemn admission of guilt by judge, hangman, and public, followed by an act of expiation.

412   The terrible things that have happened in Germany, and the moral downfall of a "nation of eighty millions," are a blow aimed at all Europeans. (We used to be able to relegate such things to "Asia!") The fact that one member of the European family could sink to the level of the

concentration camp throws a dubious light on all the others. Who are we to imagine that "it couldn't happen here"? We have only to multiply the population of Switzerland by twenty to become a nation of eighty millions, and our public intelligence and morality would then automatically be divided by twenty in consequence of the devastating moral and psychic effects of living together in huge masses. Such a state of things provides the basis for collective crime, and it is then really a miracle if the crime is not committed. Do we seriously believe that *we* would have been immune? We, who have so many traitors and political psychopaths in our midst? It has filled us with horror to realize all that man is capable of, and of which, therefore, we too are capable. Since then a terrible doubt about humanity, and about ourselves, gnaws at our hearts.

413   Nevertheless, it should be clear to everyone that such a state of degradation can come about only under certain conditions. The most important of these is the accumulation of urban, industrialized masses – of people torn from the soil, engaged in one-sided employment, and lacking every healthy instinct, even that of self-preservation. Loss of the instinct of self-preservation can be measured in terms of dependence on the State, which is a bad symptom. Dependence on the State means that everybody relies on everybody else (= State) instead of on himself. Every man hangs on to the next and enjoys a false feeling of security, for one is still hanging in the air even when hanging in the company of ten thousand other people. The only difference is that one is no longer aware of one's own insecurity. The increasing dependence on the State is anything but a healthy symptom; it means that the whole nation is in a fair way to becoming a herd of sheep, constantly relying on a shepherd to drive them into good pastures. The shepherd's staff soon becomes a rod of iron, and the shepherds turn into wolves. What a distressing sight it was to see the whole of Germany heave a sigh of relief when a megalomaniac psychopath proclaimed, "I take over the responsibility!" Any man who still possesses the instinct of self-preservation knows perfectly well that only a swindler would offer to relieve him of responsibility, for surely no one in his senses would dream of taking responsibility for the existence of another. The man who promises everything is sure to fulfil nothing, and everyone who promises too much is in danger of using evil means in order to carry out his promises, and is already on the road to perdition. The steady growth of the Welfare State is no doubt a very fine thing from one point of view, but from another it is a doubtful blessing, as it robs people of their individual responsibility and turns them into infants and sheep. Besides this, there is the danger that the capable will simply be exploited by the irresponsible, as happened on a huge scale in Germany. The citizen's instinct of self-preservation should be safeguarded at all costs, for, once a man is cut off from the nourishing roots of instinct, he becomes the shuttlecock of every wind that blows. He is then no better than a sick

animal, demoralized and degenerate, and nothing short of a catastrophe can bring him back to health.

414   I own that in saying all this I feel rather like the prophet who, according to Josephus, lifted up his voice in lamentation over the city as the Romans laid siege to Jerusalem. It proved not the slightest use to the city, and a stone missile from a Roman ballista put an end to the prophet.

415   With the best will in the world we cannot build a paradise on earth, and even if we could, in a very short time we would have degenerated in every way. We would take delight in destroying our paradise, and then, just as foolishly, marvel at what we had done. Moreover, if we happened to be a "nation of eighty millions" we would be convinced that the "others" were to blame, and our self-confidence would be at such a low ebb that we would not even think of shouldering the responsibility or taking the blame for anything.

416   This is a pathological, demoralized, and mentally abnormal condition: one side of us does things which the other (so-called decent) side prefers to ignore. This side is in a perpetual state of defence against real and supposed accusations. In reality the chief accuser is not outside, but the judge who dwells in our own hearts. Since this is nature's attempt to bring about a cure, it would be wiser not to persist too long in rubbing the noses of the Germans in their own abominations, lest we drown the voice of the accuser in their hearts – and also in our own hearts and those of our Allies. If only people could realize what an enrichment it is to find one's own guilt, what a sense of honour and spiritual dignity! But nowhere does there seem to be a glimmering of this insight. Instead, we hear only of attempts to shift the blame on to others – "no one will admit to having been a Nazi." The Germans were never wholly indifferent to the impression they made on the outside world. They resented disapproval and hated even to be criticized. Inferiority feelings make people touchy and lead to compensatory efforts to impress. As a result, the German thrusts himself forward and seeks to curry favour, or "German efficiency" is demonstrated with such aplomb that it leads to a reign of terror and the shooting of hostages. The German no longer thinks of these things as murder, for he is lost in considerations of his own prestige. Inferiority feelings are usually a sign of inferior feeling – which is not just a play on words. All the intellectual and technological achievements in the world cannot make up for inferiority in the matter of feeling. The pseudo-scientific race-theories with which it was dolled up did not make the extermination of the Jews any more acceptable, and neither do falsifications of history make a wrong policy appear any more trustworthy.

417   This spectacle recalls the figure of what Nietzsche so aptly calls the "pale criminal," who in reality shows all the signs of hysteria. He simply will not and cannot admit that he is what he is; he cannot endure his own guilt, just as he could not help incurring it. He will stoop to every kind of self-deception if only he can escape the sight of himself. It is true that this

happens everywhere, but nowhere does it appear to be such a national characteristic as in Germany. I am by no means the first to have been struck by the inferiority feelings of the Germans. What did Goethe, Heine, and Nietzsche have to say about their countrymen? A feeling of inferiority does not in the least mean that it is unjustified. Only, the inferiority does not refer to that side of the personality, or to the function, in which it visibly appears, but to an inferiority which none the less really exists even though only dimly suspected. This condition can easily lead to an hysterical dissociation of the personality, which consists essentially in one hand not knowing what the other is doing, in wanting to jump over one's own shadow, and in looking for everything dark, inferior, and culpable *in others*. Hence the hysteric always complains of being surrounded by people who are incapable of appreciating him and who are activated only by bad motives; by inferior mischief-makers, a crowd of submen who should be exterminated neck and crop so that the Superman can live on his high level of perfection. The very fact that his thinking and feeling proceed along these lines is clear proof of inferiority in action. Therefore all hysterical people are compelled to torment others, because they are unwilling to hurt themselves by admitting their own inferiority. But since nobody can jump out of his skin and be rid of himself, they stand in their own way everywhere as their own evil spirit – and that is what we call an hysterical neurosis.

418   All these pathological features – complete lack of insight into one's own character, auto-erotic self-admiration and self-extenuation, denigration and terrorization of one's fellow men (how contemptuously Hitler spoke of his own people!), projection of the shadow, lying, falsification of reality, determination to impress by fair means or foul, bluffing and double-crossing – all these were united in the man who was diagnosed clinically as an hysteric, and whom a strange fate chose to be the political, moral, and religious spokesman of Germany for twelve years. Is this pure chance?

419   A more accurate diagnosis of Hitler's condition would be *pseudologia phantastica*, that form of hysteria which is characterized by a peculiar talent for believing one's own lies. For a short spell, such people usually meet with astounding success, and for that reason are socially dangerous. Nothing has such a convincing effect as a lie one invents and believes oneself, or an evil deed or intention whose righteousness one regards as self-evident. At any rate they carry far more conviction than the good man and the good deed, or even than the wicked man and his purely wicked deed. Hitler's theatrical, obviously hysterical gestures struck all foreigners (with a few amazing exceptions) as purely ridiculous. When I saw him with my own eyes, he suggested a psychic scarecrow (with a broomstick for an outstretched arm) rather than a human being. It is also difficult to understand how his ranting speeches, delivered in shrill, grating, woman-ish tones, could have made such an impression. But the German people would never have been taken in and carried away so completely if this

figure had not been a reflected image of the collective German hysteria. It is not without serious misgivings that one ventures to pin the label of "psychopathic inferiority" on to a whole nation, and yet, heaven knows, it is the only explanation which could in any way account for the effect this scarecrow had on the masses. A sorry lack of education, conceit that bordered on madness, a very mediocre intelligence combined with the hysteric's cunning and the power fantasies of an adolescent, were written all over this demagogue's face. His gesticulations were all put on, devised by an hysterical mind intent only on making an impression. He behaved in public like a man living in his own biography, in this case as the sombre, daemonic "man of iron" of popular fiction, the ideal of an infantile public whose knowledge of the world is derived from the deified heroes of trashy films. These personal observations led me to conclude at the time (1937) that, when the final catastrophe came, it would be far greater and bloodier than I had previously supposed. For this theatrical hysteric and transparent imposter was not strutting about on a small stage, but was riding the armoured divisions of the Wehrmacht, with all the weight of German heavy industry behind him. Encountering only slight and in any case ineffective opposition from within, the nation of eighty millions crowded into the circus to witness its own destruction.

420   Among Hitler's closest associates, Goebbels and Göring stand out as equally striking figures. Göring is the good fellow and *bon vivant* type of cheat, who takes in the simple-minded with his jovial air of respectability; Goebbels, a no-less-sinister and dangerous character, is the typical *Kaffeehausliterat* and card-sharper, handicapped and at the same time branded by nature. Any one partner in this unholy trinity should have been enough to make any man whose instincts were not warped cross himself three times. But what in fact happened? Hitler was exalted to the skies; there were even theologians who looked upon him as the Saviour. Göring was popular on account of his weaknesses; few people would believe his crimes. Goebbels was tolerated because many people think that lying is inseparable from success, and that success justifies everything. Three of these types at one time were really the limit, and one is at a loss to imagine how anything quite so monstrous ever came to power. But we must not forget that we are judging from today, from a knowledge of the events which led to the catastrophe. Our judgment would certainly be very different had our information stopped short at 1933 or 1934. At that time, in Germany as well as in Italy, there were not a few things that appeared plausible and seemed to speak in favour of the regime. An undeniable piece of evidence in this respect was the disappearance of the unemployed, who used to tramp the German highroads in their hundreds of thousands. And after the stagnation and decay of the post-war years, the refreshing wind that blew through the two countries was a tempting sign of hope. Meanwhile, the whole of Europe looked on at this spectacle like Mr. Chamberlain, who was prepared at most for a heavy shower. But it is just

this extreme speciousness that is the peculiar genius of *pseudologia phantastica*, and Mussolini also had a touch of it (kept within bounds, however, while his brother Arnaldo was alive). It introduces its plans in the most innocent way in the world, finding the most appropriate words and the most plausible arguments, and there is nothing to show that its intentions are bad from the start. They may even be good, genuinely good. In the case of Mussolini, for instance, it might be difficult to draw a definite line between black and white. Where *pseudologia* is at work one can never be sure that the intention to deceive is the principal motive. Quite often the "great plan" plays the leading role, and it is only when it comes to the ticklish question of bringing this plan into reality that every opportunity is exploited and any means is good enough, on the principle that "the end justifies the means." In other words, things only become dangerous when the pathological liar is taken seriously by a wider public. Like Faust, he is bound to make a pact with the devil and thus slips off the straight path. It is even possible that this is more or less what happened to Hitler – let us give him the benefit of the doubt! But the infamies of his book, once it is shorn of its *Schwabinger*[3] brand of bombast, make one suspicious, and one cannot help wondering if the evil spirit had not already taken possession of this man long before he seized power. Round about 1936, many people in Germany were asking themselves the same question; they expressed fears that the Führer might fall a victim to "evil influences," he dabbled too much in "black magic," etc. Clearly these misgivings came much too late; but even so, it is just conceivable that Hitler himself may have had good intentions at first, and only succumbed to the use of the wrong means, or the misuse of his means, in the course of his development.

421   But I should like to emphasize above all that it is part and parcel of the pathological liar's make-up to be plausible. Therefore it is no easy matter, even for experienced people, to form an opinion, particularly while the plan is still apparently in the idealistic stage. It is then quite impossible to foresee how things are likely to develop, and Mr Chamberlain's "give-it-a-chance" attitude seems to be the only policy. The overwhelming majority of the Germans were just as much in the dark as people abroad, and quite naturally fell an easy prey to Hitler's speeches, so artfully attuned to German (and not only German) taste.

422   Although we may be able to understand why the Germans were misled in the first place, the almost total absence of any reaction is quite incomprehensible. Were there not army commanders who could have ordered their troops to do anything they pleased? Why then was the reaction totally lacking? I can only explain this as the outcome of a peculiar state of mind, a passing or chronic disposition which, in an individual, we call hysteria.

423   As I cannot take it for granted that the layman knows exactly what is meant by "hysteria," I had better explain that the "hysterical" disposition

forms a sub-division of what are known as "psychopathic inferiorities." This term by no means implies that the individual or the nation is "inferior" in every respect, but only that there is a place of least resistance, a peculiar instability, which exists independently of all the other qualities. An hysterical disposition means that the opposites inherent in every psyche, and especially those affecting character, are further apart than in normal people. This greater distance procedures a higher energic tension, which accounts for the undeniable energy and drive of the Germans. On the other hand, the greater distance between the opposites produces inner contradictions, conflicts of conscience, disharmonies of character – in short, everything we see in Goethe's Faust. Nobody but a German could ever have devised such a figure, it is so intrinsically, so infinitely German. In Faust we see the same "hungering for the infinite" born of inner contradiction and dichotomy, the same eschatological expectation of the Great Fulfilment. In him we experience the loftiest flight of the mind and the descent into the depths of guilt and darkness, and still worse, a fall so low that Faust sinks to the level of a mountebank and wholesale murderer as the outcome of his pact with the devil. Faust, too, is split and sets up "evil" outside himself in the shape of Mephistopheles, to serve as an alibi in case of need. He likewise "knows nothing of what has happened," i.e., what the devil did to Philemon and Baucis. We never get the impression that he has real insight or suffers genuine remorse. His avowed and unavowed worship of success stands in the way of any moral reflection throughout, obscuring the ethical conflict, so that Faust's moral personality remains misty. He never attains the character of reality: he is not a real human being and cannot become one (at least not in this world). He remains the German idea of a human being, and therefore an image – somewhat overdone and distorted – of the average German.

424   The essence of hysteria is a systematic dissociation, a loosening of the opposites which normally are held firmly together. It may even go to the length of a splitting of the personality, a condition in which quite literally one hand no longer knows what the other is doing. As a rule there is amazing ignorance of the shadow; the hysteric is only aware of his good motives, and when the bad ones can no longer be denied he becomes the unscrupulous Superman and *Herrenmensch* who fancies he is ennobled by the magnitude of his aim.

425   Ignorance of one's other side creates great inner insecurity. One does not really know who one is; one feels inferior somewhere and yet does not wish to know where the inferiority lies, with the result that a new inferiority is added to the original one. This sense of insecurity is the source of the hysteric's prestige psychology, of his need to make an impression, to flaunt his merits and insist on them, of his insatiable thirst for recognition, admiration, adulation, and longing to be loved. It is the cause of that loud-mouthed arrogance, uppishness, insolence, and tactlessness by which so many Germans, who at home grovel like dogs, win a bad

reputation for their countrymen abroad. Insecurity is also responsible for
their tragic lack of civic courage, criticized by Bismarck (one need only
recall the pitiable role of the German generals).

426   The lack of reality, so striking in Faust, produces a corresponding lack
of realism in the German. He merely talks of it, boasting of his "ice-cold"
realism, which in itself is enough to expose his hysteria. His realism is
nothing but a pose, a stage-realism. He merely acts the part of one who
has a sense of reality, but what does he actually want to do? He wants to
conquer the world in spite of the whole world. Of course, he has no idea
how it can be done. But at least he might know that the enterprise had
failed once before. Unfortunately a plausible reason, that explains away
the failure by means of lies, is immediately invented and believed. How
many Germans were taken in by the legend of the "stab in the back" in
1918? And how many "stab in the back" legends are floating around
today? Believing one's own lies when the wish is father to the lie is a well-
known hysterical symptom and a distinct sign of inferiority. One would
have thought that the bloodbath of the First World War would have been
enough, but not a bit of it; glory, conquest, and bloodthirstiness acted like
a smoke-screen on the German mind, so that reality, only dimly perceived
at best, was completely blotted out. In an individual we call this sort of
thing an hysterical twilight-state. When a whole nation finds itself in this
condition it will follow a mediumistic Führer over the house-tops with a
sleep-walker's assurance, only to land in the street with a broken back.

427   Supposing we Swiss had started such a war and had thrown all our
experience, all warnings and all our knowledge of the world to the winds
as blindly as the Germans, and had finally gone to the length of establishing
an original edition of Buchenwald in our country. We should no doubt feel
very disagreeably surprised if a foreigner declared that the Swiss were one
and all completely mad. No reasonable person would be surprised at such
a verdict, but can we say it about Germany? I wonder what the Germans
themselves think. All I know is that at the time of the censorship in
Switzerland we were not permitted to say these things aloud, and now it
seems we cannot say them out of consideration for Germany which is laid
so low. When on earth, I should like to ask, may one venture to form an
opinion of one's own? To my mind, the history of the last twelve years is
the case-chart of an hysterical patient. The truth should not be withheld
from him, for when the doctor makes a diagnosis he does so as part of his
effort to find the remedy, and not in order to hurt, degrade, or insult the
sufferer. A neurosis or a neurotic disposition is not a disgrace, it is a
handicap, and sometimes merely a *façon de parler.* It is not a fatal disease,
but it does grow worse to the degree that one is determined to ignore it.
When I say that the Germans are psychically ill it is surely kinder than
saying that they are criminals. I have no wish to irritate the notorious
sensitiveness of the hysteric, but there comes a time when we can no longer
afford to gloss over all the painful symptoms and to help the patient forget

what has happened, merely in order that his pathological condition should remain undisturbed. I would not like to insult the healthy-minded and decent German by suspecting him of being a coward who runs away from his own image. We should do him the honour of treating him like a man and telling him the truth, and not conceal from him that our soul is cut to the quick by the terrible things that happened in his country and were perpetrated by the Germans in Europe. We are hurt and indignant and have no particular feelings of loving-kindness – nor can any amount of determination and will-power twist these sentiments into a Christian "love of your neighbour." For the sake of the healthy-minded and decent Germans one should not attempt to do so; they would surely prefer the truth to insulting forbearance.

428   Hysteria is never cured by hushing up the truth, whether in an individual or in a nation. But can we say that a whole nation is hysterical? We can say it as much or as little of a nation as of an individual. Even the craziest person is not completely crazy; quite a number of his functions are still normal, and there may even be times when he himself is fairly normal too. This is even truer of hysteria, where there is really nothing wrong except exaggerations and excesses on the one hand, and weakness or temporary paralysis of normal functions on the other. In spite of his psychopathic condition the hysteric is very nearly normal. We may therefore expect many parts of the psychic body-politic to be entirely normal even though the overall picture can only be described as hysterical.

429   The Germans undoubtedly have their own peculiar psychology which distinguishes them from their neighbours, in spite of the many human qualities which they share with all mankind. Have they not demonstrated to the world that they consider themselves the *Herrenvolk*, with the right to disregard every human scruple? They have labelled other nations inferior and done their best to exterminate them.

430   In view of these terrible facts, it is a mere bagatelle to turn the tables on the *Herrenvolk* and apply the diagnosis of inferiority to the murderer instead of the murdered, while remaining fully conscious that one is injuring all those Germans who suffered their nation's tribulation with open eyes. It does indeed hurt one to hurt others. But, as Europeans – a brotherhood which includes the Germans – we are wounded, and if we wound in return it is not with the intention of torturing but, as I said earlier, of discovering the truth. As in the case of collective guilt, the diagnosis of its mental condition extends to the whole nation, and indeed to the whole of Europe, whose mental condition for some time past has hardly been normal. Whether we like it or not we are bound to ask: What is wrong with our art, that most delicate of all instruments for reflecting the national psyche? How are we to explain the blatantly pathological element in modern painting? Atonal music? The far-reaching influence of Joyce's fathomless *Ulysses?* Here we already have the germ of what was to become a political reality in Germany.

431   The European, or rather the white man in general, is scarcely in a position to judge of his own state of mind. He is too deeply involved. I had always wanted to see Europeans through other eyes, and eventually I was able, on my many journeys, to establish sufficiently close relationships with non-Europeans to see the European through their eyes. The white man is nervous, restless, hurried, unstable, and (in the eyes of non-Europeans) possessed by the craziest ideas, in spite of his energy and gifts which give him the feeling of being infinitely superior. The crimes he has committed against the coloured races are legion, though obviously this is no justification for any fresh crime, just as the individual is no better for being in a vast company of bad people. Primitives dread the sharply focussed stare in the eye of the European, which seems to them like the evil eye. A Pueblo chieftain once confided to me that he thought all Americans (the only white men he knew) were crazy, and the reasons he gave for this view sounded exactly like a description of people who were possessed. Well, perhaps we are. For the first time since the dawn of history we have succeeded in swallowing the whole of primitive animism into ourselves, and with it the spirit that animated nature. Not only were the gods dragged down from their planetary spheres and transformed into chthonic demons, but, under the influence of scientific enlightenment, even this band of demons, which at the time of Paracelsus still frolicked happily in mountains and woods, in rivers and human dwelling-places, was reduced to a miserable remnant and finally vanished altogether. From time immemorial, nature was always filled with spirit. Now, for the first time, we are living in a lifeless nature bereft of gods. No one will deny the important role which the powers of the human psyche, personified as "gods," played in the past. The mere act of enlightenment may have destroyed the spirits of nature, but not the psychic factors that correspond to them, such as suggestibility, lack of criticism, fearfulness, propensity to superstition and prejudice – in short, all those qualities which make possession possible. Even though nature is depsychized, the psychic conditions which breed demons are as actively at work as ever. The demons have not really disappeared but have merely taken on another form: they have become unconscious psychic forces. This process of reabsorption went hand in hand with an increasing inflation of the ego, which became more and more evident after the sixteenth century. Finally we even began to be aware of the psyche, and, as history shows, the discovery of the unconscious was a particularly painful episode. Just when people were congratulating themselves on having abolished all spooks, it turned out that instead of haunting the attic or old ruins the spooks were flitting about in the heads of apparently normal Europeans. Tyrannical, obsessive, intoxicating ideas and delusions were abroad everywhere, and people began to believe the most absurd things, just as the possessed do.

432   The phenomenon we have witnessed in Germany was nothing less than the first outbreak of epidemic insanity, an irruption of the unconscious into

what seemed to be a tolerably well-ordered world. A whole nation, as well as countless millions belonging to other nations, were swept into the blood-drenched madness of a war of extermination. No one knew what was happening to him, least of all the Germans, who allowed themselves to be driven to the slaughterhouse by their leading psychopaths like hypnotized sheep. Maybe the Germans were predestined to this fate, for they showed the least resistance to the mental contagion that threatened every European. But their peculiar gifts might also have enabled them to be the very people to draw helpful conclusions from the prophetic example of Nietzsche. Nietzsche was German to the marrow of his bones, even to the abstruse symbolism of his madness. It was the psychopath's weakness that prompted him to play with the "blond beast" and the "Superman." It was certainly not the healthy elements in the German nation that led to the triumph of these pathological fantasies on a scale never known before. The weakness of the German character, like Nietzsche's, proved to be fertile soil for hysterical fantasies, though it must be remembered that Nietzsche himself not only criticized the German Philistine very freely but laid himself open to attack on a broad front. Here again the Germans had a priceless opportunity for self-knowledge – and let it slip. And what could they not have learned from the suet-and-syrup of Wagner!

433   Nevertheless, with the calamitous founding of the Reich in 1871, the devil stole a march on the Germans, dangling before them the tempting bait of power, aggrandizement, national arrogance. Thus they were led to imitate their prophets and to take their words literally, but not to understand them. And so it was that the Germans allowed themselves to be deluded by these disastrous fantasies and succumbed to the age-old temptations of Satan, instead of turning to their abundant spiritual potentialities, which, because of the greater tension between the inner opposites, would have stood them in good stead. But, their Christianity forgotten, they sold their souls to technology, exchanged morality for cynicism, and dedicated their highest aspirations to the forces of destruction. Certainly everybody else is doing much the same thing, but even so there really are chosen people who have no right to do such things because they should be striving for higher treasures. At any rate the Germans are not among those who may enjoy power and possessions with impunity. Just think for a moment what anti-Semitism means for the German: he is trying to use others as a scapegoat for his own greatest fault! This symptom alone should have told him that he had got on to a hopelessly wrong track.

434   After the last World War the world should have begun to reflect, and above all Germany, which is the nerve-centre of Europe. But the spirit turned negative, neglected the decisive questions, and sought solutions in its own negation. How different it was at the time of the Reformation! Then the spirit of Germany rose manfully to the needs of Christendom, though the answer – as we might expect from the German tension of opposites – was somewhat too extreme. But at least this spirit did not

shrink from its own problems. Goethe, too, was a prophet when he held up before his people the example of Faust's pact with the devil and the murder of Philemon and Baucis. If, as Burckhardt says, Faust strikes a chord in every German soul, this chord has certainly gone on ringing. We hear it echoing in Nietzsche's Superman, the amoral worshipper of instinct, whose God is dead, and who presumes to be God himself, or rather a demon "six thousand feet beyond good and evil." And where has the feminine side, the soul, disappeared to in Nietzsche? Helen has vanished in Hades, and Eurydice will never return. Already we behold the fateful travesty of the denied Christ: the sick prophet is himself the Crucified, and, going back still further, the dismembered Dionysus-Zagreus. The raving prophet carries us back to the long-forgotten past: he had heard the call of destiny in the shrill whistling of the hunter, the god of the rustling forests, of drunken ecstasy, and of the berserkers who were possessed by the spirits of wild animals.

435   While Nietzsche was prophetically responding to the schism of the Christian world with the art of thinking, his brother in spirit, Richard Wagner, was doing the same thing with the art of music. Germanic prehistory comes surging up, thunderous and stupefying, to fill the gaping breach in the Church. Wagner salved his conscience with *Parsifal*, for which Nietzsche could never forgive him, but the Castle of the Grail vanished into an unknown land. The message was not heard and the omen went unheeded. Only the orgiastic frenzy caught on and spread like an epidemic. Wotan the storm-god had conquered. Ernst Jünger sensed that very clearly: in his book *On the Marble Cliffs* a wild huntsman comes into the land, bringing with him a wave of possession greater than anything known even in the Middle Ages. Nowhere did the European spirit speak more plainly than it did in Germany, and nowhere was it more tragically misunderstood.

436   Now Germany has suffered the consequences of the pact with the devil, she has experienced madness and is torn in pieces like Zagreus, she has been ravished by the berserkers of her god Wotan, been cheated of her soul for the sake of gold and world-mastery, and defiled by the scum rising from the lowest depths.

437   The Germans must understand why the whole world is outraged, for our expectations had been so different. Everybody was unanimous in recognizing their gifts and their efficiency, and nobody doubted that they were capable of great things. The disappointment was all the more bitter. But the fate of Germany should not mislead Europeans into nursing the illusion that the whole world's wickedness is localized in Germany. They should realize that the German catastrophe was only one crisis in the general European sickness. Long before the Hitler era, in fact before the First World War, there were symptoms of the mental change taking place in Europe. The medieval picture of the world was breaking up and the metaphysical authority that ruled it was fast disappearing, only to reappear

in man. Did not Nietzsche announce that God was dead and that his heir was the Superman, that doomed rope-dancer and fool? It is an immutable psychological law that when a projection has come to an end it always returns to its origin. So when somebody hits on the singular idea that God is dead, or does not exist at all, the psychic God-image, which is a dynamic part of the psyche's structure, finds its way back into the subject and produces a condition of "God-Almightiness," that is to say all those qualities which are peculiar to fools and madmen and therefore lead to catastrophe.

438   This, then, is the great problem that faces the whole of Christianity: where now is the sanction for goodness and justice, which was once anchored in metaphysics? Is it really only brute force that decides everything? Is the ultimate authority only the will of whatever man happens to be in power? Had Germany been victorious, one might almost have believed that this was the last word. But as the "thousand-year Reich" of violence and infamy lasted only a few years before it collapsed in ruins, we might be disposed to learn the lesson that there are other, equally powerful forces at work which in the end destroy all that is violent and unjust, and that consequently it does not pay to build on false principles. But unfortunately, as history shows, things do not always turn out so reasonably in this world of ours.

439   "God-Almightiness" does not make man divine, it merely fills him with arrogance and arouses everything evil in him. It produces a diabolical caricature of man, and this inhuman mask is so unendurable, such a torture to wear, that he tortures others. He is split in himself, a prey to inexplicable contradictions. Here we have the picture of the hysterical state of mind, of Nietzsche's "pale criminal." Fate has confronted every German with his inner counterpart: Faust is face to face with Mephistopheles and can no longer say, "So that was the essence of the brute!" He must confess instead: "That was my other side, my *alter ego*, my all too palpable shadow which can no longer be denied."

440   This is not the fate of Germany alone, but of all Europe. We must all open our eyes to the shadow who looms behind contemporary man. We have no need to hold up the devil's mask before the Germans. The facts speak a plainer language, and anyone who does not understand it is simply beyond help. As to what should be done about this terrifying apparition, everyone must work this out for himself. It is indeed no small matter to know of one's own guilt and one's own evil, and there is certainly nothing to be gained by losing sight of one's shadow. When we are conscious of our guilt we are in a more favourable position – we can at least hope to change and improve ourselves. As we know, anything that remains in the unconscious is incorrigible; psychological corrections can be made only in consciousness. Consciousness of guilt can therefore act as a powerful moral stimulus. In every treatment of neurosis the discovery of the shadow is indispensable, otherwise nothing changes. In this respect, I rely on those

parts of the German body-politic which have remained sound to draw conclusions from the facts. Without guilt, unfortunately, there can be no psychic maturation and no widening of the spiritual horizon. Was it not Meister Eckhart who said: "For this reason God is willing to bear the brunt of sins and often winks at them, mostly sending them to people for whom he has prepared some high destiny. See! Who was dearer to our Lord or more intimate with him than his apostles? Not one of them but fell into mortal sin, and all were mortal sinners."[4]

441   Where sin is great, "grace doth much more abound." Such an experience brings about an inner transformation, and this is infinitely more important than political and social reforms which are all valueless in the hands of people who are not at one with themselves. This is a truth which we are forever forgetting, because our eyes are fascinated by the conditions around us and riveted on them instead of examining our own heart and conscience. Every demagogue exploits this human weakness when he points with the greatest possible outcry to all the things that are wrong in the outside world. But the principal and indeed the only thing that is wrong with the world is man.

442   If the Germans today are having a hard time of it outwardly, fate has at least given them a unique opportunity of turning their eyes inward to the inner man. In this way they might make amends for a sin of omission of which our whole civilization is guilty. Everything possible has been done for the outside world: science has been refined to an unimaginable extent, technical achievement has reached an almost uncanny degree of perfection. But what of man, who is expected to administer all these blessings in a reasonable way? He has simply been taken for granted. No one has stopped to consider that neither morally nor psychologically is he in any way adapted to such changes. As blithely as any child of nature he sets about enjoying these dangerous playthings, completely oblivious of the shadow lurking behind him, ready to seize them in its greedy grasp and turn them against a still infantile and unconscious humanity. And who has had a more immediate experience of this feeling of helplessness and abandonment to the powers of darkness than the German who fell into the clutches of the Germans?

443   If collective guilt could only be understood and accepted, a great step forward would have been taken. But this alone is no cure, just as no neurotic is cured by mere understanding. The question remains: How am I to live with this shadow? What attitude is required if I am to be able to live in spite of evil? In order to find valid answers to these questions a complete spiritual renewal is needed. And this cannot be given gratis, each man must strive to achieve it for himself. Neither can old formulas which once had a value be brought into force again. The eternal truths cannot be transmitted mechanically; in every epoch they must be born anew from the human psyche.

NOTES

1 [First published as "Nach der Katastrophe," *Neue Schweizer Rundschau* (Zurich), n.s., XIII (1945), 67–88; reprinted in *Aufsätze zur Zeitgeschichte* (Zurich, 1946), pp. 73–116. Previously trans. by Elizabeth Welsh in *Essays on Contemporary Events* (London, 1947), pp. 45–72. – EDITORS.]
2 [See previous paper.]
3 [Schwabing is the bohemian quarter of Munich. EDITORS.]
4 *Works*, trans. by Evans, II, pp. 18–19.

Sources and acknowledgements

'A Letter to Freud' from *The Freud/Jung Letters: The correspondence between Sigmund Freud and C.G. Jung*, edited by William McGuire, translated by Ralph Mannheim and R.F.C. Hull (London: Hogarth/Rougledge, 1974; Princeton: Princeton University Press, 1974), no. 178J, pp. 293–4.

'Introduction to the religious and psychological problems of alchemy', *Collected Works*, Vol. 12, paras 22–43.

'The spirit Mercurius', *Collected Works*, Vol. 13, paras 247–72.

'The problem of the fourth', *Collected Works*, Vol. 11, paras 243–85.

'Two letters to Father Victor White' from *C.G. Jung: Letters* Vol. 2 (1951–1961), selected and edited by Gerhard Adler in collaboration with Aniela Jaffé, translations from the German by R.F.C. Hull (London: Routledge, 1976; Princeton: Princeton University Press, 1953), pp. 58–61 and pp. 163–74.

'Good and evil in analytical psychology', *Collected Works*, Vol. 10, paras 858–86.

'The shadow', *Collected Works*, Vol. 9ii, paras 13–19.

'North Africa' from *Memories, Dreams, Reflections*, recorded and edited by Aniela Jaffé, translated by Richard and Clara Winston (London: Fontana/HarperCollins Publishers Ltd., 1977), pp. 238–46.

'A psychological view of conscience', *Collected Works*, Vol. 10, paras 825–57.

'Answer to Job', *Collected Works*, Vol. 11, paras 553–608, 628–42, 649–82, 688–717, 736–47.

'The fight with the shadow', *Collected Works*, Vol. 10, paras 444–57.

'After the catastrophe', *Collected Works*, Vol. 10, paras 400–43.

Index